Postcard History Series

# *Claremore*

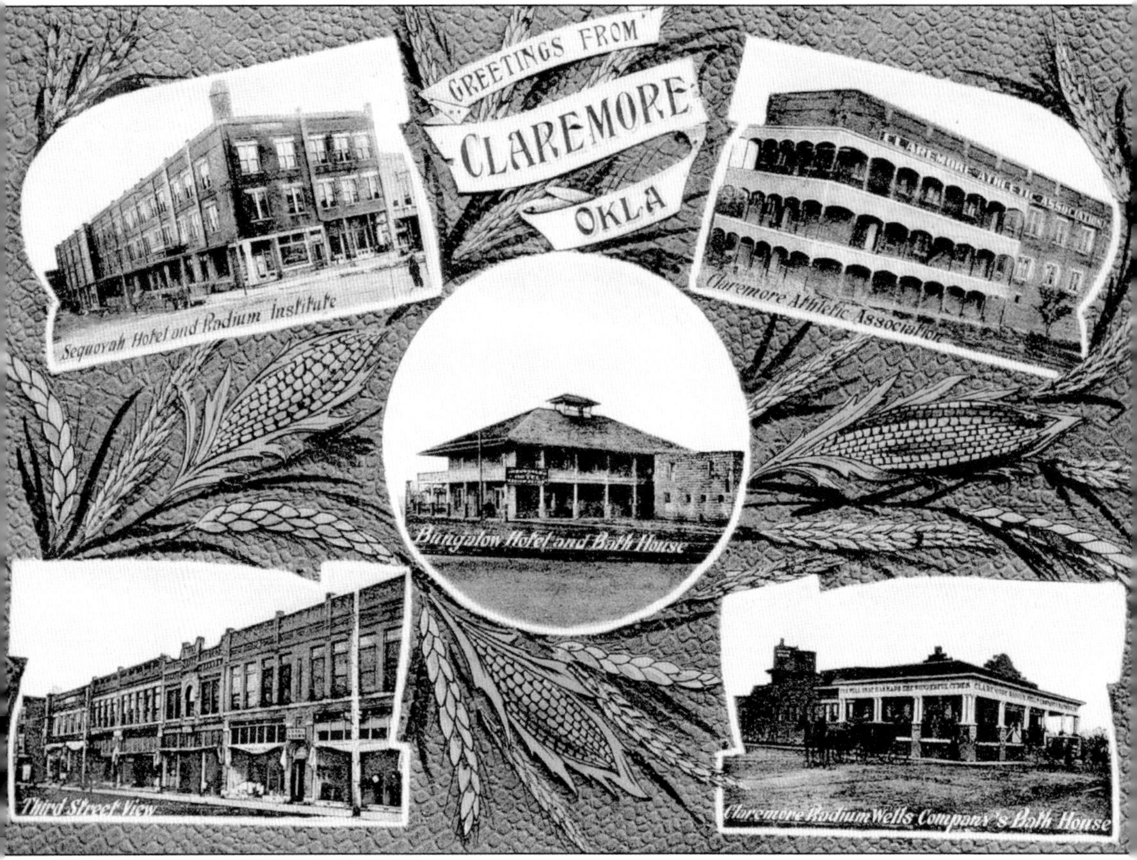


This postcard depicts multiple views of Claremore during a prosperous time in the city's history.

*On the front cover*: This postcard of Claremore was taken around 1918 and appears to be of either a funeral procession or a parade. The reverse of this card states that the population of Claremore was 5,000 and that it was a "modern and progressive city." The building in the foreground on the left housed Wilson's Hardware, and above that building, Robson Lawyers can be seen written on the window. Across the street from the hardware store can be seen the Farmers Bank. Other noticeable stores would be a grocery and the Scmitz building, which became the Twin Oaks Hotel. (Courtesy of April Churchill.)

*On the back cover*: The Sequoyah Hotel was built by John M. Bayless in 1901 on the southwest corner of what today is Will Rogers Boulevard and Missouri Street. Bayless established a bank in the front corner of the hotel named the National Bank of Claremore. This corner view of the hotel offers a view of an abstract and loan company as well as a dental office in front of the hotel next to the bank. The building was razed and RCB Bank currently stands at that location. (Courtesy of Dorothy Kizer-Dennis.)

POSTCARD HISTORY SERIES

# *Claremore*

*April Churchill and Dorothy Kizer-Dennis*

ARCADIA
PUBLISHING

ISBN 978-0-7385-5056-5

Published by Arcadia Publishing
Charleston, South Carolina

Printed in the United States of America

Library of Congress Catalog Card Number: 2007926281

For all general information contact Arcadia Publishing at:
Telephone 843-853-2070
Fax 843-853-0044
E-mail sales@arcadiapublishing.com
For customer service and orders:
Toll-Free 1-888-313-2665

Visit us on the Internet at www.arcadiapublishing.com

*To our husbands, Robert and Jack, for showing us constant support and encouragement during our long hours of research. To Rebecca and Ryan Churchill for being a source of joy and inspiration. Don't ever be afraid to accomplish your dreams. To Mike, Jennifer, Mica, Matthew, and Makenna, just because we love you.*

# Contents

# ACKNOWLEDGMENTS

A project of this magnitude cannot be done single-handedly. We would like to thank the following individuals for their generosity in sharing postcards, photographs, and recollections: Butch and Renee Shaver, Ralph and Mary Bridwell, Pam Crume, Mike Washburn, Elwynn Isaacs, Carol Low, Ella Mae Cheek-Dennis, and Sandra Dennis-Irwin.

A special thank-you to the Will Rogers Memorial and Museum and the Rogers County Historical Society.

# INTRODUCTION

Claremore is a small town with a population of 16,000 steeped in history. It is the county seat for Rogers County and sits in the heart of the Cherokee Nation. Claremore's foundation dates to prestatehood when it was known as Claremore, Indian Territory.

Originally there were three different Claremores. The first was settled in 1802 by Chief Claremont and his tribe of Osage Indians. It was located near Claremore Mound just north of present-day Claremore. It was the first recognized and official village of Indian Territory.

The Battle of Claremore Mound took place in October 1817. The Cherokee people had tried for several years to take the Osage land. That October day, while the Osage men were on a hunting trip, the Cherokee attacked the village. With the men away, the village was defenseless. The Osage were shown no mercy when the Cherokee attacked, killing 14 older men, 69 boys, and several women and children. The village was burned, and the remaining 104 Osage were taken prisoner. Chief Claremont passed away in 1828, and in 1838, the Osage tribe was driven out of its ancient lands into Kansas.

The second Claremore was organized in 1844 at the same site as the original settlement. The village had over 150 dwellings. The first official store was a general merchandise store owned by John Bullette, a Delaware Indian.

In 1882, the third and present-day Claremore was organized. The St. Louis and San Francisco Railroad, more commonly known as the Frisco Railroad, was moving into Indian Territory. John Bullette quickly moved his store and family to the nearest railroad stop. Joe Chambers had already started a store since the railroad stop was practically at his front door. These were the first two stores in present-day Claremore. John Bullette's daughter Zoe was the first child born in Claremore.

The original intention was to name the town Claremont after the Osage chief. There is a little confusion over how the name was changed. One story says that the telegraph operator misspelled the name and it stuck.

The Frisco Railroad and the St. Louis, Iron Mountain and Southern Railroad, also known as the Missouri Pacific and Iron Mountain Railroad, both came roaring into Indian Territory in the late 1800s: the Frisco in 1882 and the St. Louis, Iron Mountain and Southern in 1889. Towns and cities began to form as businesses sprang up at each railroad stop. The two railroads provided easy access to the towns for shipment of merchandise as well as tourists. Claremore soon became the fastest-growing site along the railroad route. The Frisco depot was situated on the west side of town, and the Missouri Pacific and Iron Mountain located on the east side.

George Washington Eaton was one of the founding fathers of Claremore. Eaton was born in 1845 in Arkansas. After the Civil War, he was intent on returning home to Texas when he met and fell in love with a young Cherokee woman in Claremore. Eaton built many of the residences and buildings in early-day Claremore. The old Wilson's Hardware building still bears a stone at the top that reads, "Eaton 1902."

Eaton is also to be credited for first bringing tourism to Claremore. In 1903, while drilling for oil, he discovered a foul-smelling liquid. This substance was originally discarded into a local creek. It was then discovered that a dog was cured of mange after swimming in the same creek. Eaton sent the water to Dr. Edward Keister at Washington University in St. Louis, Missouri, for a chemical analysis. The results showed the water contained hydrogen sulfide and sulfur. Eaton named his discovery radium water. The name radium water was a misnomer as the water itself was proven to have no radium content whatsoever. Eaton began to promote the water as a cure for rheumatism, stomach problems, eczema, and "whatever ailed you." It was his entrepreneurial spirit in marketing this water that helped form Claremore into the city it is today.

The first radium bathhouse was built in 1904 and several more followed. This section of town became known as Radium Town. Radium Town at that time was located outside Claremore, so most bathhouses offered taxi service from the train depots to the bathhouses. People traveled from all over the world to take baths in these amazing healing waters. Perhaps one of the more interesting people to travel to Claremore seeking health was Princess Stephania Kaunitz from Vienna, Austria. She traveled here in March 1913 after sending her personal physician to substantiate the health claims. While in Claremore, the princess stayed at the Sequoyah Hotel. The Pittsburgh Pirates also happened to be in Claremore during the same time. The princess asked to meet the famous "Flying Dutchman" of Pirates fame.

Some questioned the validity of the health claims; however, many testimonials were sent verifying the water's ability. One woman from Tulsa visited on a regular basis for her smoking habit. Having taken her bath, she would be given a white towel in order to dry herself. She stated that the white towel would turn black from the nicotine drawn out of her body by the water.

The Radium Town area is located between the present-day streets of Seminole and Dorothy Avenues on Ninth Street. A few buildings still stand in Radium Town, although none of the bathhouses are in operation. The radium wells remain capped, waiting for the next generation of health seekers.

By 1904, Claremore was considered the most stable town in Indian Territory. It had five debt-free churches, hotel accommodations, an opera house, two banks, a flour mill, two newspapers, a U.S. court, and 29 rock and brick business buildings. Most of the private residences were built along Fourth Street to begin with. Those living on Fourth Street in the early 1900s included Judge William Hall, Dr. Minor Gordon, Earnest Feland, Sidney Vinson (Vinson Drug Store), George Davis, Sen. Tom Brown, the Braden family, John M. Bayless, and John Quincy Adams.

Claremore's first city hall was built in 1911. In front of that building was a wading pool and amphitheater. There was also a small park with monkey cages. A time capsule was set into the cornerstone of the building containing a Bible, an 1893 copy of the *Claremore Progress*, current issues of the *Claremore Messenger*, and several coins.

Besides Claremore Regional Hospital and the United States Indian Hospital, Claremore at one time had two other hospitals. The first, Claremore General Hospital, was directed by Dr. Ralph C. Meloy and was located on Main Street. The other hospital was the Franklin Hospital. Both buildings still stand.

There were almost more general merchandise stores in early Claremore than there are today. Early stores included, but were not limited to, the Haas Department Store, the Boston Store, Walker Brothers Department Store, the New York 5 and 10¢ Store, the Globe, and Laderer-Davis Clothing Company. Several other specialty shops existed in Claremore, including furniture stores, grocery stores, jewelers, drugstores, and hardware stores, to name a few.

Most do not realize the entertainment opportunities that came to Claremore in the early days. In 1899, the Lemen Brothers' circus came to Claremore, drawing 5,000 curious onlookers to the town. At that time, Claremore itself had a population of less than 500.

An opera house was originally located at the site of Claremore Laundry. This would have been in the empty lot next to the current location of the Claremore Progress. John M. Bayless then built the Windsor Opera House in the early 1900s across from the Sequoyah Hotel.

Theaters in Claremore have been a longtime attraction. In 1909, the Lyric Theatre and the Pastime Theatres were known to be in existence. By 1918, the Electric Theatre, the Lyric, the Claremore Theatre, and the Yale Theatre were all in existence. The Electric Theatre claimed to be the only one that offered moving pictures only. Vaudeville acts came into Claremore to play at the other theaters. In later years the Yale, the Cadet, and the Palace were the three theaters in town.

Two newspapers operated in Claremore during the early 1900s, the *Claremore Messenger* and the *Claremore Progress*, both beginning before statehood. The *Messenger* operated through the 1940s, and the *Progress* remains today to give one the latest news around the town and county. A. L. Kates was the first editor of the *Progress*, and J. J. Sanders was first known editor of the *Messenger.*

Claremore continued to grow and at one time was larger in size and population than nearby Tulsa. In 1945, there were seven hotels on Main Street alone. The Main Street hotels included the B&R Hotel, the Berwick Hotel, the Mason Hotel, the Reed Hotel, the Sequoyah Hotel, the Will Rogers Hotel, and the New Worth Hotel. The Bungalow and the Wayne Hotels were also listed in Claremore in 1945.

The city had its own country club at the present-day location of Lowe's. The nearby road was named Country Club Road. Claremore also had a park called Perrier's Park. The park contained a large swimming pool and a baseball field. The Lincoln, Nebraska, Links trained in there. According to a baseball advertisement in the *Claremore Messenger,* "All Roads Lead to Claremore."

Sports have always played a large part in Claremore. The first baseball team was organized in 1912 and was originally named the Radium City League. Claremore's football field is named Lantow Field in honor of former players Robert and Norman Lantow. The Lantow brothers were paratroopers who lost their lives during the Normandy and Holland invasions of 1944.

Citizens of Claremore are proud of their heritage. The hit Broadway musical *Oklahoma!* was based on Claremore and its people. The screenplay for this musical *Green Grow the Lilacs* was written by Claremore native Lynn Riggs. Many famous people have called Claremore home, including Will Rogers, Patti Page, and NASA astronaut Stuart Roosa. The town also had its share of outlaws, including bootleggers, car thieves, murderers, and the famous outlaw Belle Starr.

Claremore's population has always been a mixture of Native American, Caucasian, and African American. As with many towns during the early years, tensions between the races were strained to say the least. Claremore was literally divided by the railroad tracks. The west side was considered "the wrong side of the tracks." There was also a section of town on the west side known as "colored town." This area had its own bathhouses, churches, and school. The Lincoln School building still stands but is used as school maintenance building. Things were very different during those days; one department store even required men and women to enter by separate doors.

Claremore has a very rich history that the authors are excited to share and preserve through this collection of over 200 historic postcards, pictures, and memorabilia. The city has seen many changes in the 100 years since statehood.

In researching this book, many hours have been spent physically looking at the architecture of Main Street in Claremore as well as buildings in other areas of town. Although a large portion of the buildings no longer exist as they once did, some are still recognizable. It is our hope that this book revives an interest in Claremore's historic districts before they are lost forever. Progress is a necessity of life; however, that progress must not destroy the past.

Perhaps Noel Kaho expressed Claremore best in his booklet *The Will Rogers Country*:

> They are the heights and depths of a group of people who have built and live in a place unlike any other in the whole world. It is filled with richness and true character. It is alive. And it looks upon the days of its international fame as a nobleman might remember his first youthful trip abroad. The accents are not upon the past but upon the future. It is old in name and being, but it is new in spirit. It looks very young to be so old; and quite grown up to be so young.

This is more than a pictorial history book. When reading it, a magnifying glass is a highly recommended tool. Things that are not seen at first glance are usually picked up if given a second or third look.

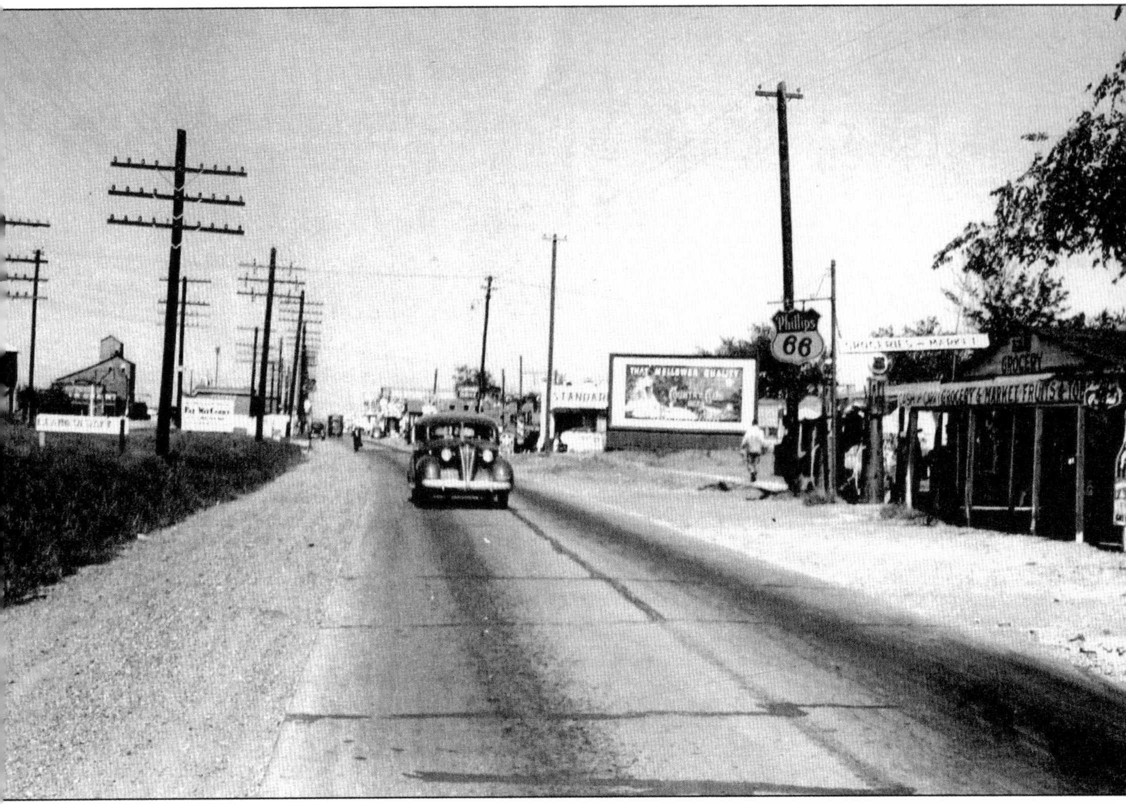


Historic Route 66 runs north to south through Claremore. This 1940s photograph is facing north. This portion of old Route 66 still exists; however, it has been renamed JM Davis Boulevard. A newer four-lane highway was built one block east to accommodate additional traffic. Businesses in this photograph include the Cash and Carry Grocery and Market and the Standard gas station. The Frisco depot can be seen on the left along with a feed and grain store.

# *One*

# Street Scenes

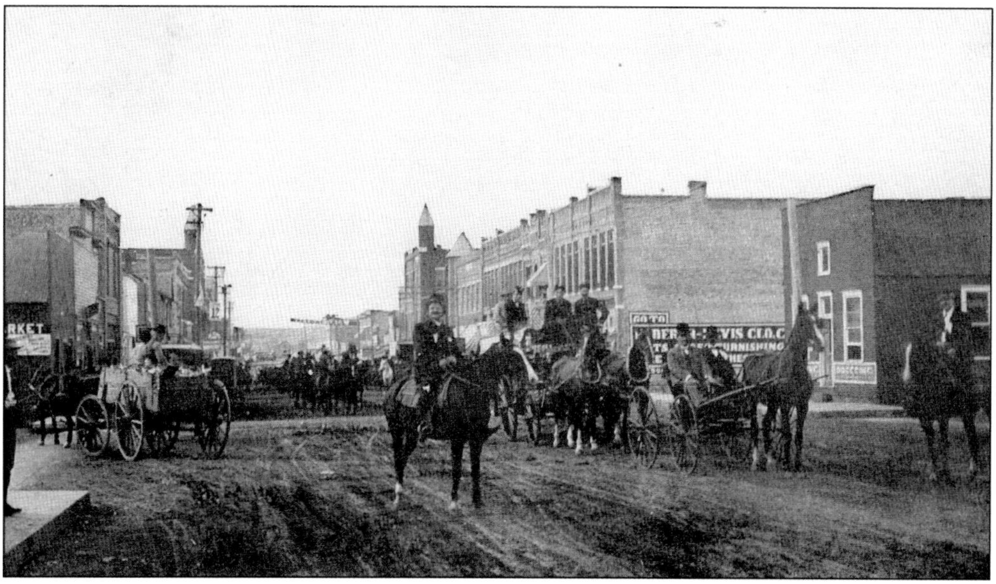

This parade is dated October 23, 1907, and took place in Claremore, Indian Territory. Take note of the Welcome banner in the background. The two tallest buildings in the photograph were built by John M. Bayless. The one on the left was the Sequoyah Hotel, and the one on the right was the opera house. The black building on the right at one time housed the Claremore Progress. The photograph was taken facing west toward what is now Rogers State University.

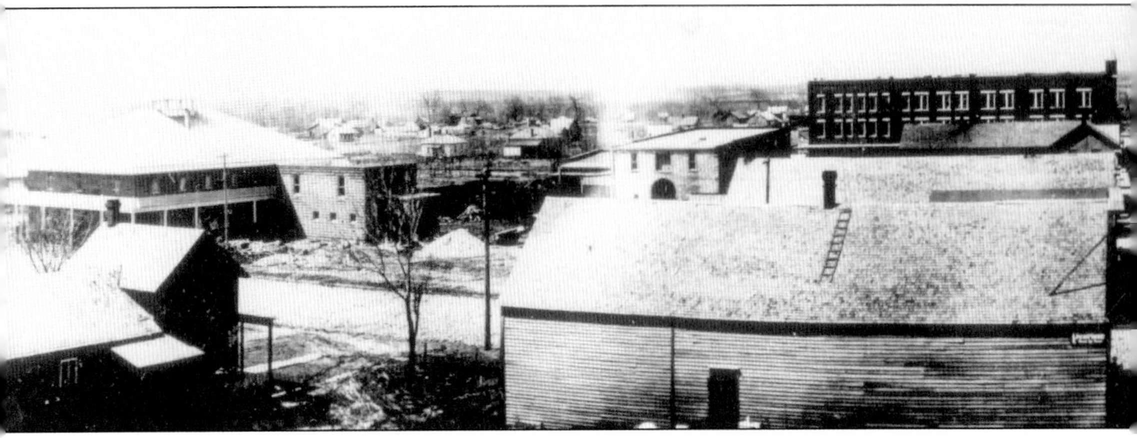

This photograph of Claremore, Indian Territory, was taken on March 26, 1906. This was just one year before Indian Territory became the state of Oklahoma. It was taken facing west. The long building in the background on the left was the Sequoyah Hotel. Across the street from the Sequoyah is a portion of the Windsor Opera House, built by John M. Bayless. The two-story building on the far left, with the balcony, was the Bungalow Bath House. During this time

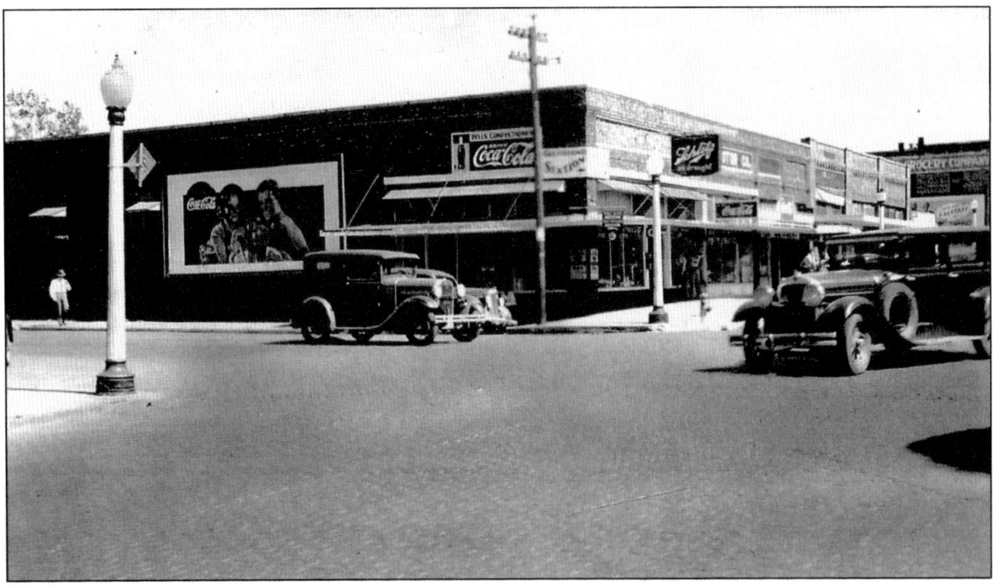


Brick streets, corner streetlamps, painted advertisements on buildings, and various businesses made up Claremore's Third Street, or Main Street in the 1920s. The building on the corner with the Coca-Cola sign was Bell's Confectionary, located at 322 Third Street. Bell's was a soda fountain and popular gathering spot for youth. According to the sign on the building, it was also the Greyhound station during that time period. Nell's Café can be seen toward the middle of the block. Nell's was later sold and has been home to Dot's Café for many years. The taller building in the background was a grocery company, later home to Ward's Rooms.

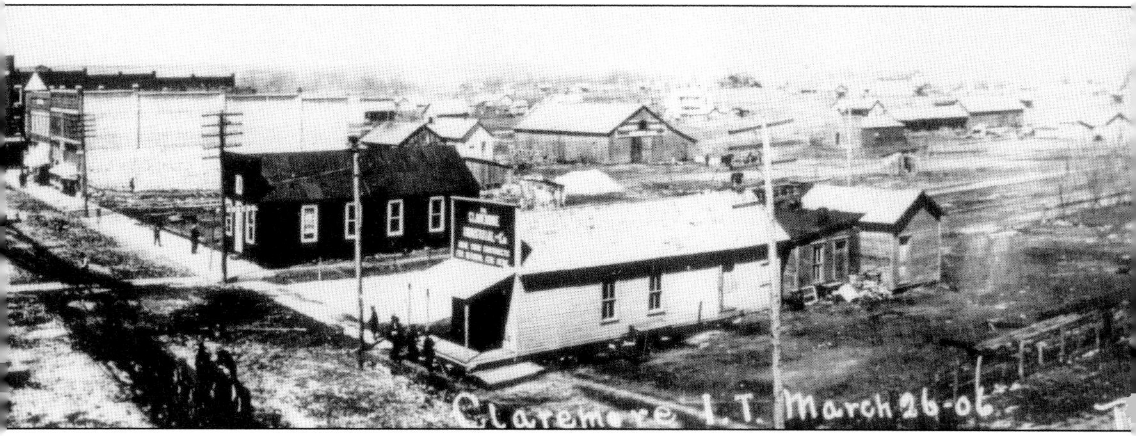

period, Clem Rogers, father of Will, was advocating for Oklahoma statehood, John M. Bayless and George Washington Eaton were the foremost builders in town, and radium bathhouses were the main attraction. Two weekly newspapers served Claremore at this time, the *Claremore Progress* and the *Claremore Messenger.*

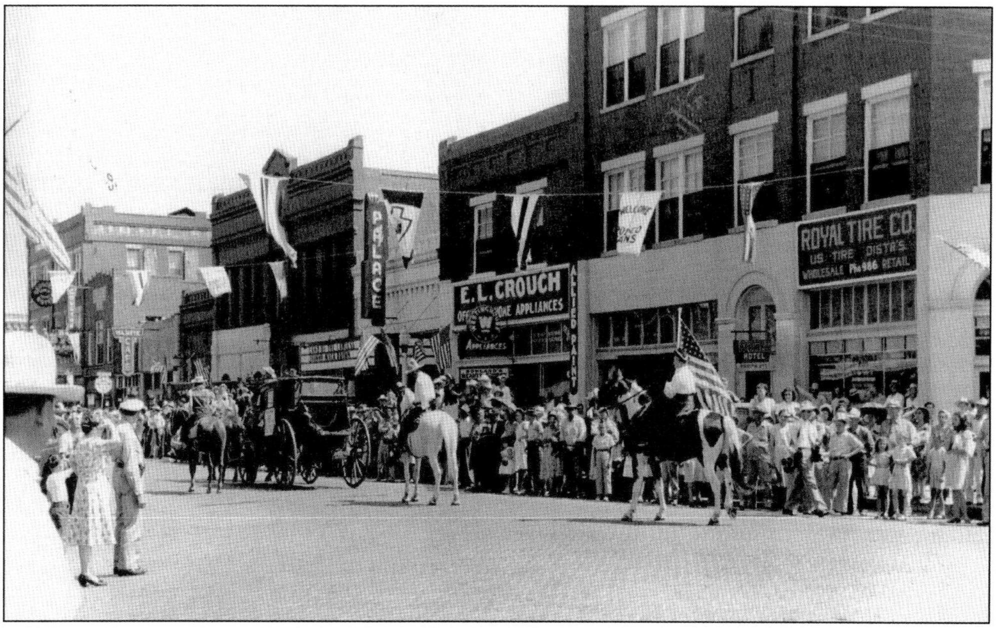

Claremore citizens turn out for all types of parades. This rodeo parade was held in 1947. The photograph is of the south side of the 500 block of Third Street, commonly known as Main Street. The first building, Royal Tire Company, was also once home to the Odd Fellows hall. Heading east down the street are the following businesses: the Berwick Hotel, Allied Paint, E. L. Crouch Office and Home Appliances, Rowland's Beauty Shoppe, the Palace Theatre, Majestic Cafe, Collins Drug Store, and the Sequoyah Hotel. An interesting note is that the spire of the Sequoyah has been removed. Showing at the Palace is *Land of the Lawless*, starring Johnny Mack Brown.

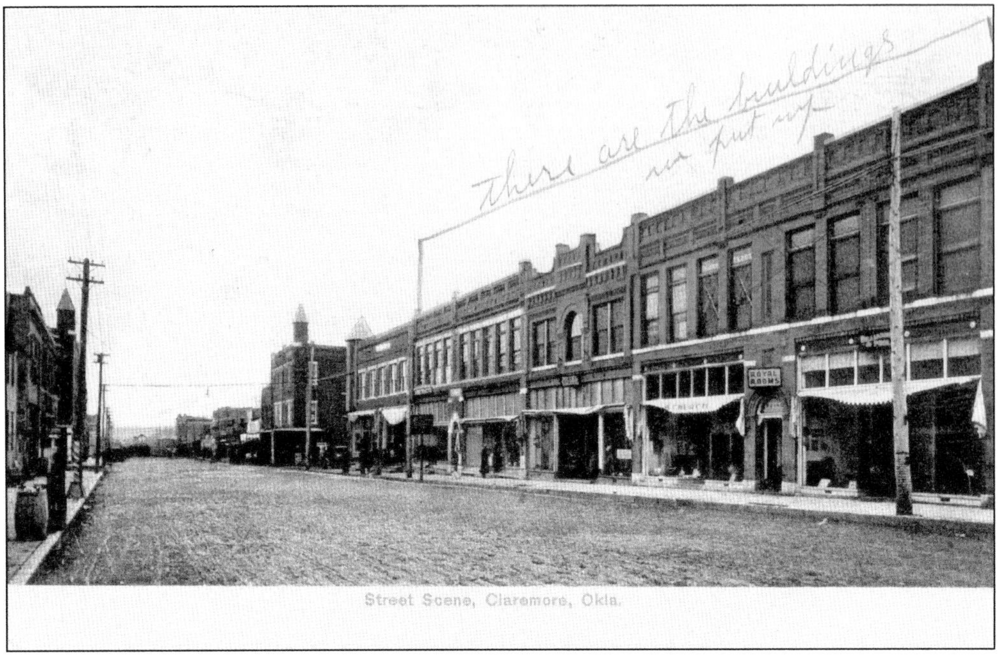


These postcards show the middle block of Third Street, also known as Main Street, as it appeared in 1908. Both views were taken toward the west. Close examination of the postcards reveal an M. B. Church department store, an abstract office, Royal Rooms, and a billiards and pool establishment. The building with the oval window was also a hotel; the upper level of this building no longer exists, although the other buildings remain.

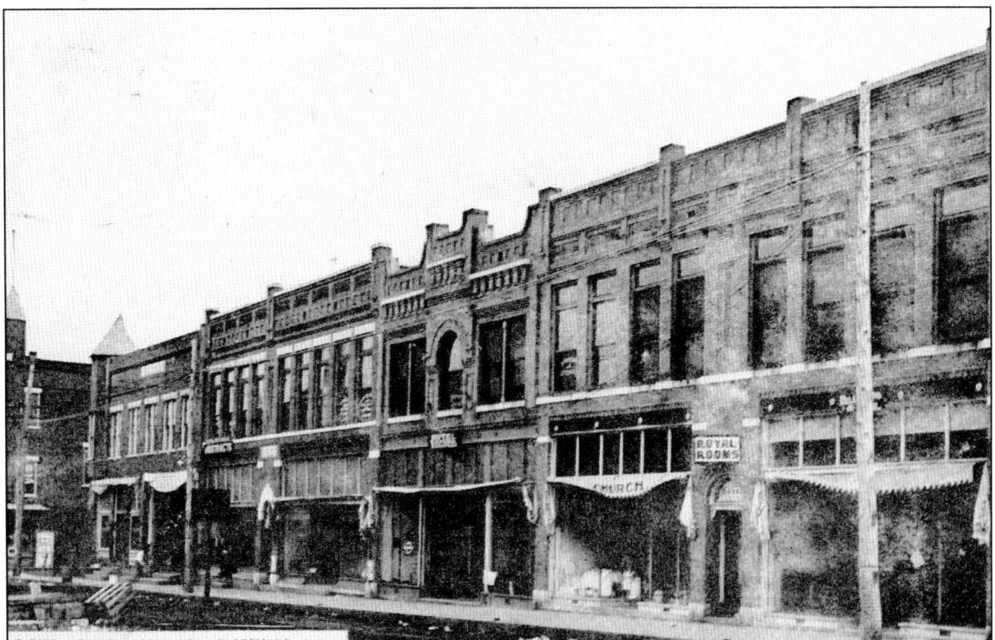

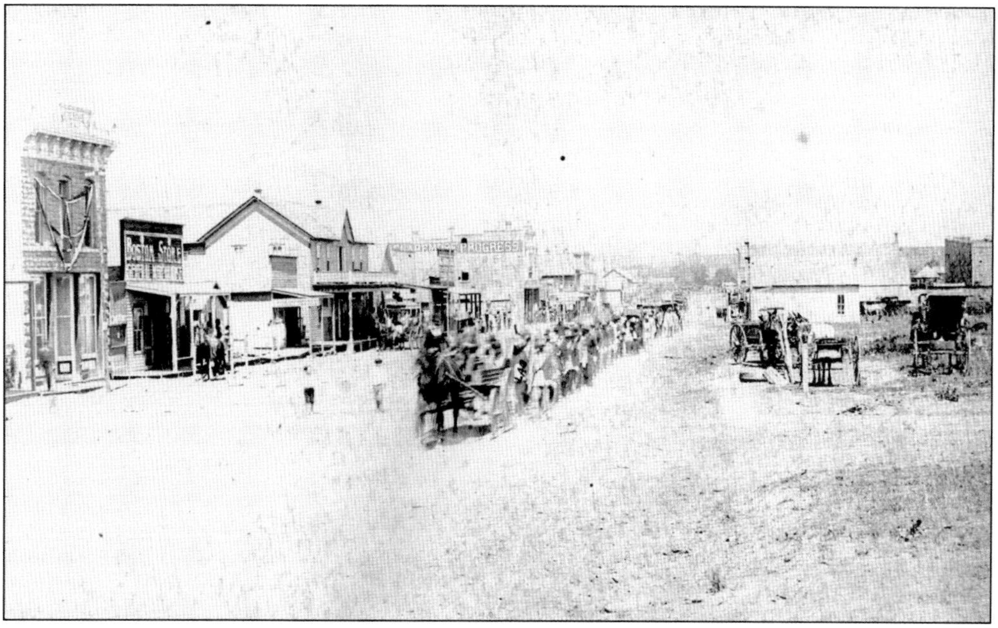

Seen here is the funeral procession of James Musgrove on June 5, 1895, in Claremore, Indian Territory. On the left in the background can be seen the City Drug Store, which also housed the Claremore Progress. This was located in the first block of Main Street where RCB Bank is today. In the foreground is the Boston Store, which sold general merchandise. Both the City Drug Store and the Boston Store continued to operate in the 1900s.

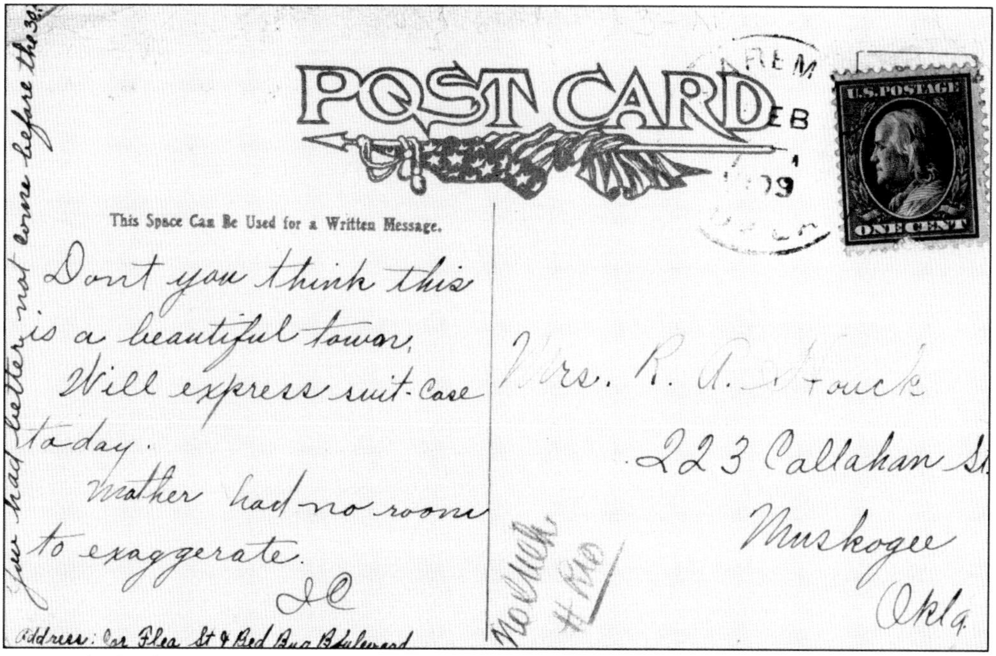


Postmarked February 1909, this postcard was mailed to Mrs. R. A. Houck in Muskogee. It reads, "Don't you think this is a beautiful town. Will express suit-case today. Mother had no room to exaggerate. You had better not come before the 30th." The author must have had a sense of humor as he or she noted the address as "Flea St. & Bed Bug Boulevard."

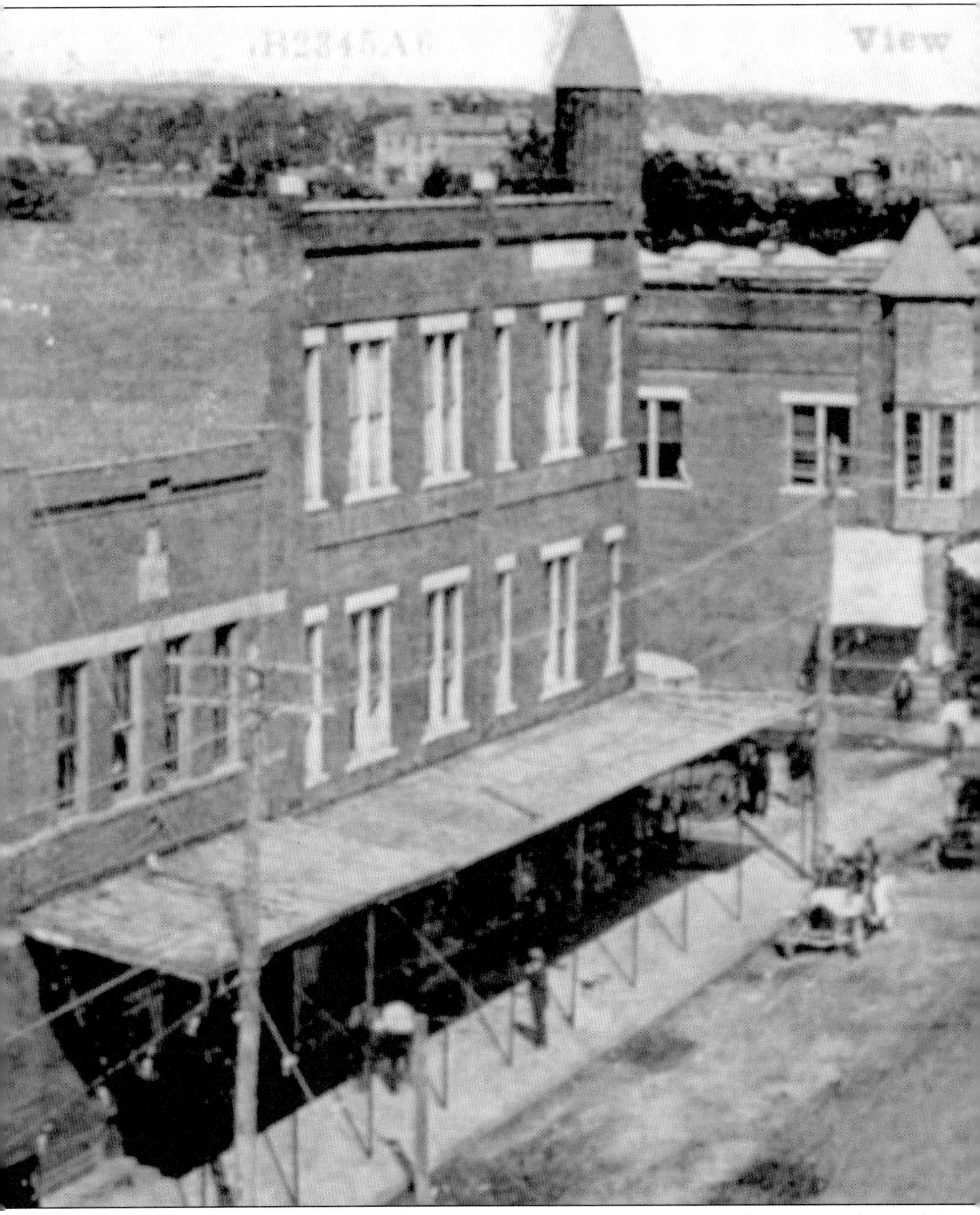

This view of Third Street, more commonly known as Main Street, faces east. The card is postmarked 1910. The photograph for the card is believed to have been taken from the top of the Odd Fellows hall. In the foreground, the first building on the left housed the first Masonic lodge. Next to the Masonic lodge was the Windsor Opera House built by John M. Bayless. Missouri Street separated the opera house from the Eaton building. The Sequoyah Hotel is the

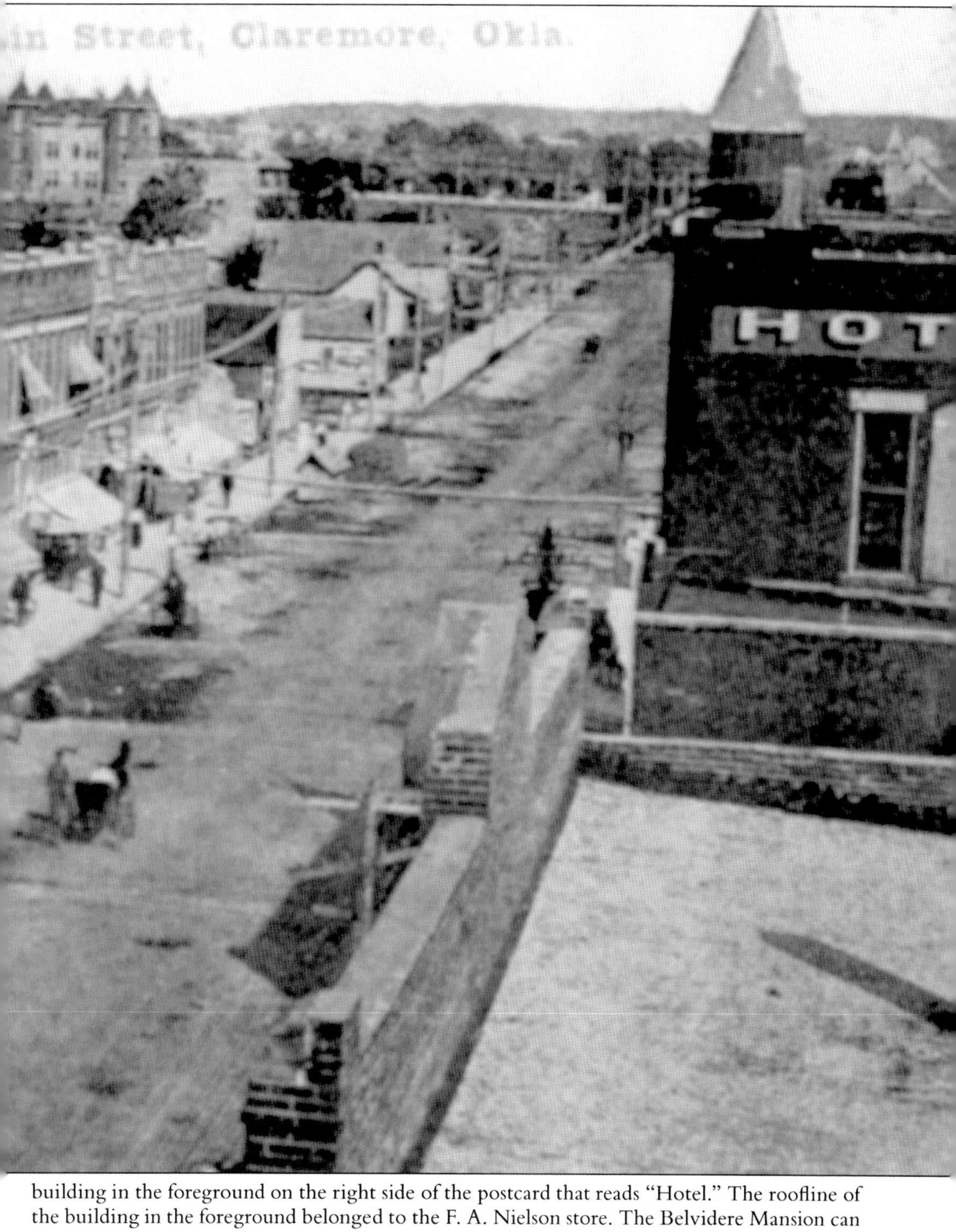


building in the foreground on the right side of the postcard that reads "Hotel." The roofline of the building in the foreground belonged to the F. A. Nielson store. The Belvidere Mansion can be seen prominently in the background. The steeple of First Baptist Church can be seen in the distance behind the Sequoyah Hotel. The rock building beside the Belvidere is the Presbyterian church. To the left of the Windsor Opera House spire is the Hiawatha School.

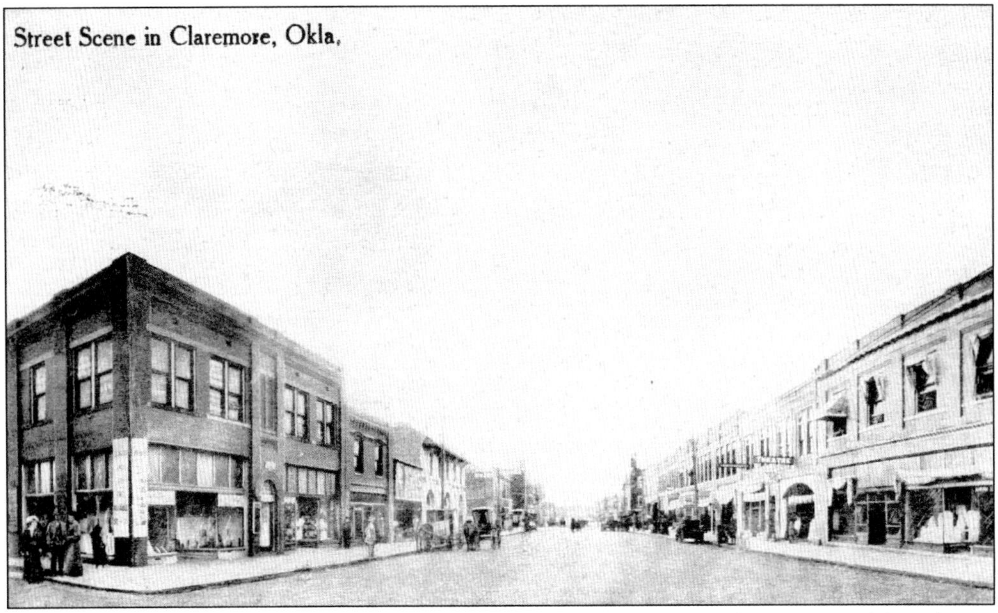


This view of Third Street, more commonly known as Main Street, faces west. Although it is hard to tell what some of these buildings housed during this time period, some structures can be recognized by the architecture. The building in the foreground on the left was Claremore's first hospital, established by Dr. Ralph C. Meloy. It currently houses Ann's Cleaners. The second building on that side currently houses a bakery. It is said the original business was also a bakery, called Priest's Bakery. Also notice the theater across the street. This appears to have been the Lyric Theater.

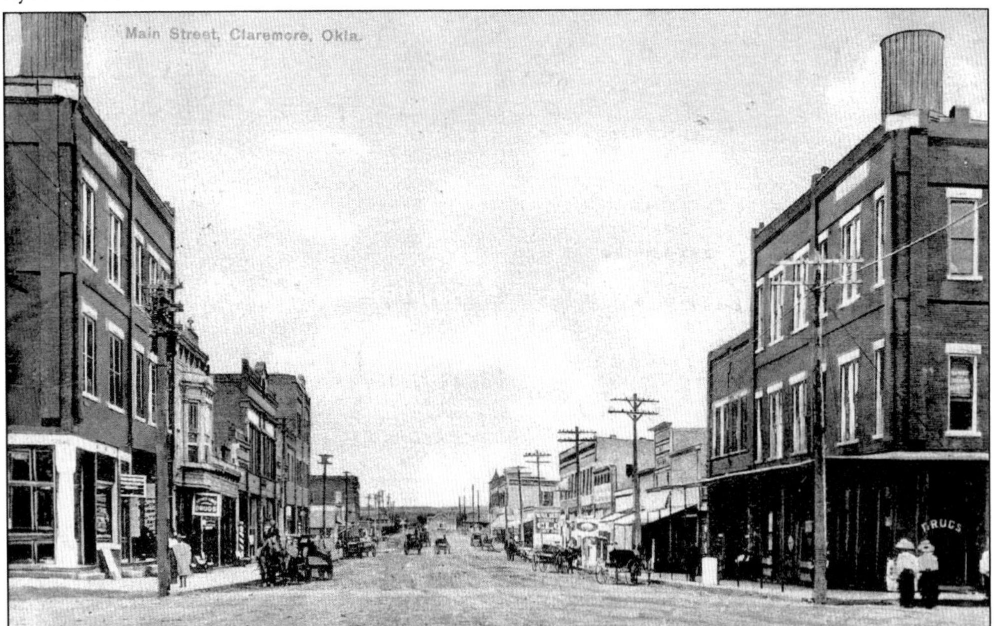


Claremore was a bustling and fast-growing town in the years surrounding statehood. People came from all over the nation to bathe in the healing mineral waters; this fact along with two major railroads crossing town caused Claremore to be larger than nearby Tulsa for a time.

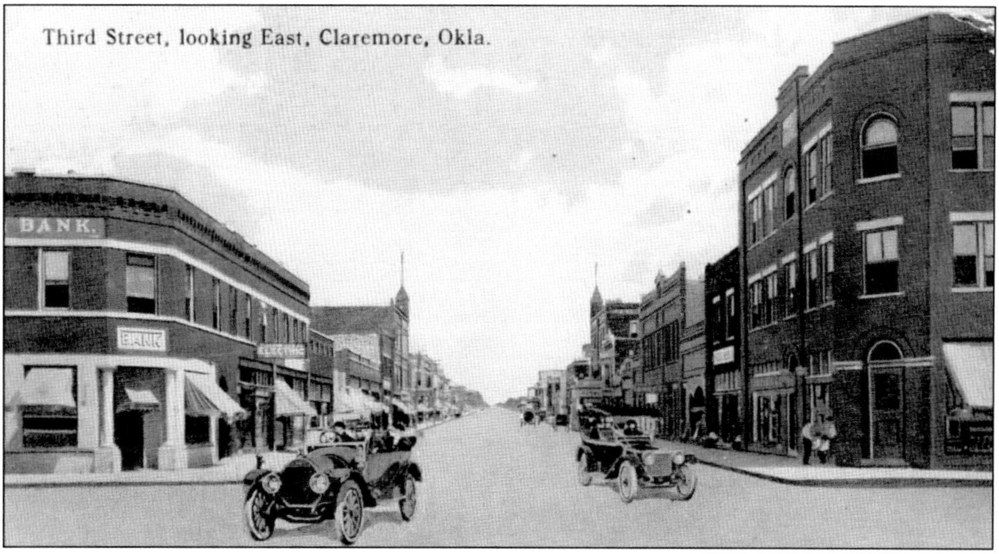


This rare view of Claremore pictures an area of town that for the most part no longer exists. The buildings have been torn down to make way for newer, more modern businesses. The photograph shows the first block of Third Street, commonly known as Main Street, as it appeared prior to 1930. The building in the foreground on the left was First National Bank built by Clem Rogers. It stood where the Will Rogers Hotel is today. The buildings on the right have all been razed. The large building on the right was originally the Odd Fellows hall. At the time of this postcard, Carleton Tire and Supply occupied the space. Other businesses in that block were the Palace Theater and the Berwick Hotel. RCB Bank occupies that block today. The spires of the Windsor Opera House and the Sequoyah Hotel can be seen in the background.

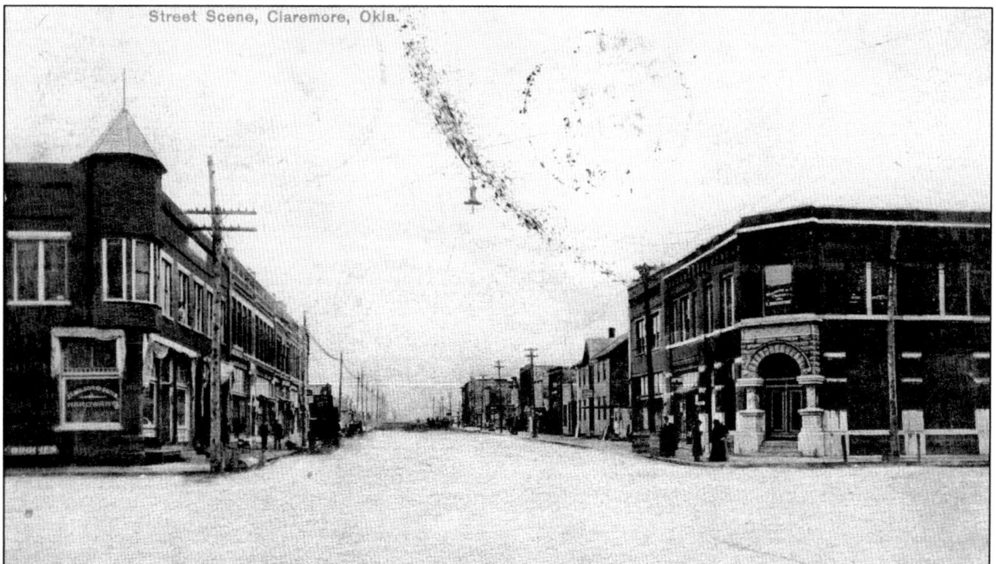


Looking east, the sun can be seen rising over Claremore's Third Street, also known as Main Street, in 1907. Store owners are getting ready for their busy day to follow. On the right, customers are seen waiting for the Farmers Bank to open for the day. The building on the left housed J. L. Wilson and Sons Hardware. Wilson's Hardware remained a fixture in Claremore until the family sold the business in 1985.

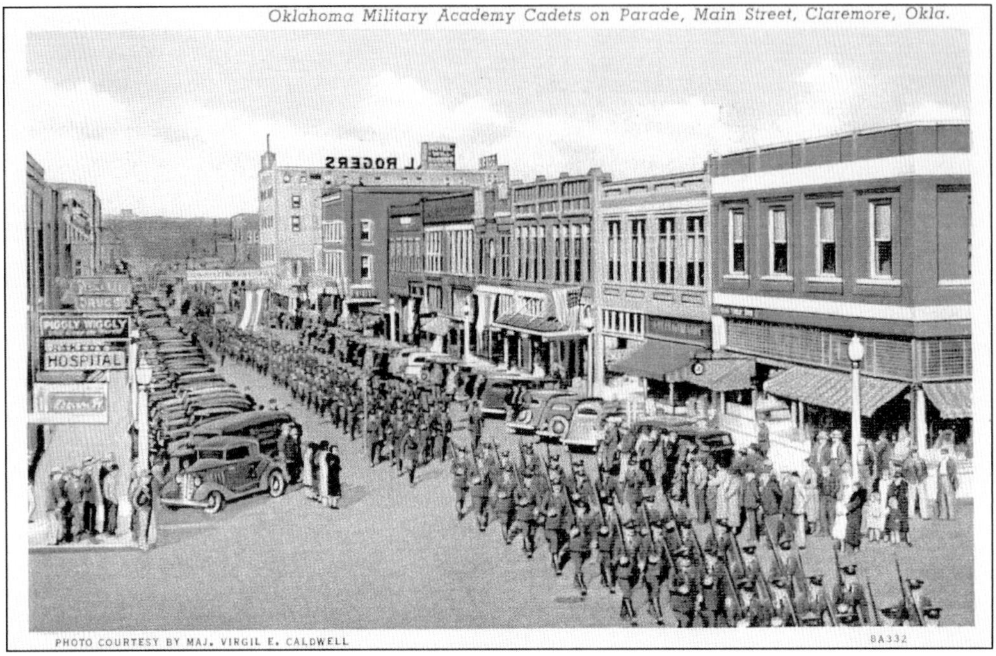


The cadets of Oklahoma Military Academy practiced their skills by marching through downtown Claremore every Saturday. This particular Saturday in 1940 was full of activity. The left side of the postcard reveals the hospital, Piggly Wiggly (grocery store), Rexall Drug, and a bakery.

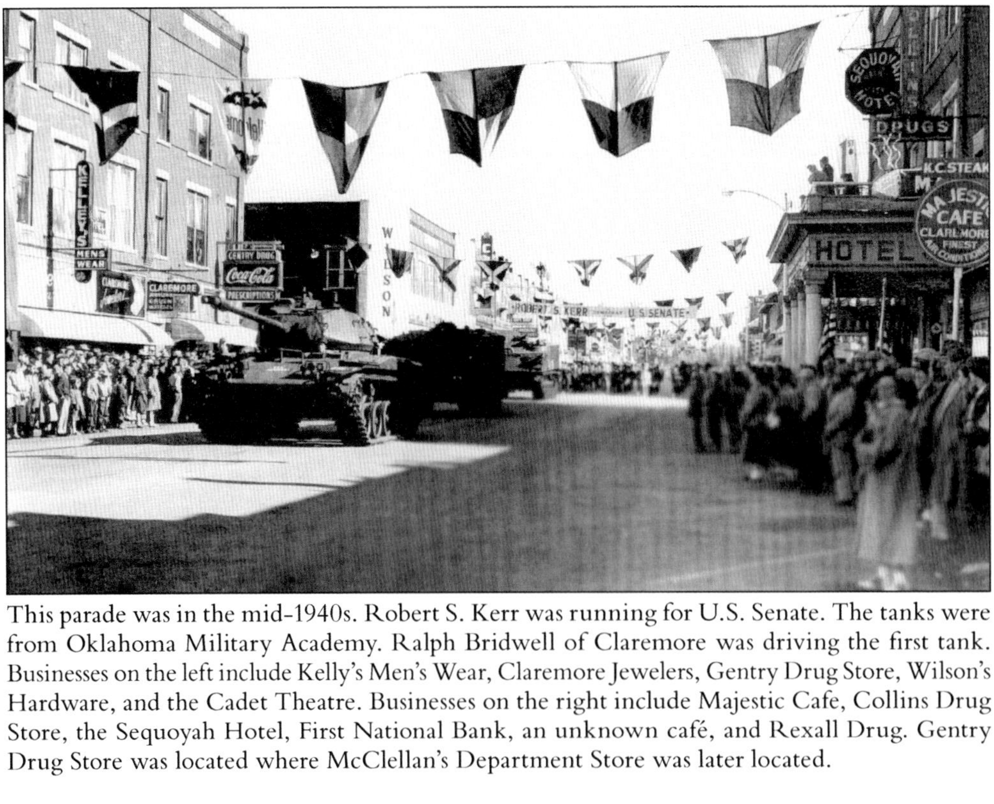


This parade was in the mid-1940s. Robert S. Kerr was running for U.S. Senate. The tanks were from Oklahoma Military Academy. Ralph Bridwell of Claremore was driving the first tank. Businesses on the left include Kelly's Men's Wear, Claremore Jewelers, Gentry Drug Store, Wilson's Hardware, and the Cadet Theatre. Businesses on the right include Majestic Cafe, Collins Drug Store, the Sequoyah Hotel, First National Bank, an unknown café, and Rexall Drug. Gentry Drug Store was located where McClellan's Department Store was later located.

# *Two*

# Businesses, Hotels, and Residences

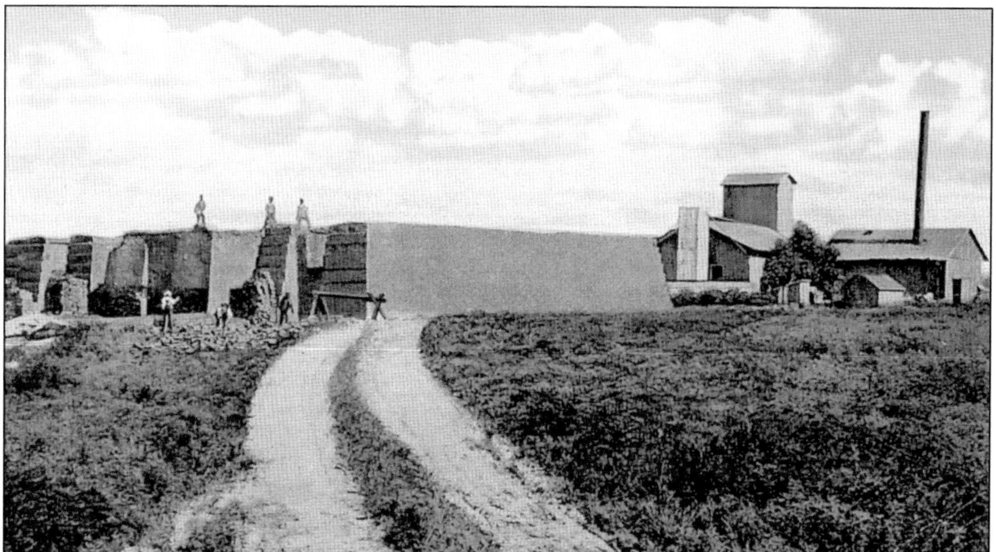

The Howard Brick and Tile Plant was located on what today is West Blue Starr Drive, near Hydro Hoist. The brick plant was once Claremore's most important industrial concern. In 1910, the plant closed for several months but then reopened in February 1911 for a short time. No evidence of the brick plant remains today.

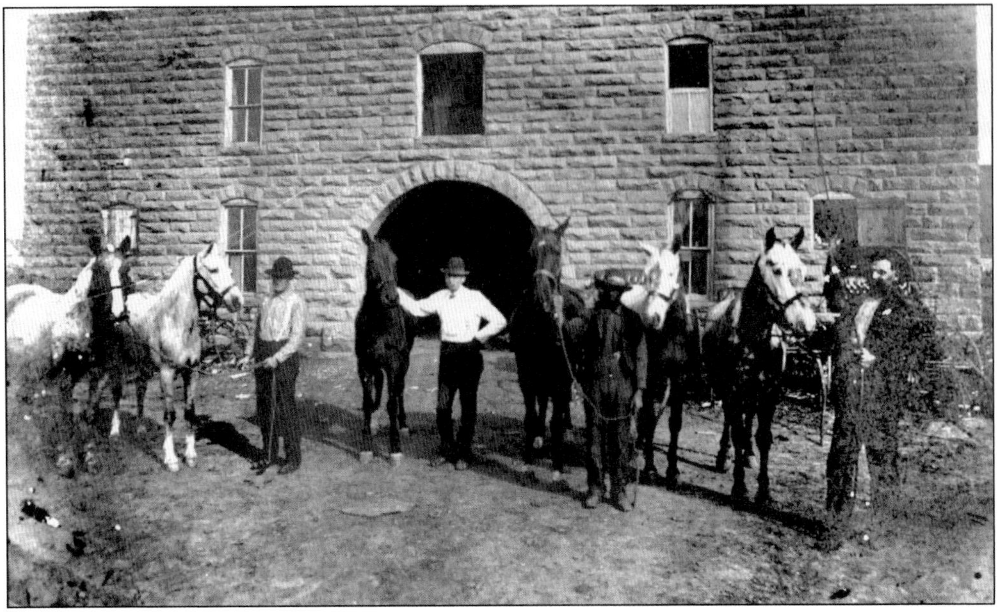

This livery stable, owned by Clem Rogers, was one of the earlier buildings in Claremore. The stable was located on Missouri Street between Will Rogers Boulevard and Patti Page Boulevard. The land was sold and a post office was built on that site (now the federal building) as well as the Yale Theatre. Several years later, a portion of the facade of the Yale fell, revealing the entrance to the old livery stable. The stable's original cornerstone was set into the old Claremore Library, which now houses the Lynn Riggs Memorial.

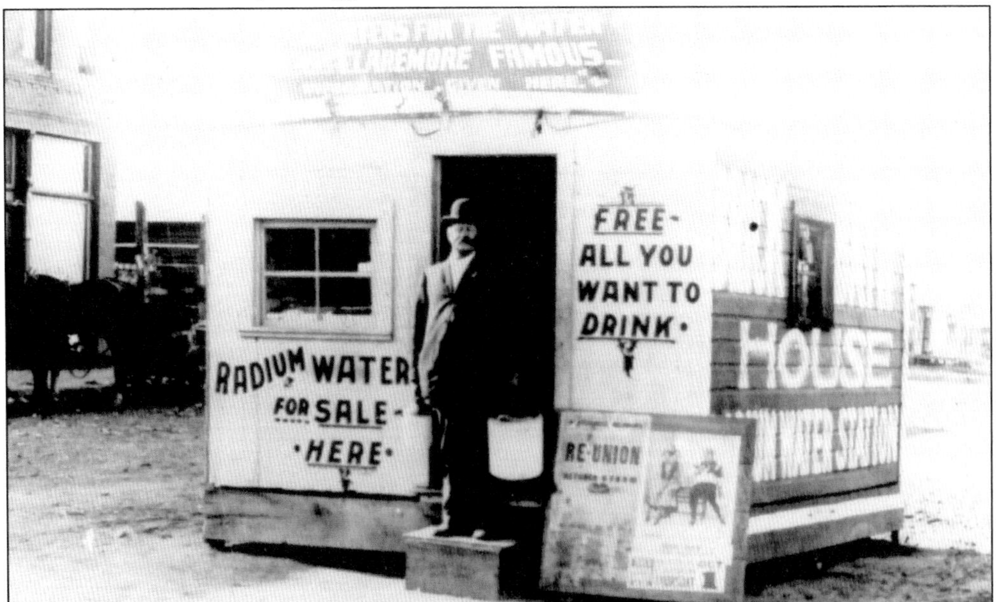


People went into business wherever possible in the early 1900s to sell Claremore's most precious commodity, radium water. This small makeshift building was set up in the middle of the street. The sign on top reads, "Headquarters for the Water That Made Claremore Famous. Information Given Here." The side of the building appears to read, "Brick Bath House Radium Water Station."

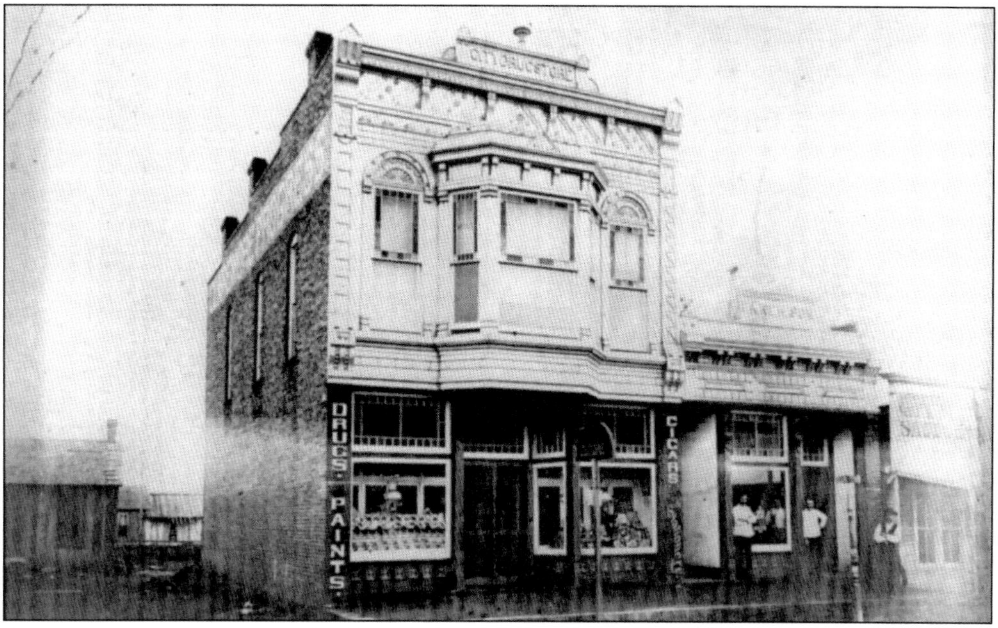


City Drug was a very ornate building located in the first block of Third Street, also known as Main Street, where RCB Bank is now located. The photograph was taken prior to 1906. The Claremore Progress was also housed in this building. The Sequoyah Hotel was eventually built just to the left of the building. On the right was F. A. Nielsons's Mercantile and then Campbell's Saddle and Harness Shop. The drugstore changed names over the years and was also known as Haynes and Davis Drug Store, the Owl Drug Store, and Collins Drug Store.

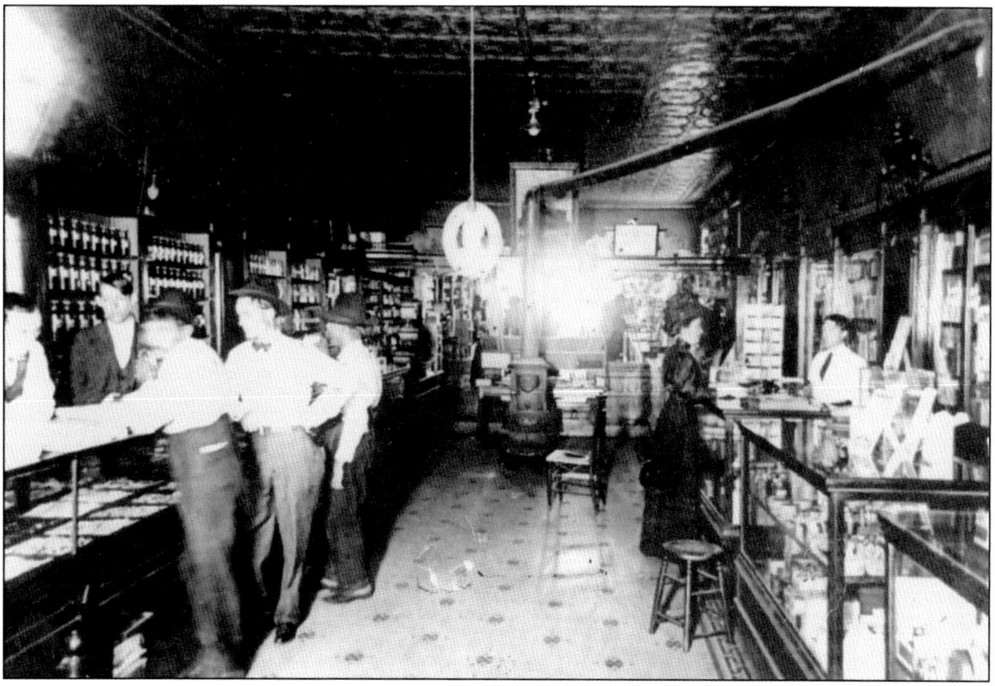

Pictured here is the interior of the above store after it became Collins Drug Store. This store became a popular gathering spot for people of the town.

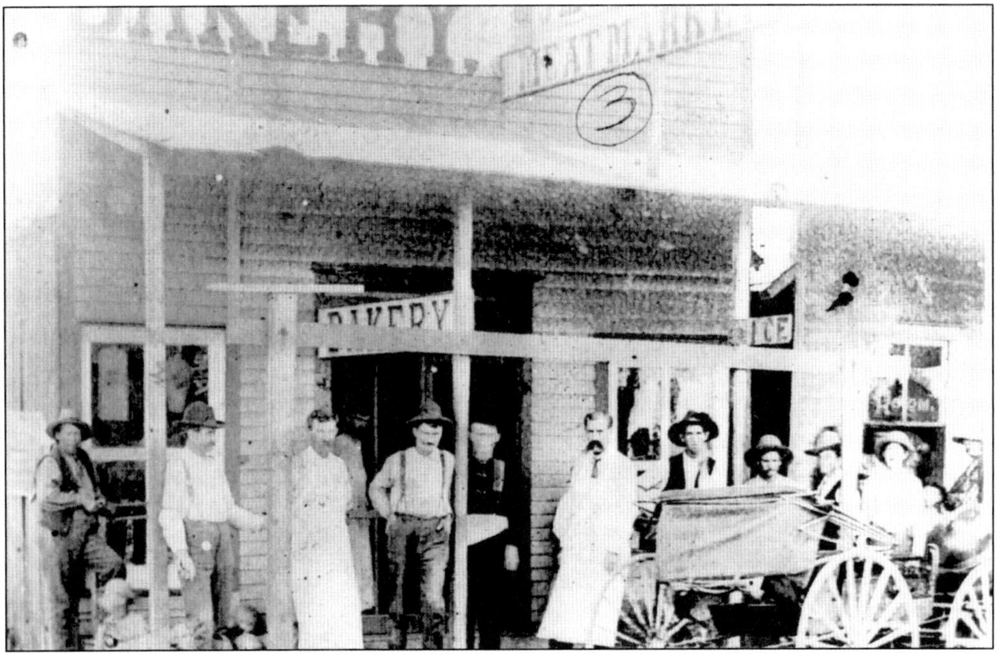


The name of this bakery is unknown. It was located next to Allton Meat Market. According to a sign in a window on the right, there appears to have been a boardinghouse next to the meat market.

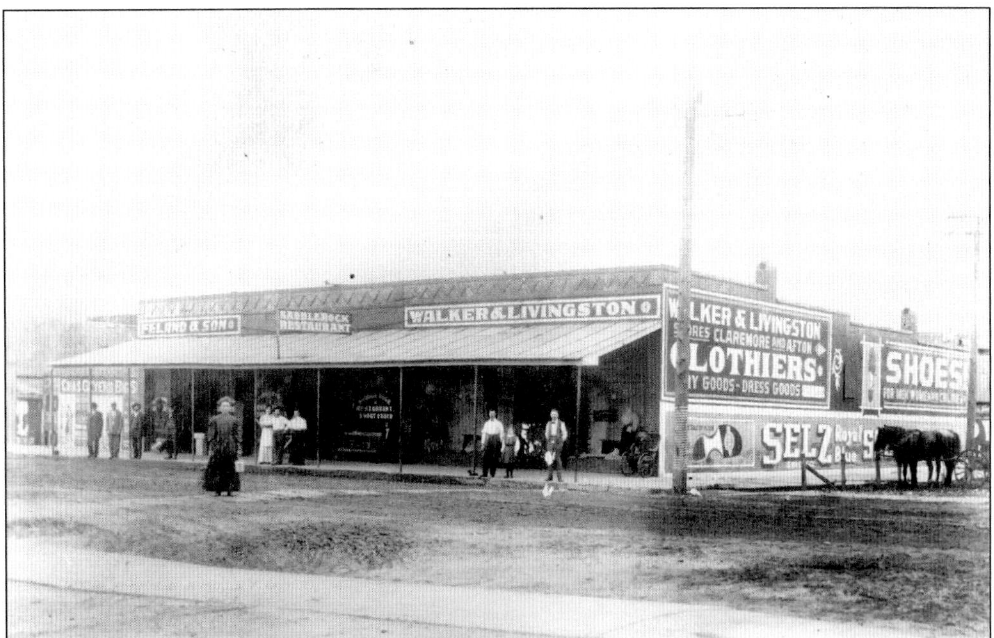


Walker and Livingston Clothiers sold dress goods and dry goods. It also advertised a complete line of Selz Shoes. Directly to the left of Walker and Livingston was the Saddlerock Restaurant and then Feland and Sons. The Hotel Elk was located west of these buildings. These buildings are believed to have existed in the 600 block of Third Street, commonly known as Main Street.

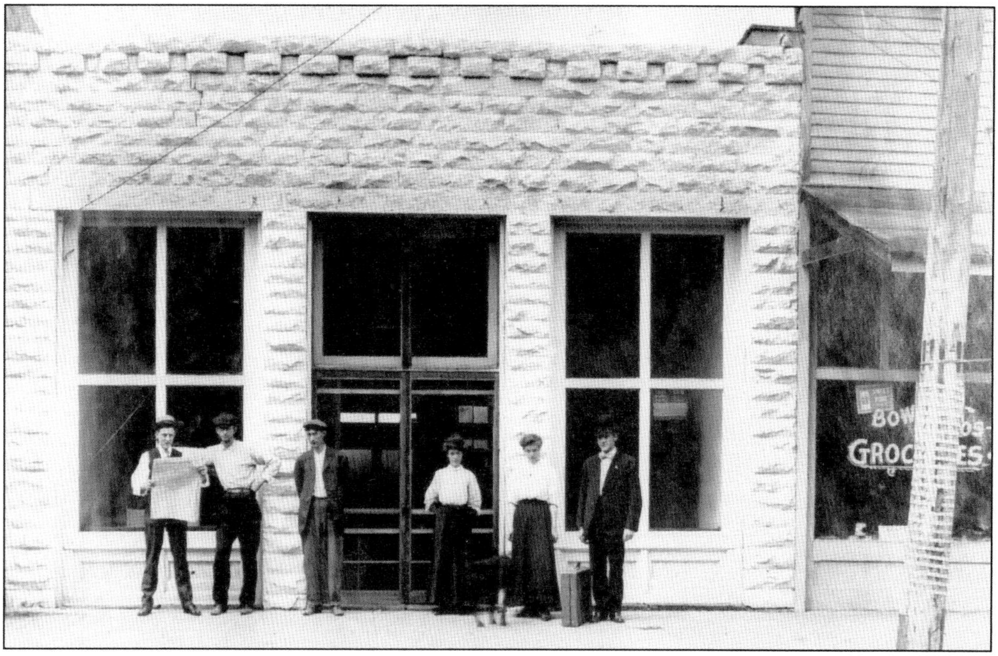

Bowers Grocery was located at 318 East Seventh Street. It was in operation prior to April 1945. It went out of business by June 1947.

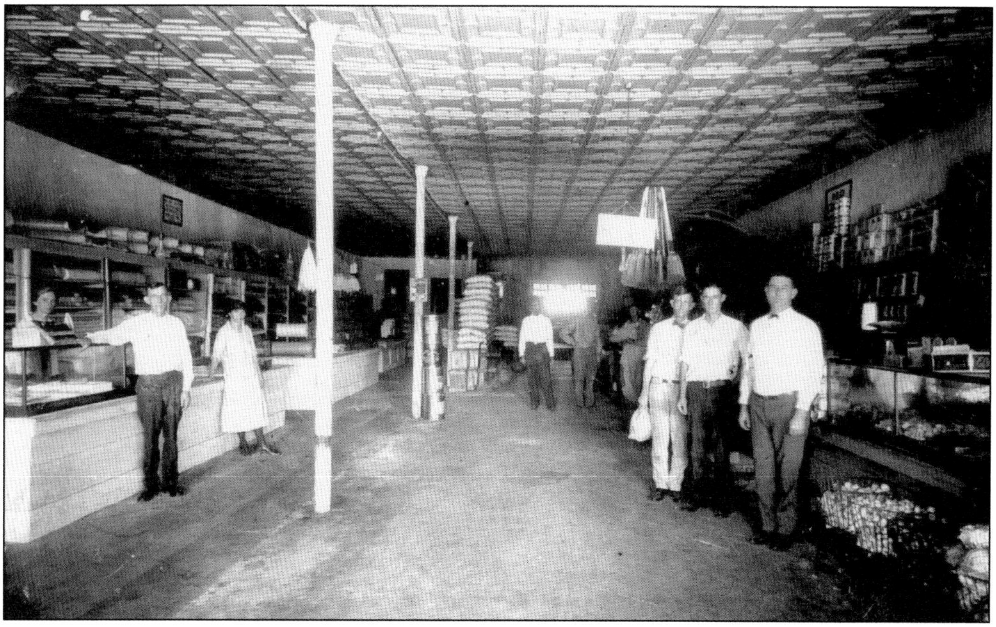

This interior view of Mouton and Stone's Grocery was taken in 1930. Jim Stone was the proprietor of this general merchandise and grocery store. A lady, known only as Mrs. Mason, is standing in front of the counter. She sold women's dresses. The store was located on Missouri Street, possibly in the present-day Rogers County Printing building. Missouri Street was at one time also known as Wall Street because the menfolk liked to sit on benches along the wall up and down the street. Ministers would stand at the corners of Third and Missouri Streets to preach the gospel.

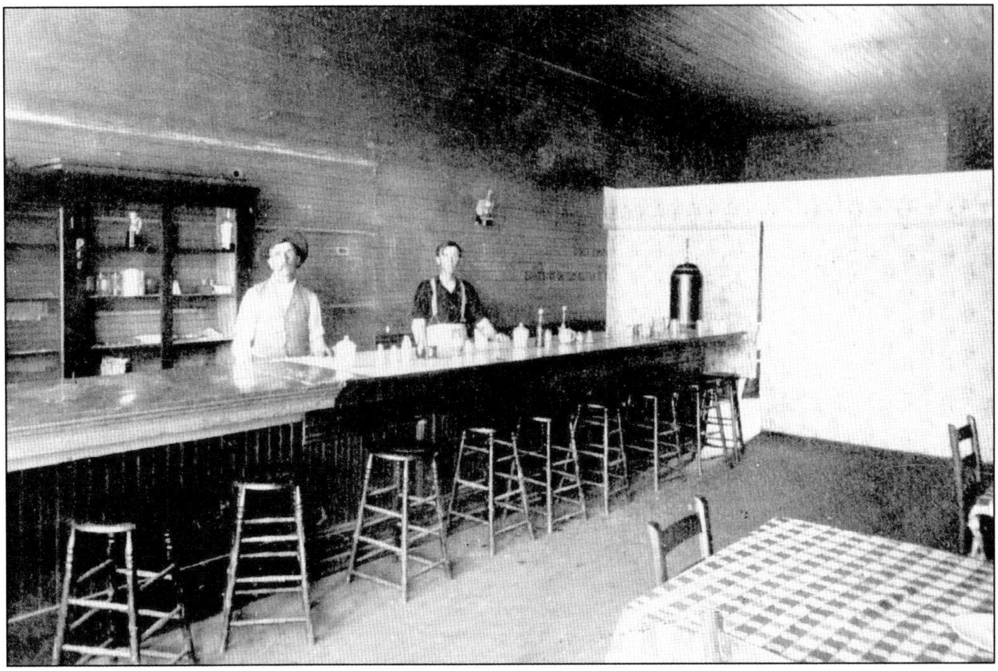

The Little Jewel Café was located across the street from the Mason Hotel. This picture of the interior was taken in 1893. Manager of the café was Richard Rose. The café was famous for "Uncle Dick's Chili."

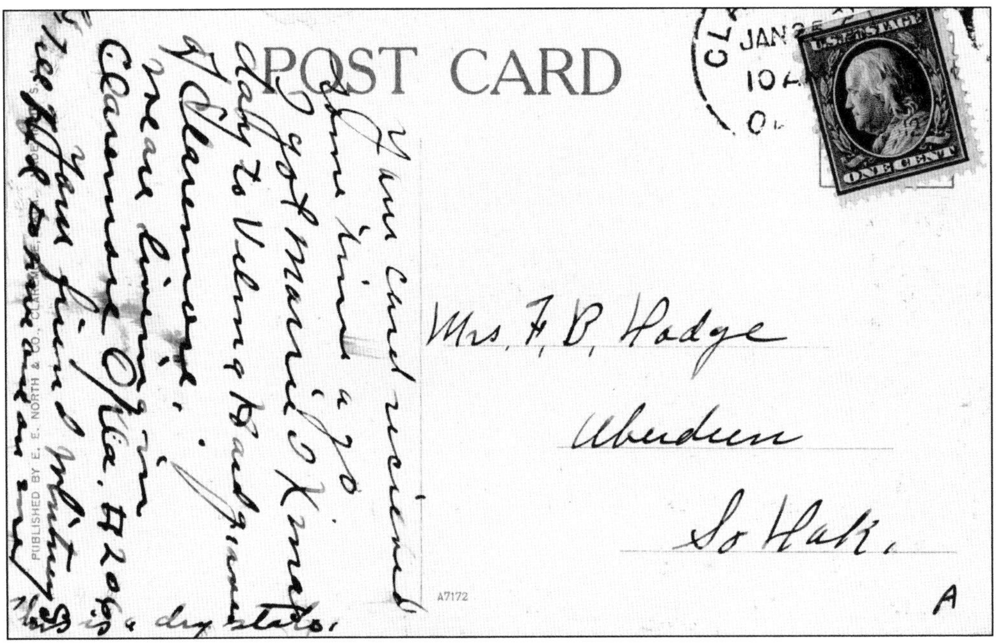


This humorous postcard was written to Mrs. F. B. Hodge in Aberdeen, South Dakota. It states, "Your card received some time ago. I got married Xmas day to Velma Hardgraves of Claremore. We are living in Claremore Okla. # 206. Your friend, Whitney. P.S. Tell Fred to have one on me. This is a dry state."

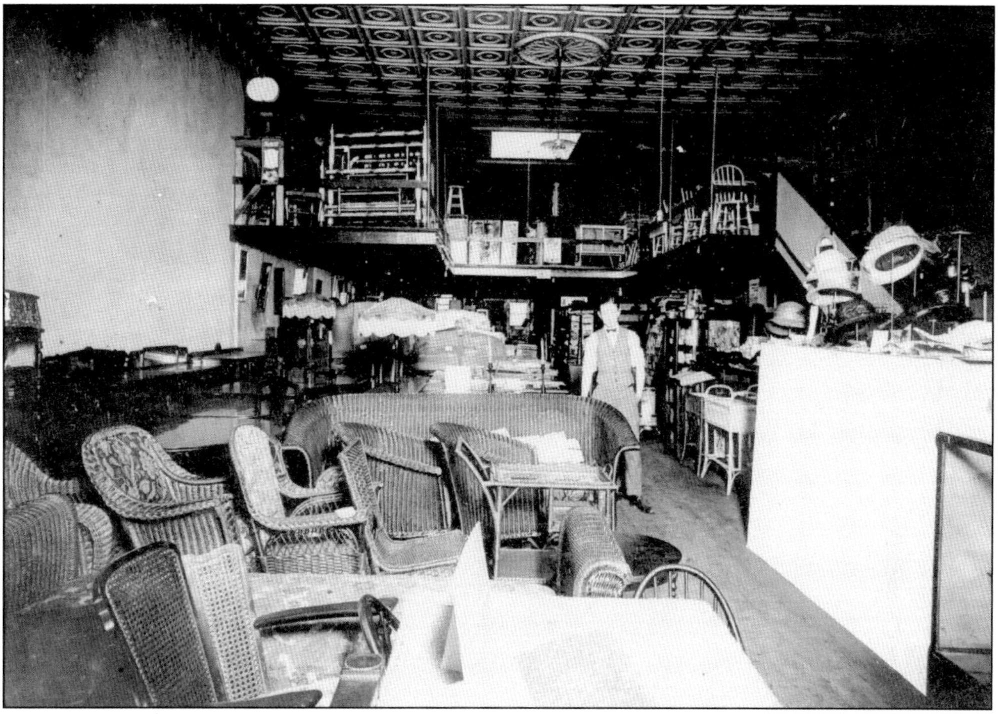

Seen here is an interior view of Nowlin-Feezell Furniture Company, located at 315 West Third Street. It was known to be in operation as early as 1918. By 1947, the store was apparently sold to Clark D. Mason, shown in the picture. The name of the store was changed to Mason Furniture. By May 1962, the store was again sold and the name changed to Smith Furniture and Appliance Company.

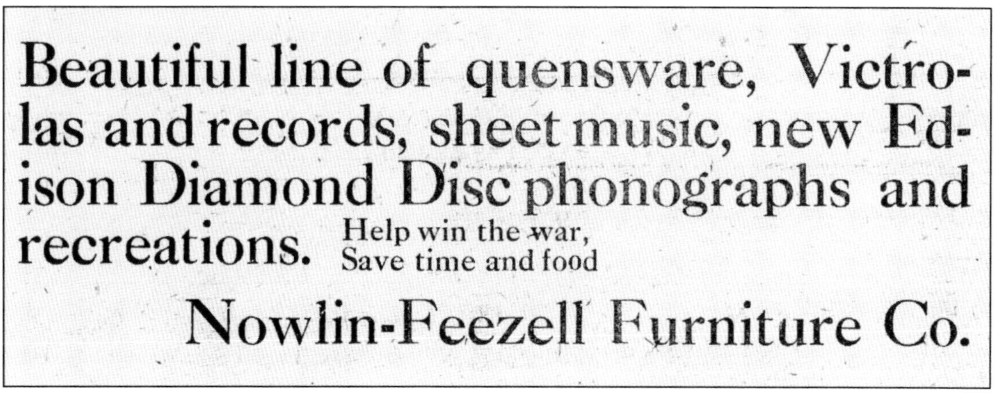

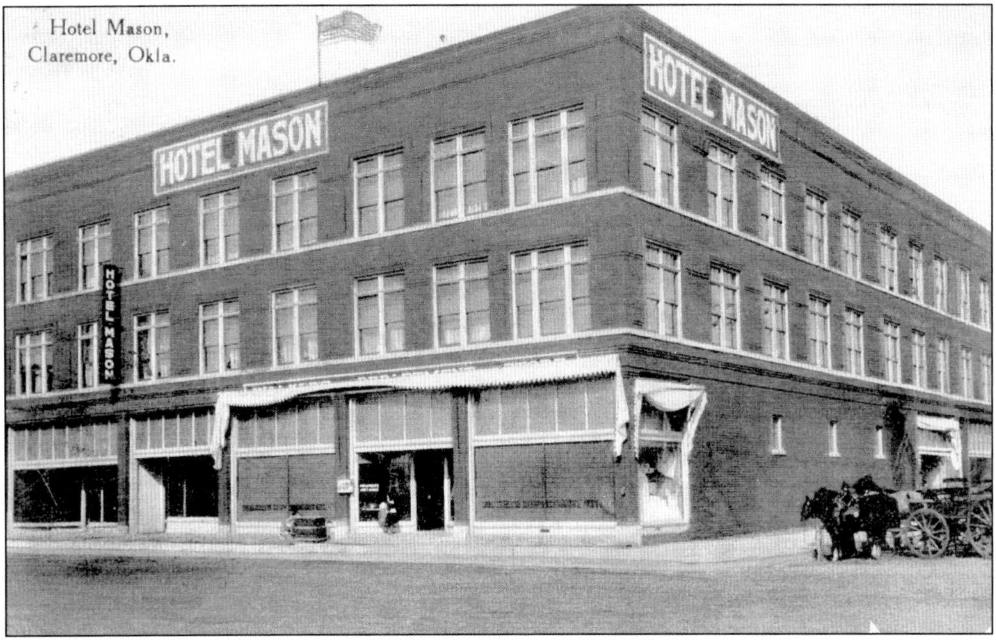


Walker's Department Store was located just west of the Will Rogers Hotel in the corner of the Mason Hotel building. The department store was out of business by 1947; however, the Walker brothers operated a furniture store in the back portion of the building for several years after that.

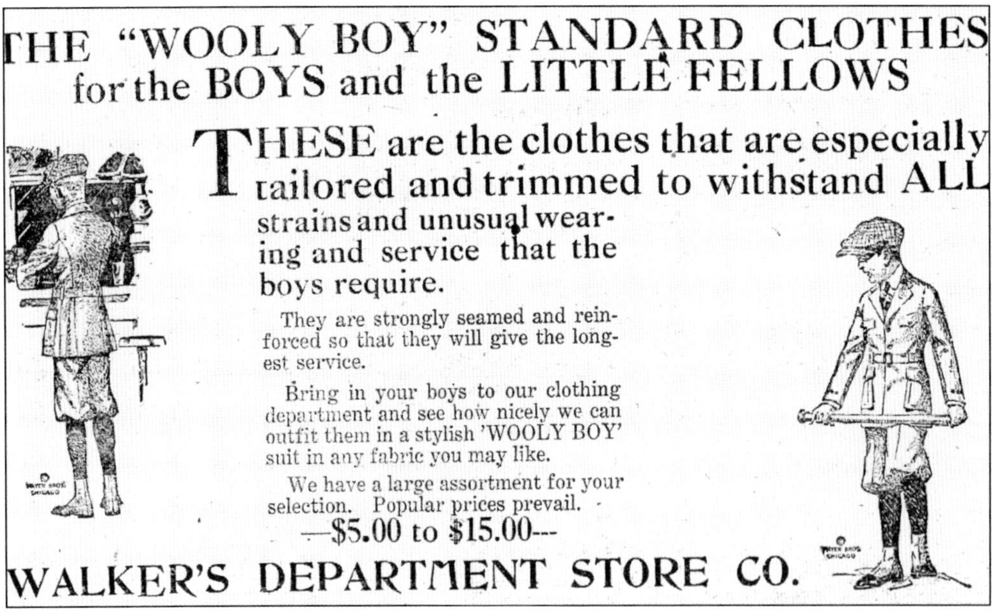

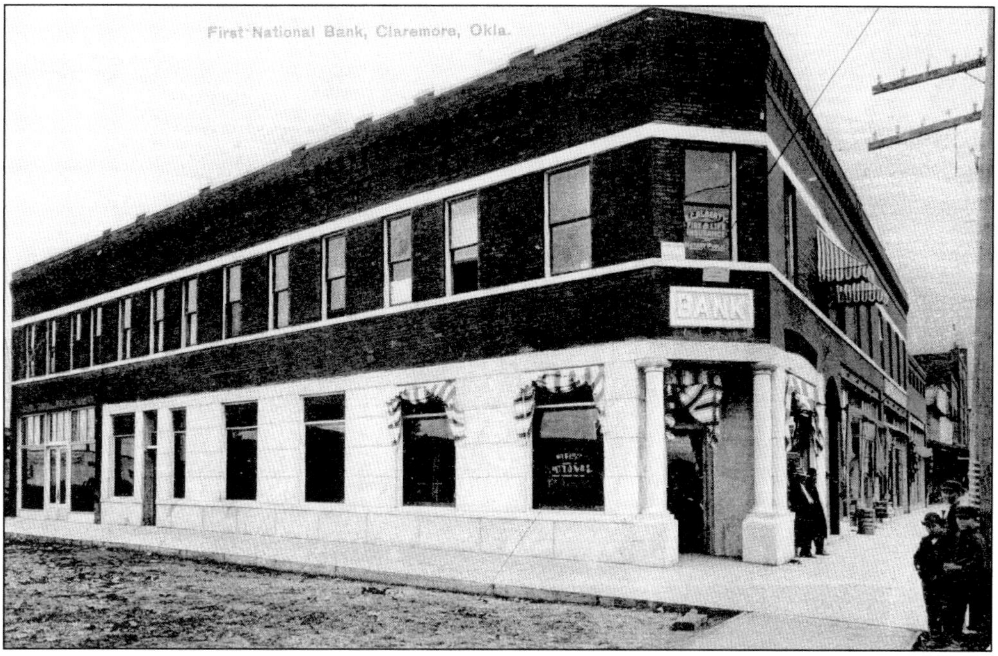


A few leading men with interests in the bank at Vinita contacted Clem Rogers and decided to create a branch of the bank at Vinita. The group first looked at sites in Chelsea, Wagoner, and Tulsa before deciding on Claremore. The bank was built on Main Street across from the St. Louis and San Francisco Railroad (also known as the Frisco Railroad) tracks. Rogers was named executive vice president, and Charl Godbey from the bank at Vinita became the cashier. The creation of the bank solidified Rogers's decision to move into town. He enjoyed sitting in the back room, or "board room," with his feet on the table, watching the people who passed the large window. The window above the bank reads "E. C. Alberty Fire & Life Insurance, Notary Public."

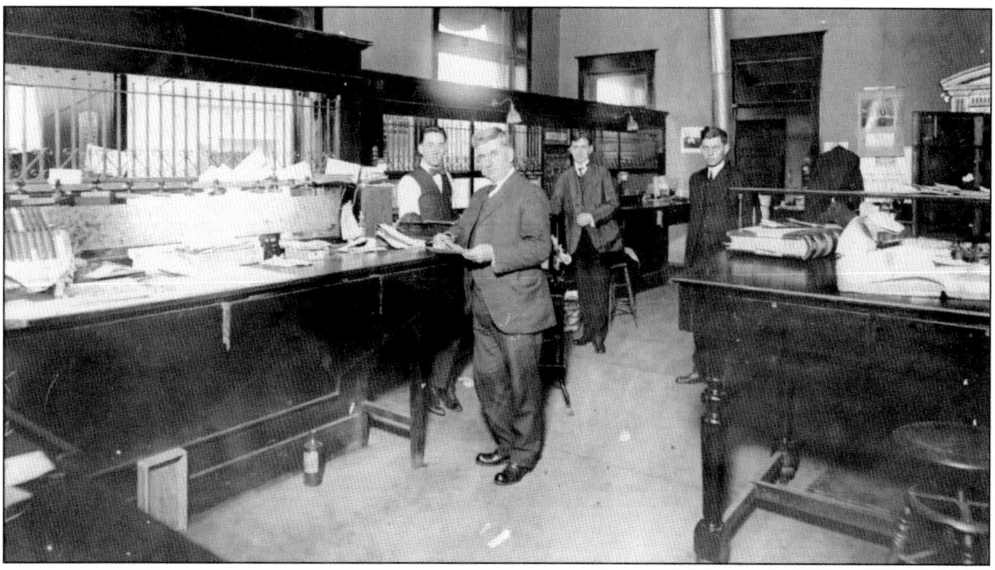

This is an interior view of the above First National Bank. Standing in the foreground in front of the counter is Charl Godbey, a bank cashier.

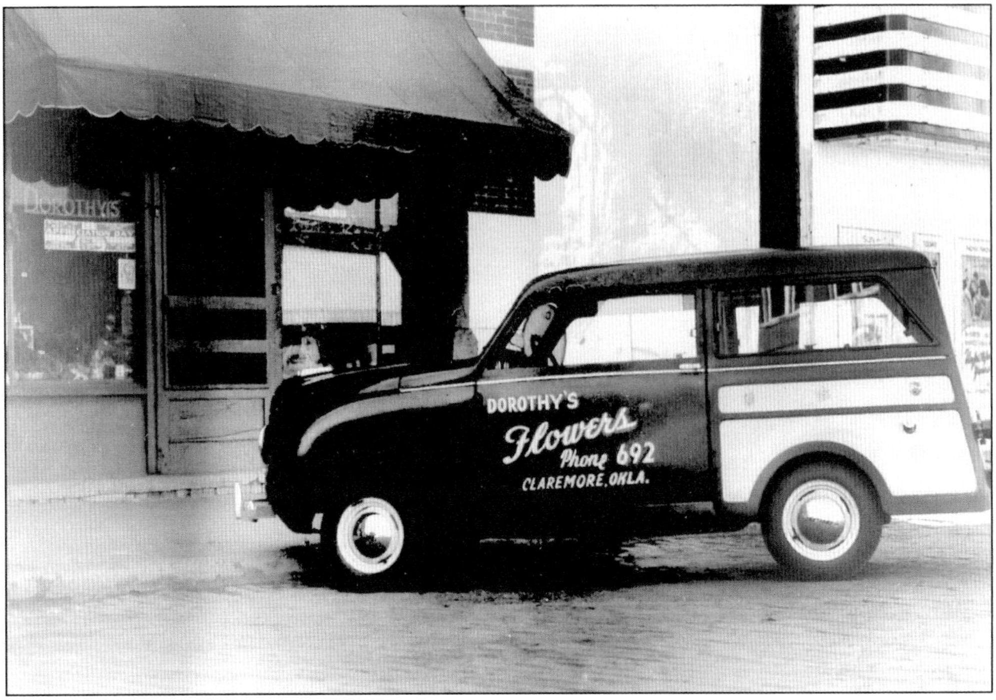


Dorothy's Flowers has been a longtime fixture in Claremore. The theater on the right was the Yale Theatre. Dorothy's Flowers and the Yale were both located on Missouri Street. Judging by the movie poster for *Unfaithfully Yours*, this photograph would have been taken in December 1948. The movie starred Rex Harrison.

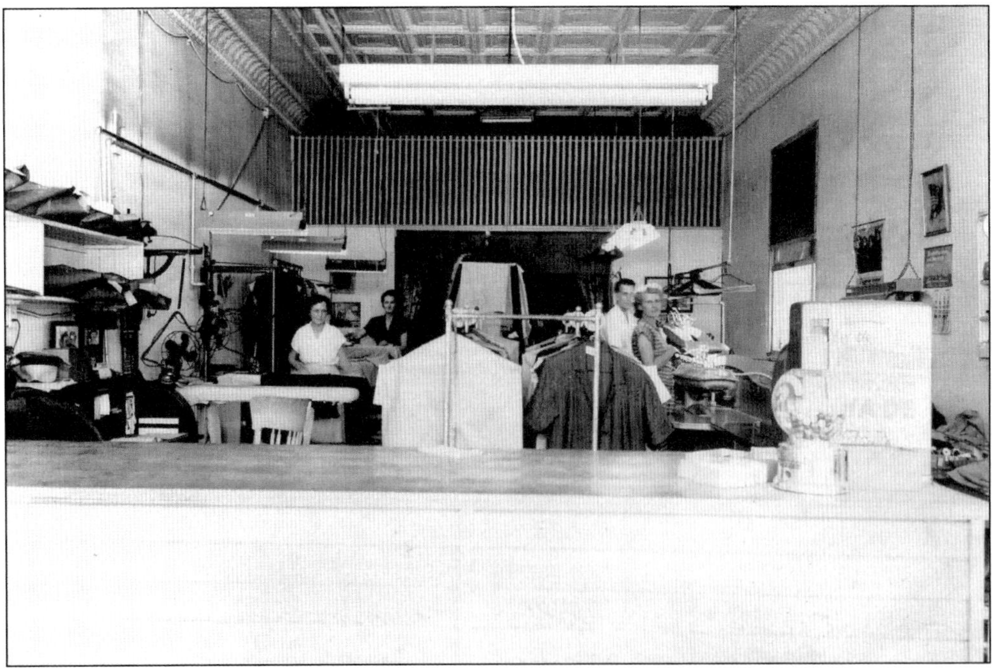

Streeter Cleaners was located at 300 West Third Street. It was in operation prior to April 1945. Although it is out of business today, it was still operating as of May 1964.

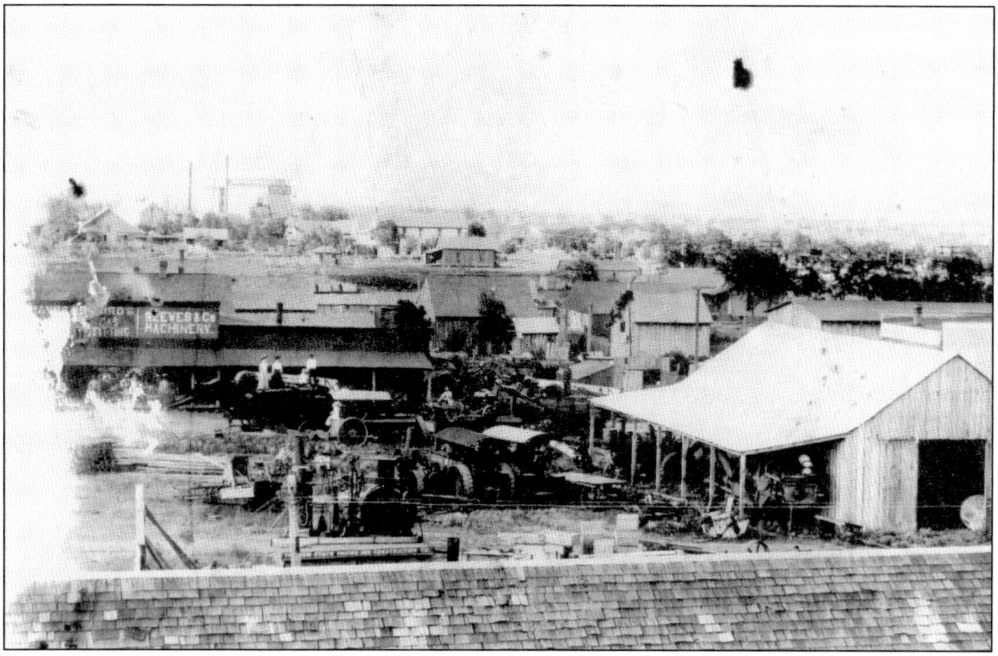


This machine shop was built in 1901 by John M. Mayberry and his brother Harvey. The Mayberrys put a cement floor in their original shop so they could take care of "gasoline hosses."

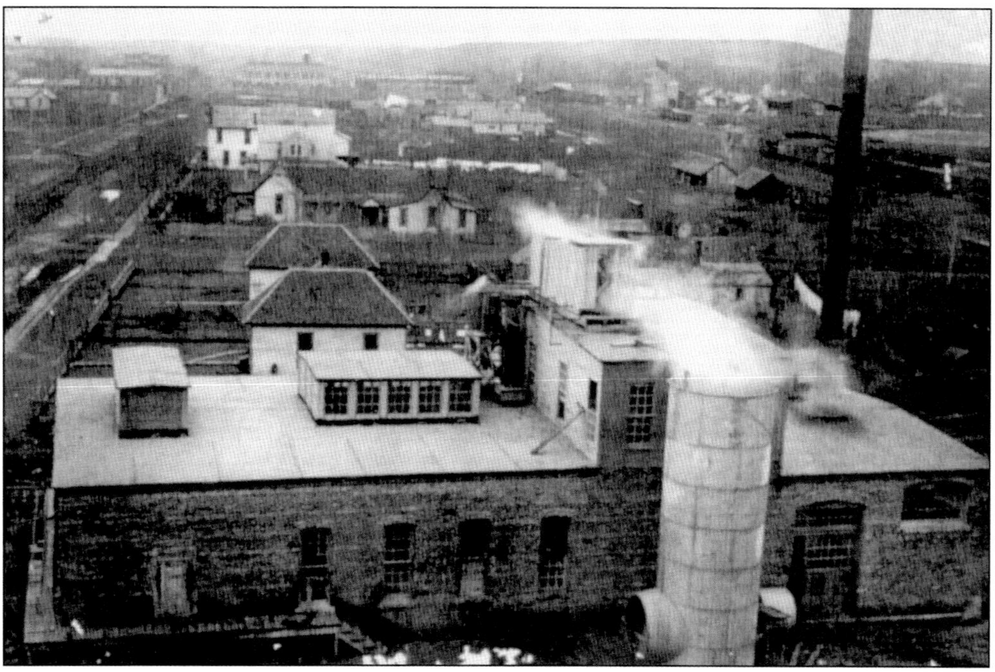

The Southwest Ice Plant and Dairy Products was located at 505 North Catalayah Street. Sometime between 1945 and 1956, the ice plant changed to Central Dairy Products.

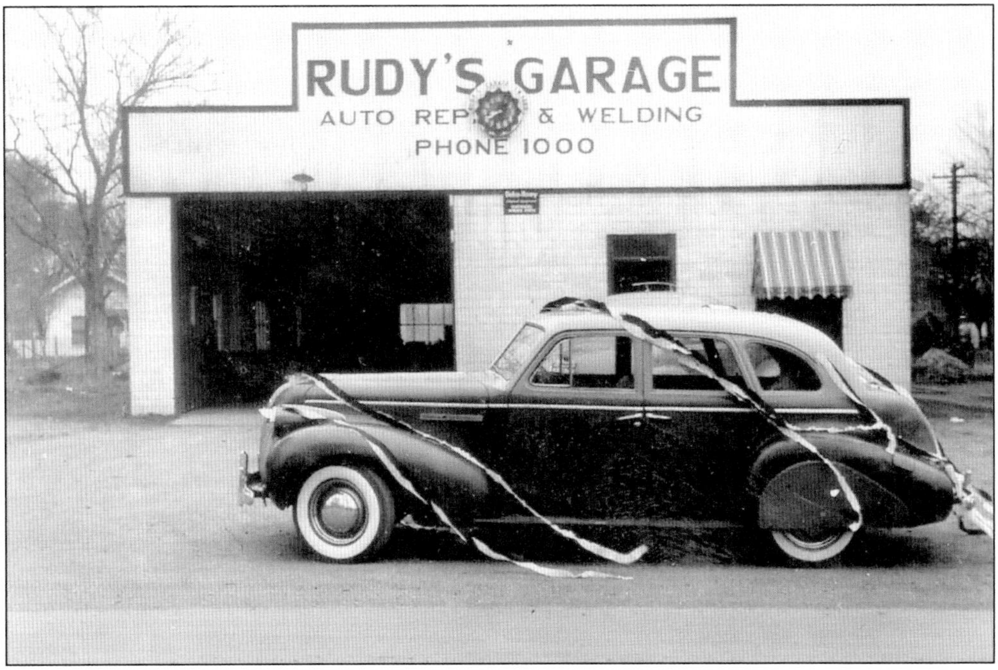


This garage was owned and operated by Rudy Sutter. The garage was located at 514 East Will Rogers Boulevard. This is near the wye as it intersects with Patti Page Boulevard. The photograph was taken in 1949, although the garage was known to be in existence in 1947. The car is decorated for Claremore Senior Day.

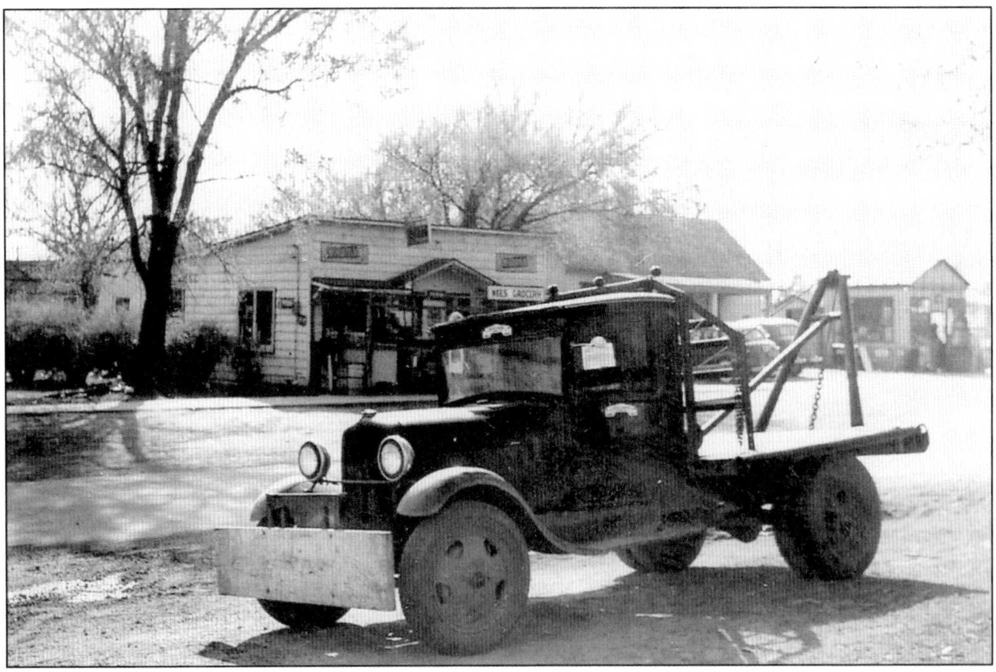


"Rudy's Wrecker," as it was affectionately known about town, was a familiar site. Those with car trouble could call on Sutter for a quick tow to his garage. Nee's Grocery can be seen in the background behind the wrecker.

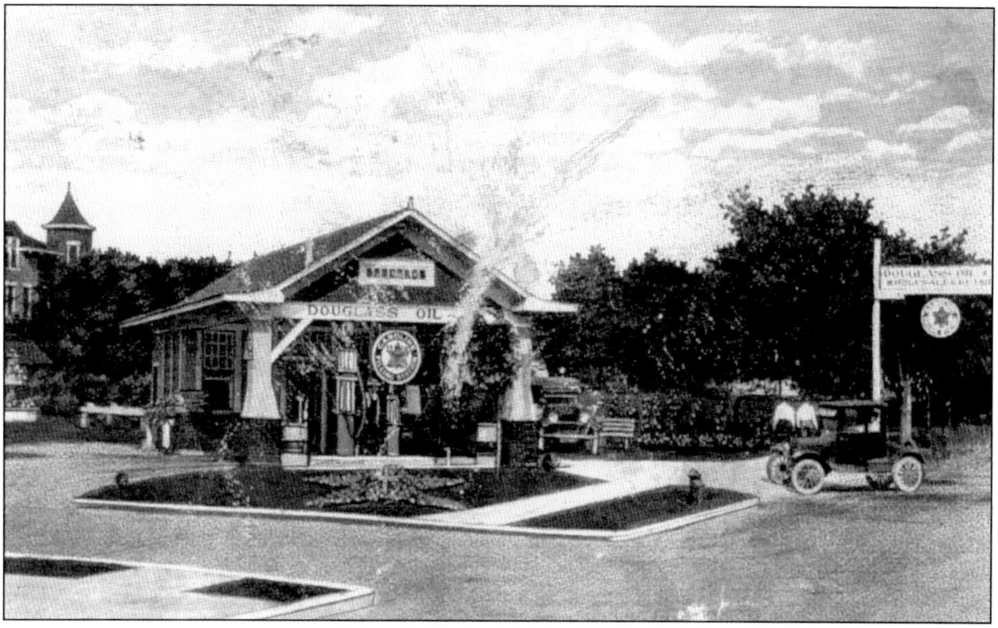


Douglass Oil Company sat diagonal from the Rummage Oil Company. The Belvidere Mansion can be seen in the background. Douglass was located near the Missouri Pacific Railroad station and across from city hall.

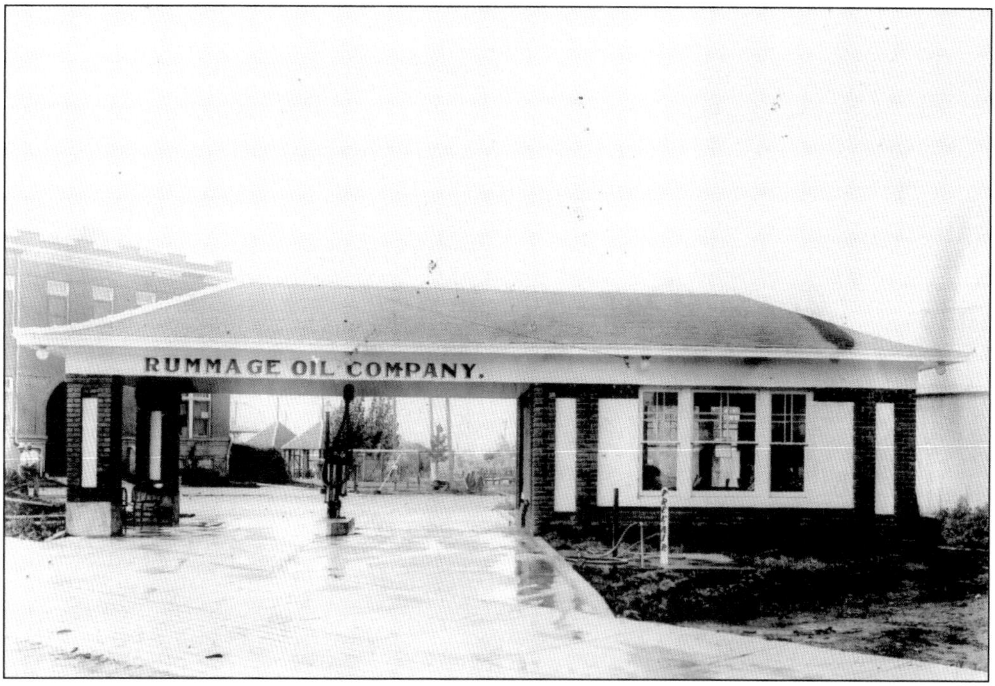


Rummage Oil Company was the first gas station in Claremore. It was located on the corner of Third Street and Muskogee Avenue in 1925. Perry Tilden was the proprietor. The building on the left was Claremore City Hall, which also housed the fire department. The Claremore City Park can be seen in the background. The tentlike structures were monkey cages.

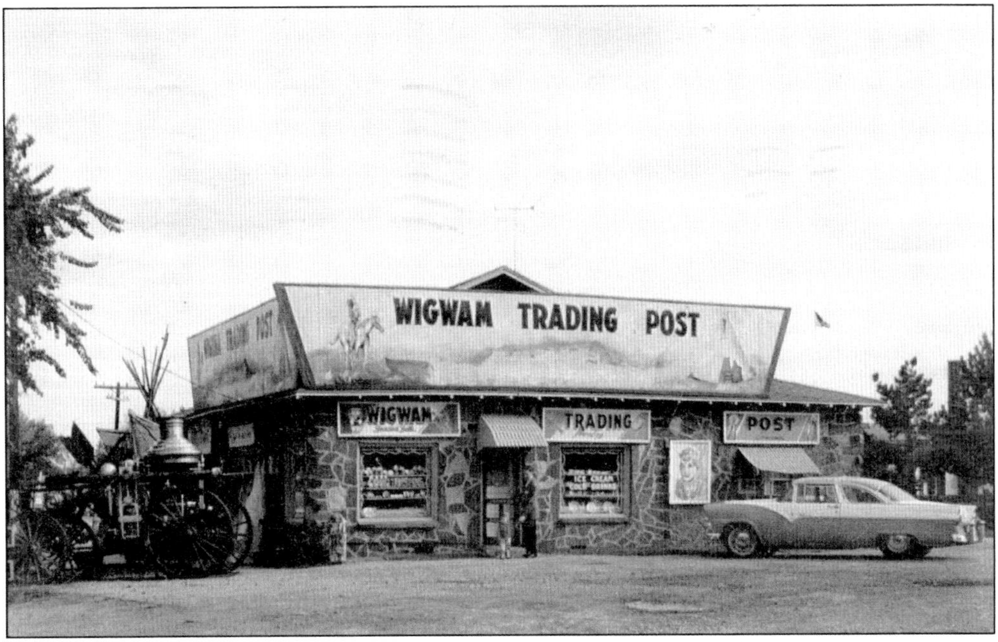


The Wigwam Trading Post was owned by longtime Claremore resident John Denbo. It was located at the wye just east of the Will Rogers Memorial. The store offered Will Rogers and American Indian souvenirs. A portion of the authentic American Indian teepee is visible in the background. The building still exists today.

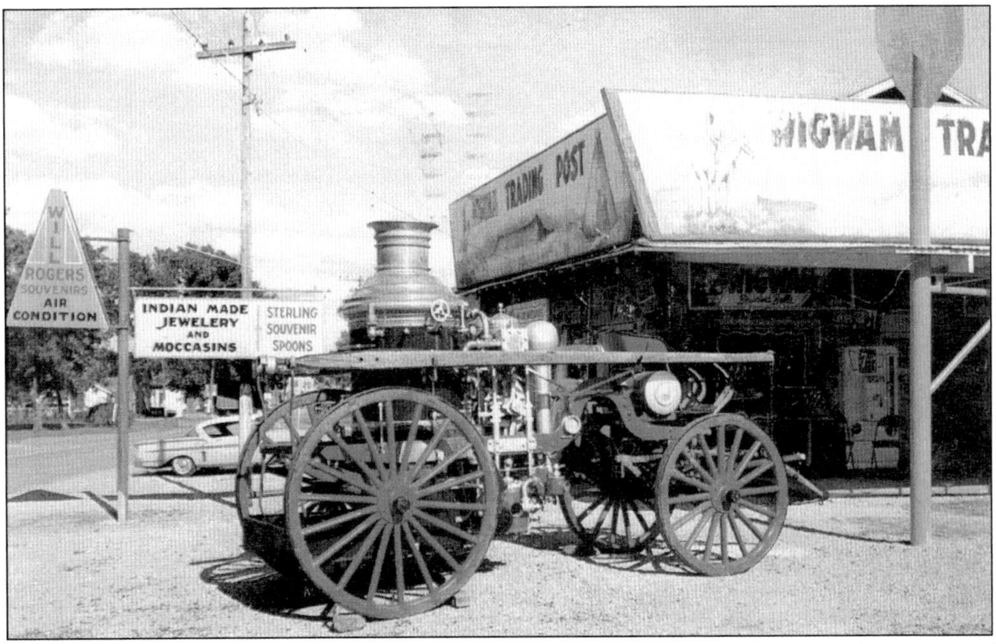


This antique red fire engine stood for years outside the Wigwam Trading Post. The reverse of the card states, "Little Jana Denbo says to take as many pictures of her big red fire engine as you like."

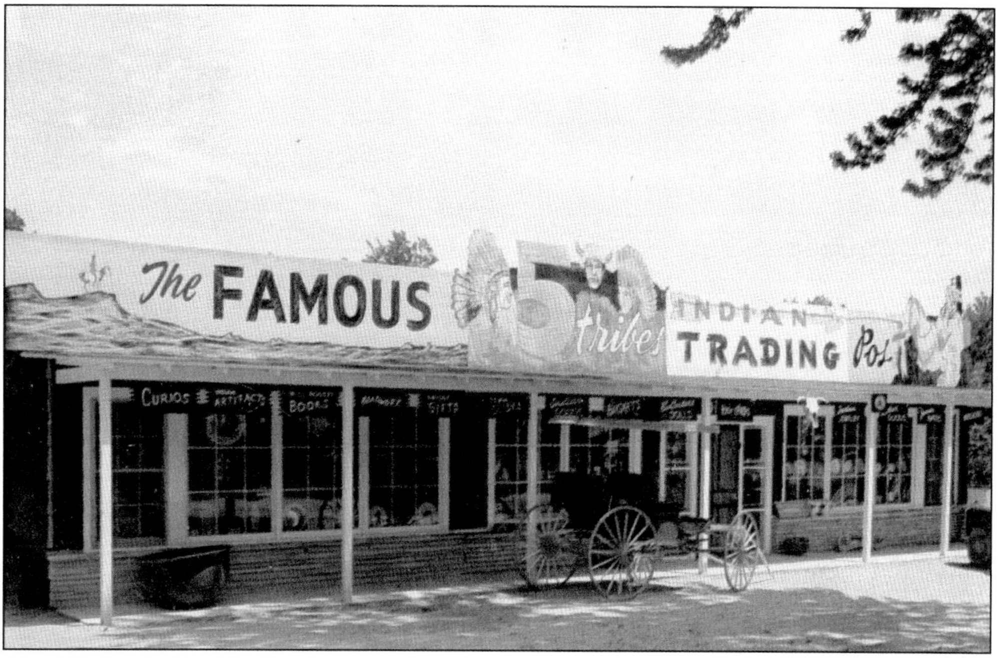


The 5 Tribes Indian Trading Post stood on the property of Hammett House Restaurant. It was an authentic trading post owned and operated by the Cherokee tribe. It specialized in American Indian goods and Will Rogers souvenirs.

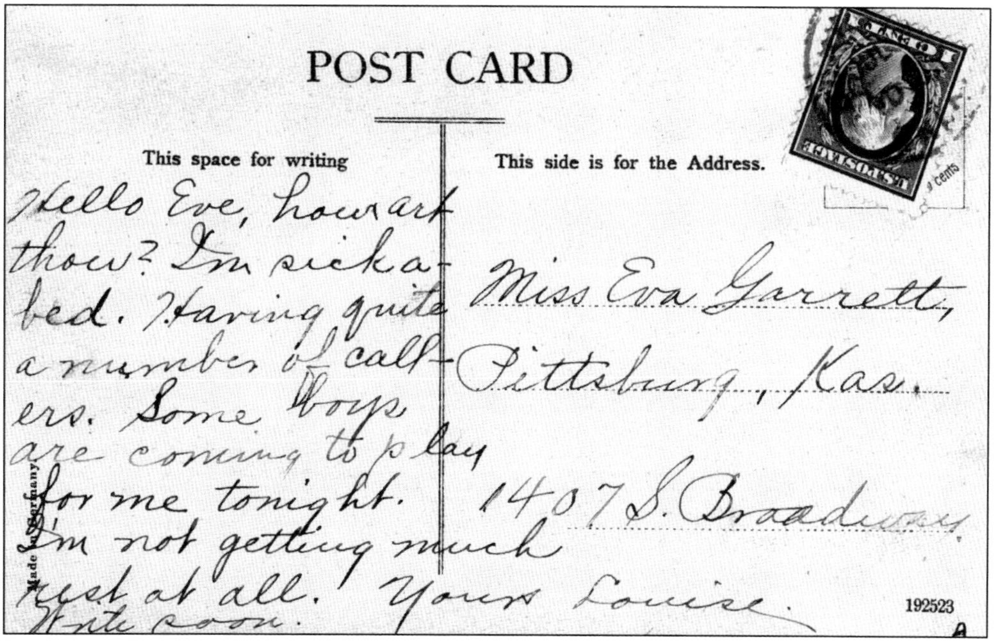

POST CARD

This space for writing

This side is for the Address.

Hello Eve, how art thou? I'm sick abed. Having quite a number of callers. Some boys are coming to play for me tonight. I'm not getting much rest at all. Yours Louise. Write soon.

Miss Eva Garrett, Pittsburg, Kas. 1407 S. Broadway

Made in Germany

192523

This postcard was mailed to Eva Garrett of Pittsburg, Kansas. It states, "Hello Eve, how art thou? I'm sick abed. Having quite a number of callers. Some boys are coming to play for me tonight. I'm not getting much rest at all. Write soon. Yours Louise."

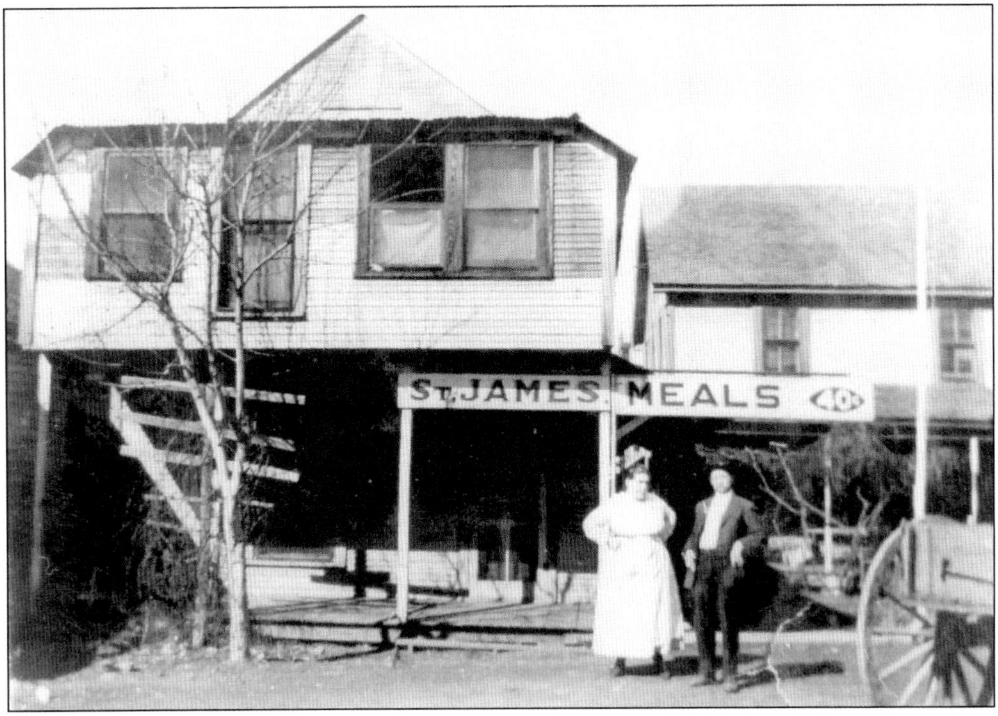


St. James Hotel Restaurant was owned by Jimmie Riggs about 1908. Riggs is shown here along with Martha Thompson in front of the restaurant. The banner advertises 40¢ meals.

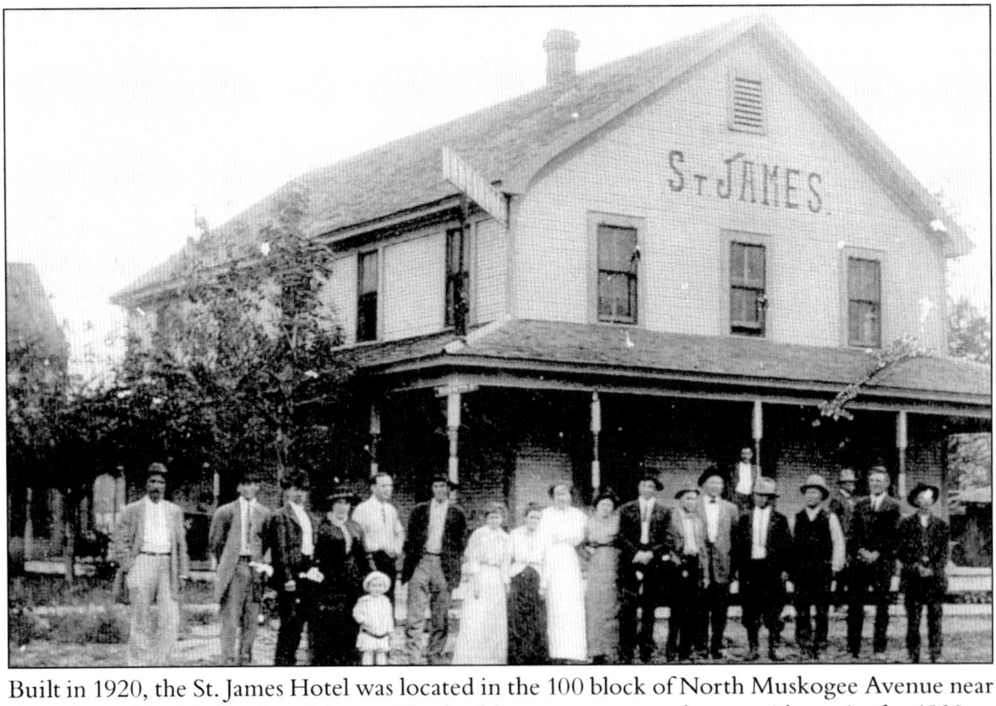


Built in 1920, the St. James Hotel was located in the 100 block of North Muskogee Avenue near the Missouri Pacific Railroad depot. The building was converted to a residence in the 1930s.

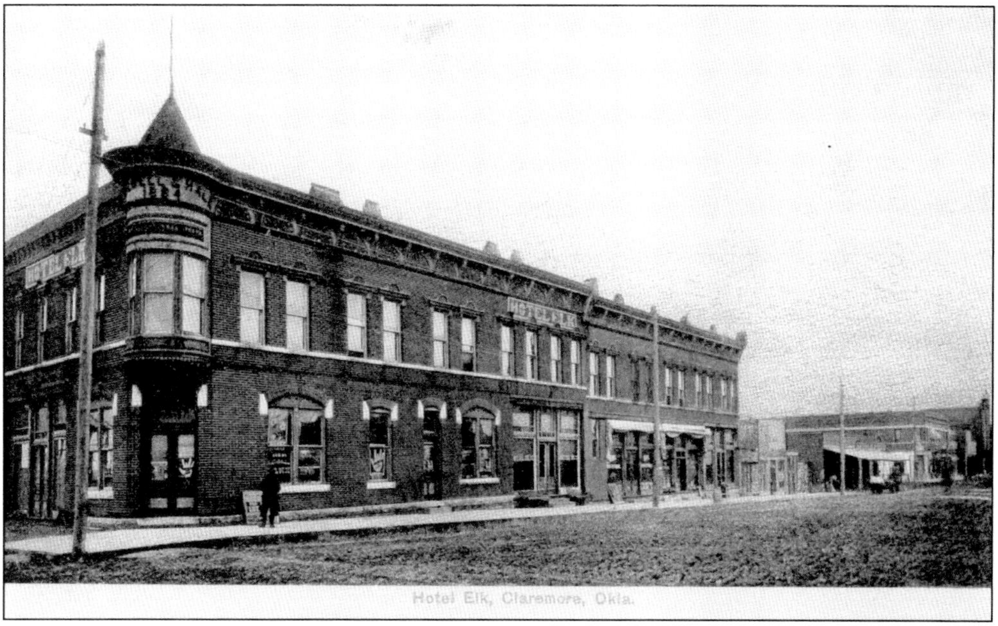


Not much is known about the Hotel Elk. According to the stonework on the building, it was built in 1884 by Hale and Halsell, two cattlemen from Vinita. It was also known at one time as the Hotel Main. In the background can be seen a sign for the Saddlerock Restaurant. Next to the Saddlerock was the Walker and Livingston store. These buildings would have existed in the 600 block of Main Street. The Mason Hotel was later built beside the two larger buildings.

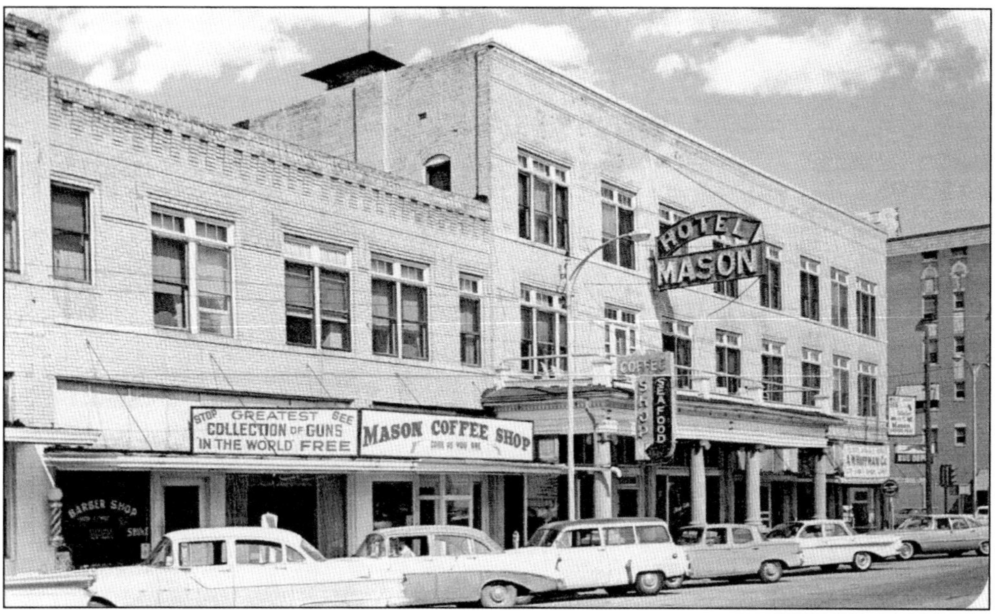


This front view of the Mason Hotel was taken in the mid-1950s. The Mason building took up most of the block.

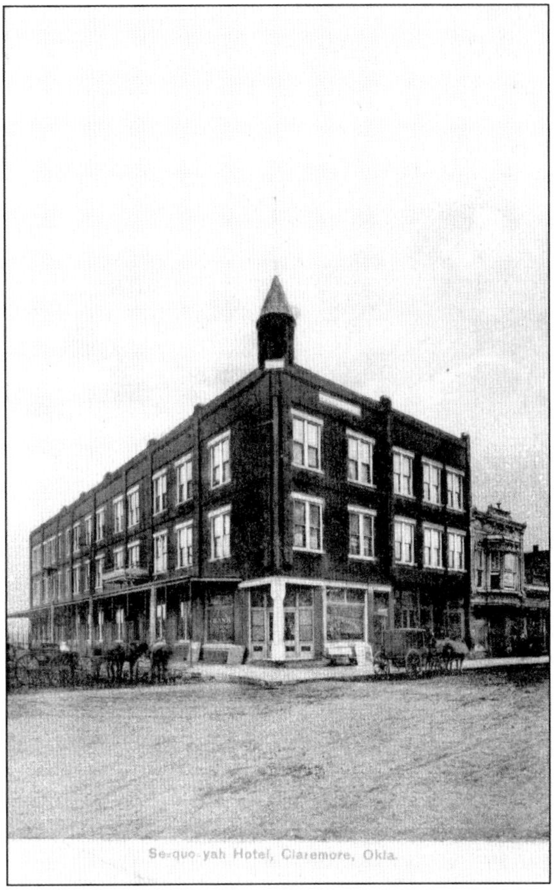


The Sequoyah Hotel was built in 1901. Radium baths were added to the hotel in 1905. The building to the right of the hotel was the City Drug Store, next to it was F. A. Nielson's Mercantile, and then Campbell's Saddle and Harness Shop. It was located on the southwest corner of Missouri and Third Streets. Although it is not clear how long the hotel was in business, it was still in existence in 1960. It was no longer listed in the telephone directory after 1960. The building was eventually torn down, and RCB Bank now stands at that location.

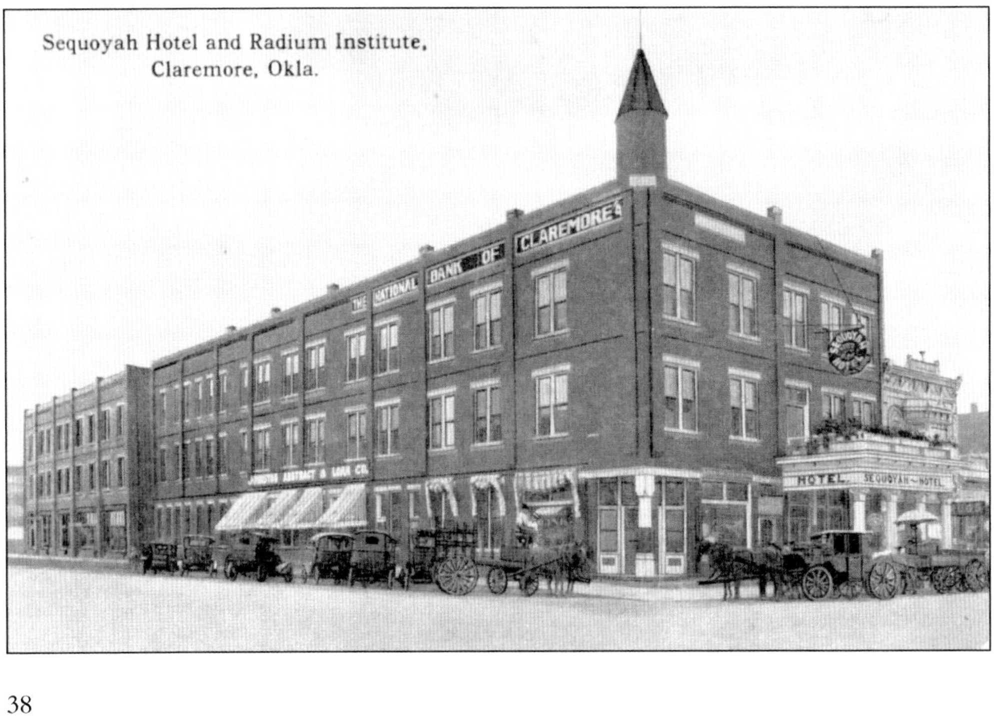

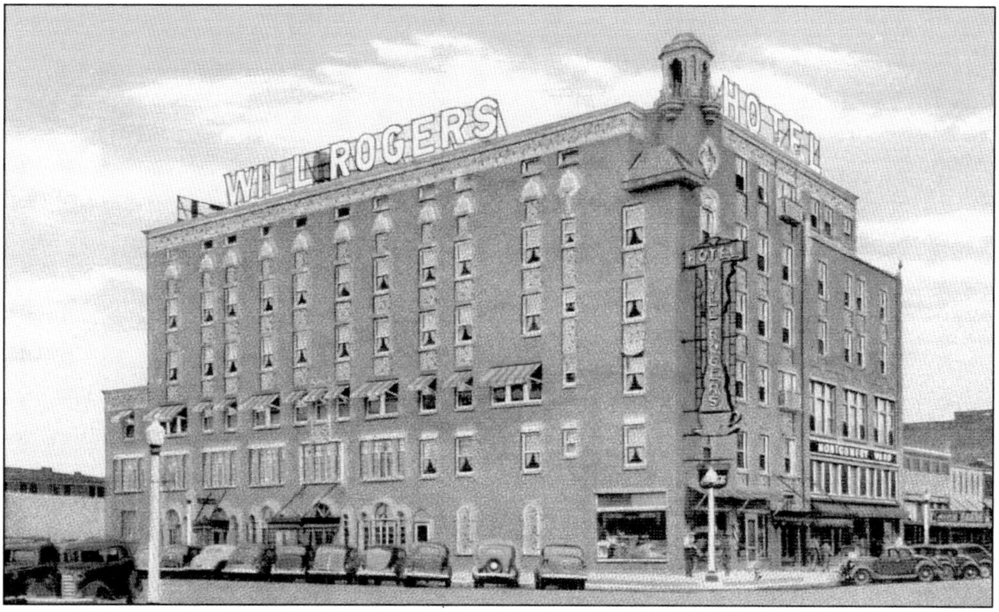


The Will Rogers Hotel was dedicated on February 7, 1930. The fireproof structure of concrete and steel, along with furnishings, cost $321,000. It was built by Louis Abram, Walter Krumrei, and Morton Harrison. Louis's father, Joe Abram, had been cured of rheumatism in Claremore and fell in love with the city but felt it lacked in suitable hotel facilities. The six-story hotel contains 78 rooms and seven apartments. During World War II, it was designated as a bomb shelter. Will Rogers had a permanent suite in the hotel for his trips to town. It was known for eastern atmosphere, western welcome, and southern hospitality.

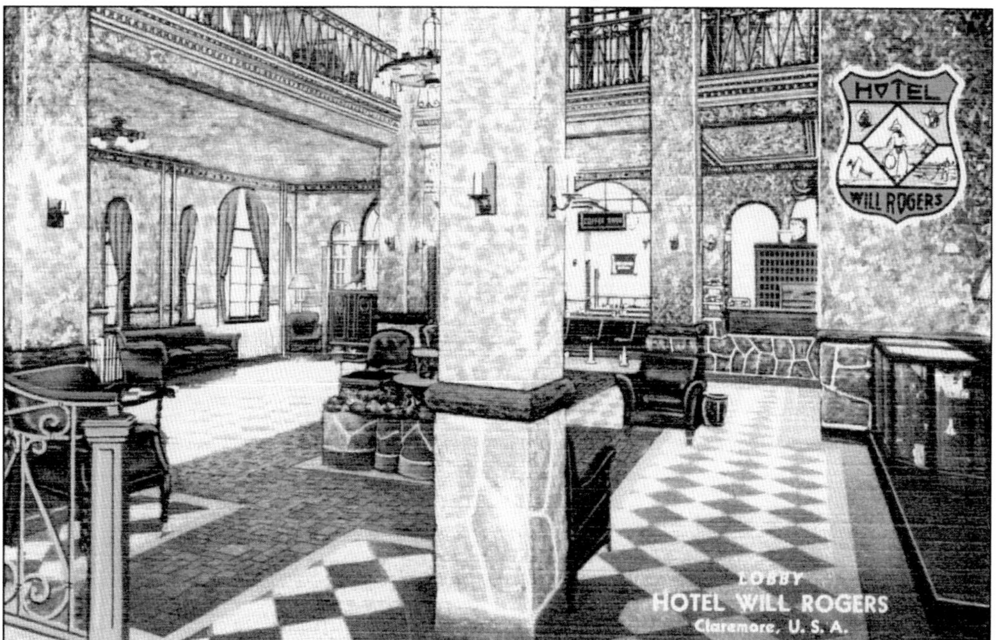

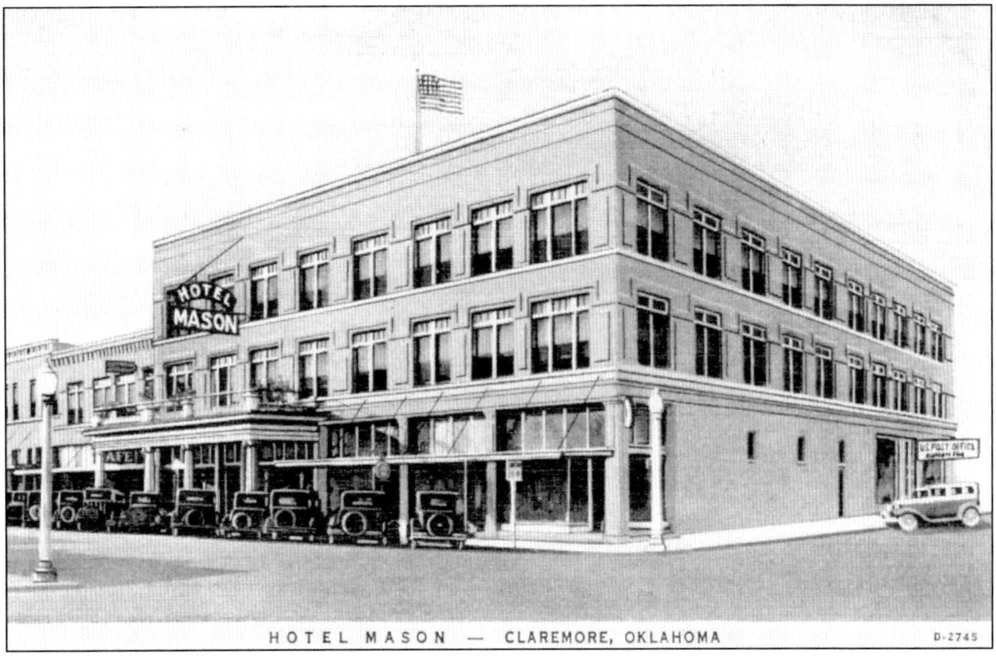


The Mason Hotel was located at the intersection of Route 66 and Highway 20. It was built in 1910 by Dr. John Rucker, who traded it to J. M. Davis in 1916 for land in Arkansas. The hotel boasted 116 rooms and a coffee shop. The postcard above shows the post office in the back of the hotel.

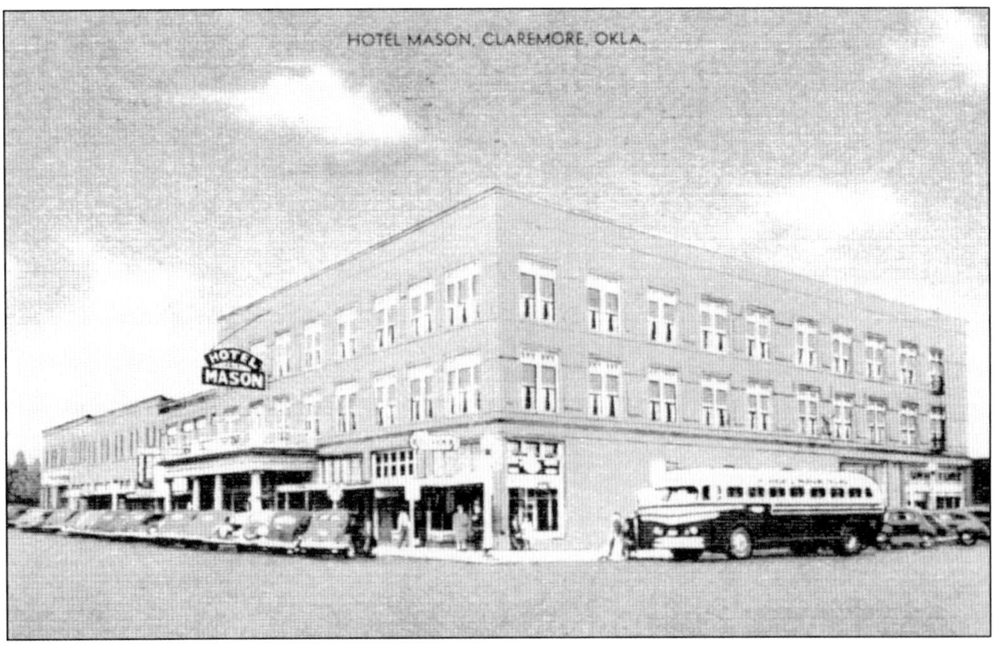

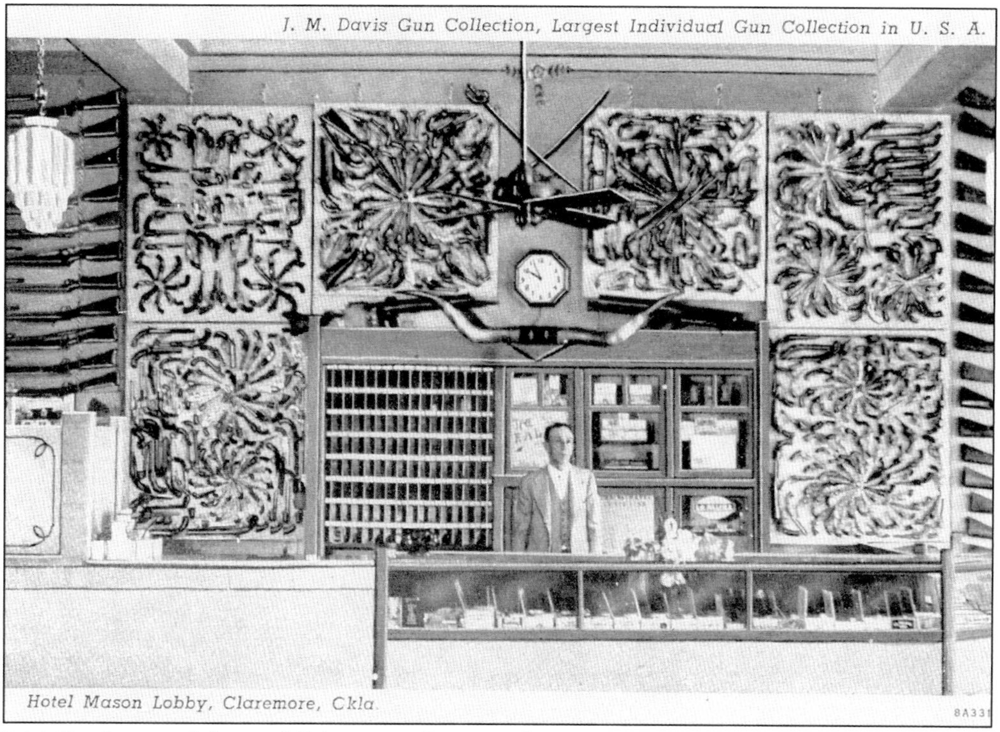


J. M. Davis owned the world's largest collection of guns. The collection was at one time housed on the interior of the Mason Hotel. Davis displayed his collection on the walls of the lobby, ball room, hallways, and even in the private rooms.

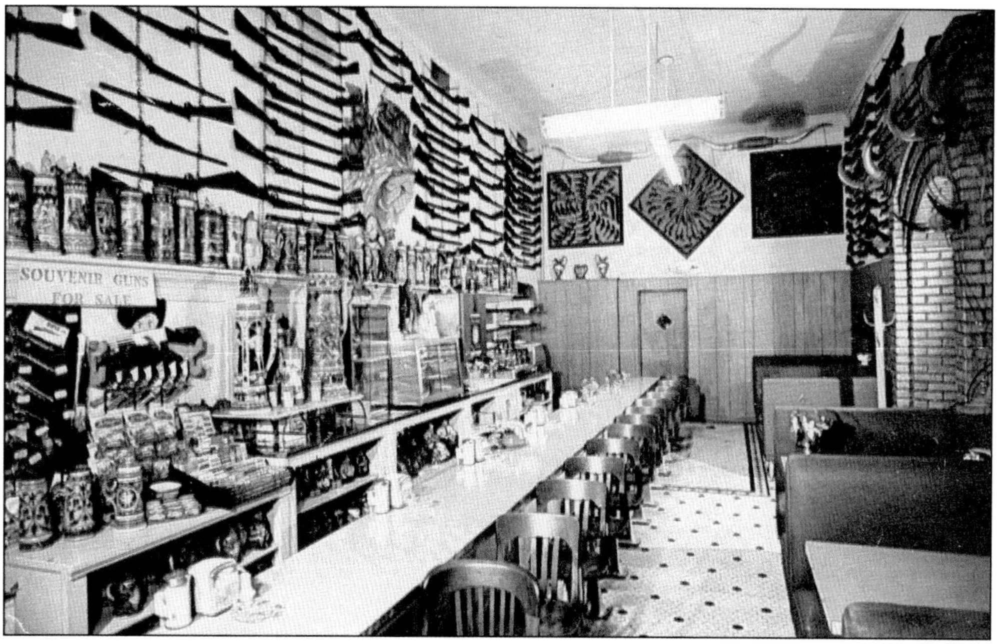


The Mason Hotel Coffee Shop was once a favorite gathering spot for Claremore citizens to sit and shoot the breeze.

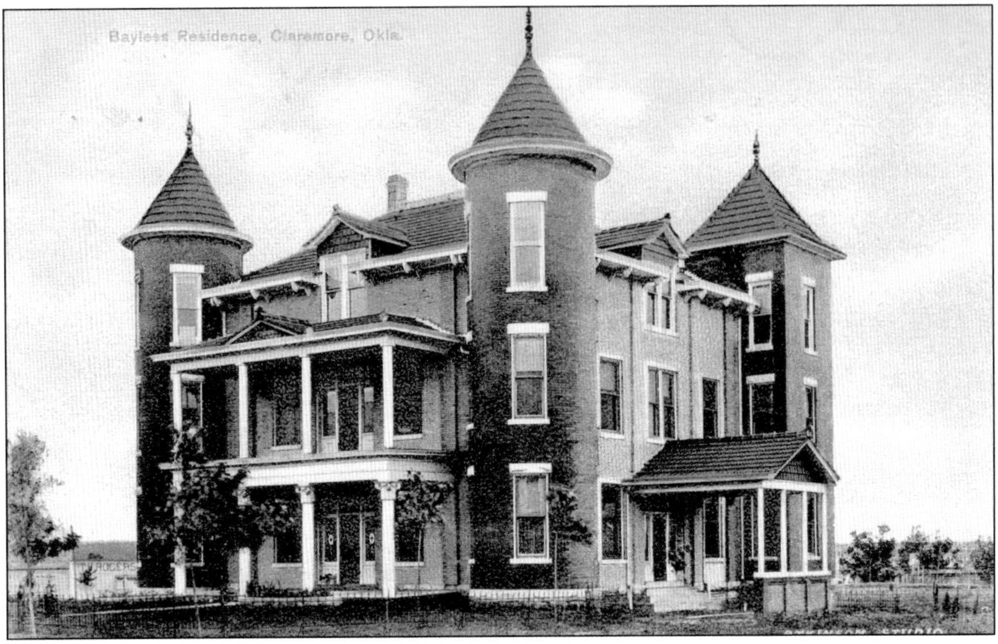


This stately mansion known as the Belvidere Mansion was built in Claremore in 1907 by John M. Bayless. Bayless passed away from appendicitis just before work on the mansion was completed. The residence has three floors, the top of which is a ballroom. People came from all over the county to attend the grand galas at the Bayless home. The mansion is in the process of being restored to its original grandeur by the Rogers County Historical Society. It is open four days a week for tours.

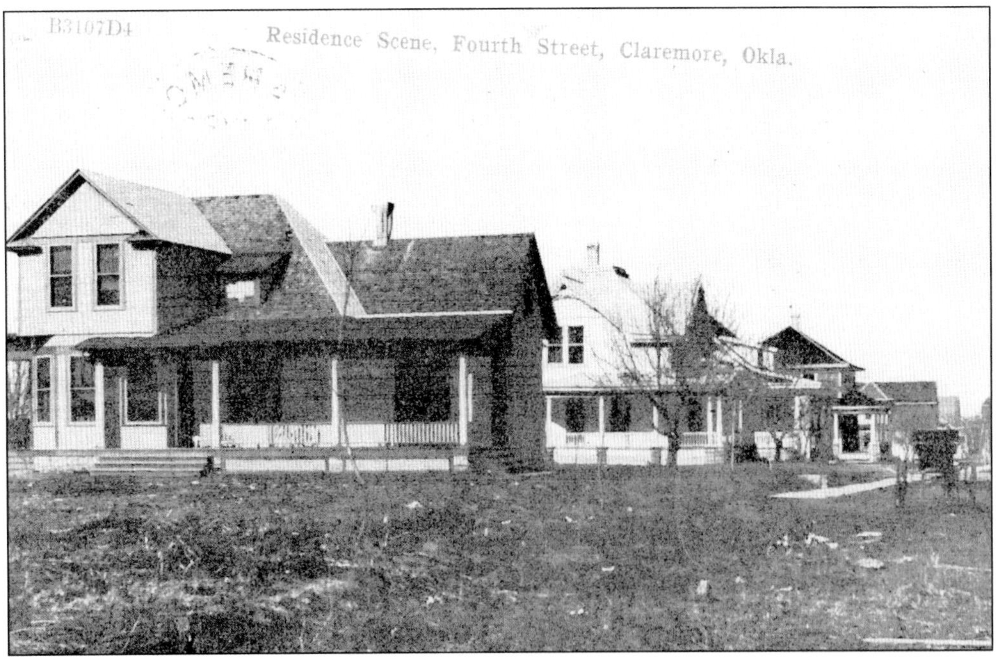


These private residences lined Fourth Street in Claremore. This was typical of the residences in Claremore in 1912. Many of the city's influential people lived on Fourth Street.

# *Three*

# Radium Bathhouses

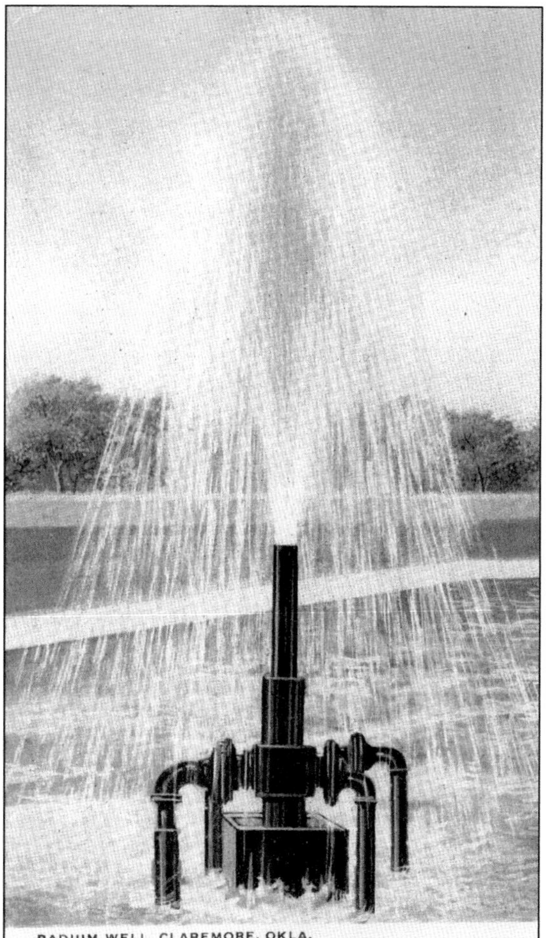


In 1903, while drilling for oil, George Washington Eaton discovered water with a foul-smelling odor. Tests run on the water showed it to have medicinal value. Eaton named the water radium water, although tests proved the water did not contain radium. Soon bathhouses sprang up all over town. By 1930, thousands of afflicted people visited Claremore each year for the baths. The water was especially recommended for rheumatism, eczema, stomach trouble, and skin diseases.

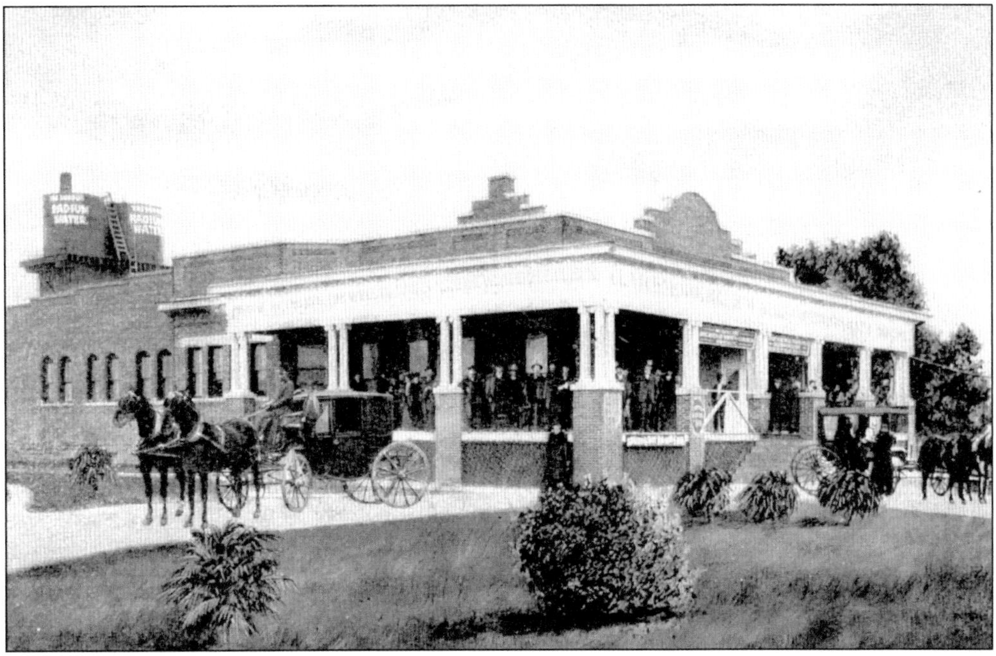

The Claremore Radium Wells Company bathhouse was built by J. S. Flippin. It was one of the first bathhouses built in Radium Town. It was later sold to William Jasper Perdue of Salem, Indiana.

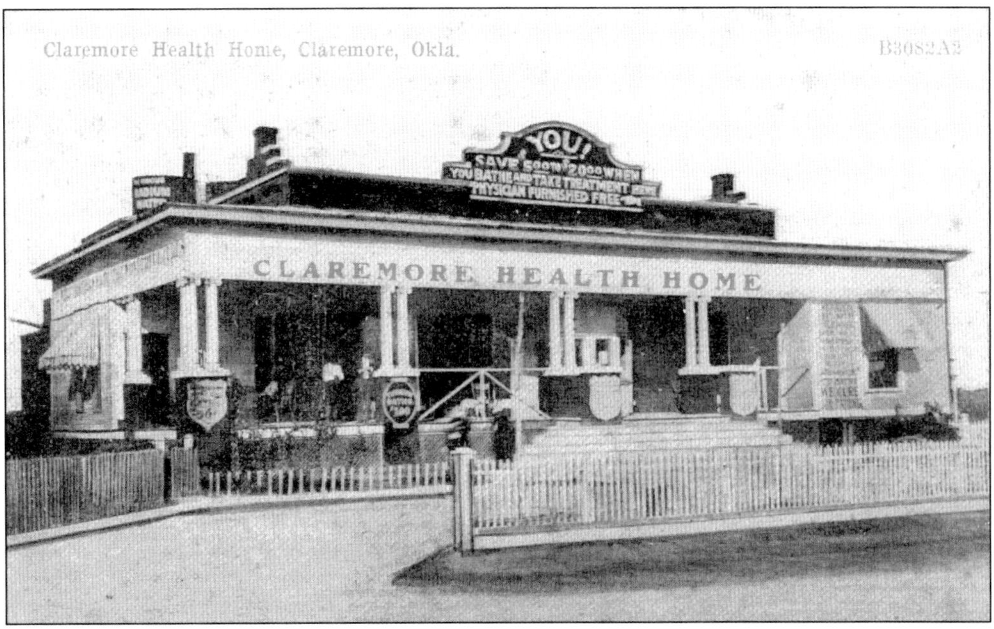


Claremore Health Home was the same building as the Claremore Radium Wells Company and the Perdue Bathhouse. It is unclear if the name was changed to Claremore Health Home before or after it was known as the Perdue.

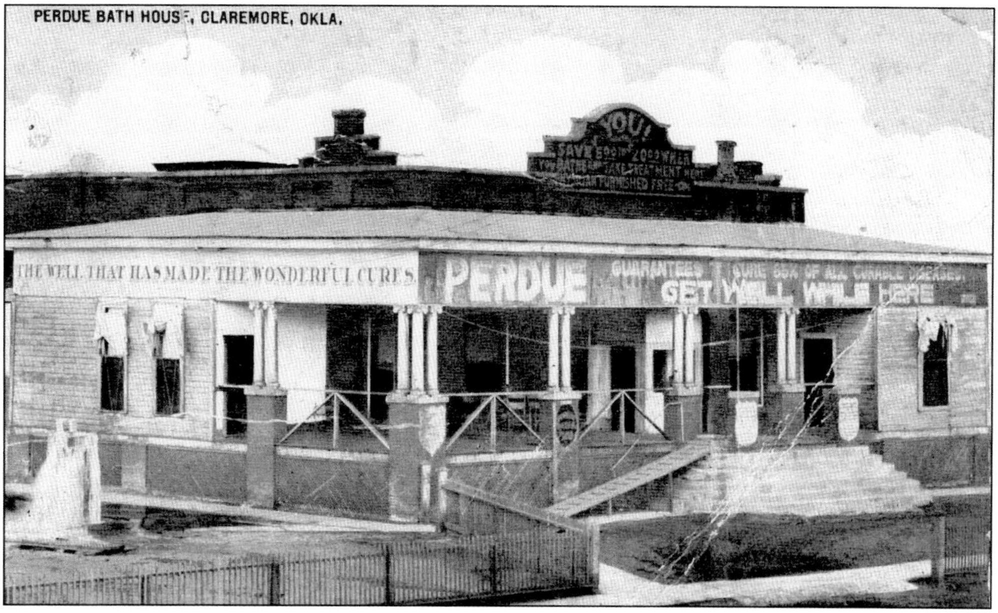


In 1904, William Jasper Perdue of Salem, Indiana, purchased this bathhouse from J. S. Flippin. Perdue renamed the bathhouse the Perdue Bathhouse. The well, pictured beside the bathhouse, was one of the original wells in Radium Town. It supplied the Perdue with a continual supply of mineral water for its business.

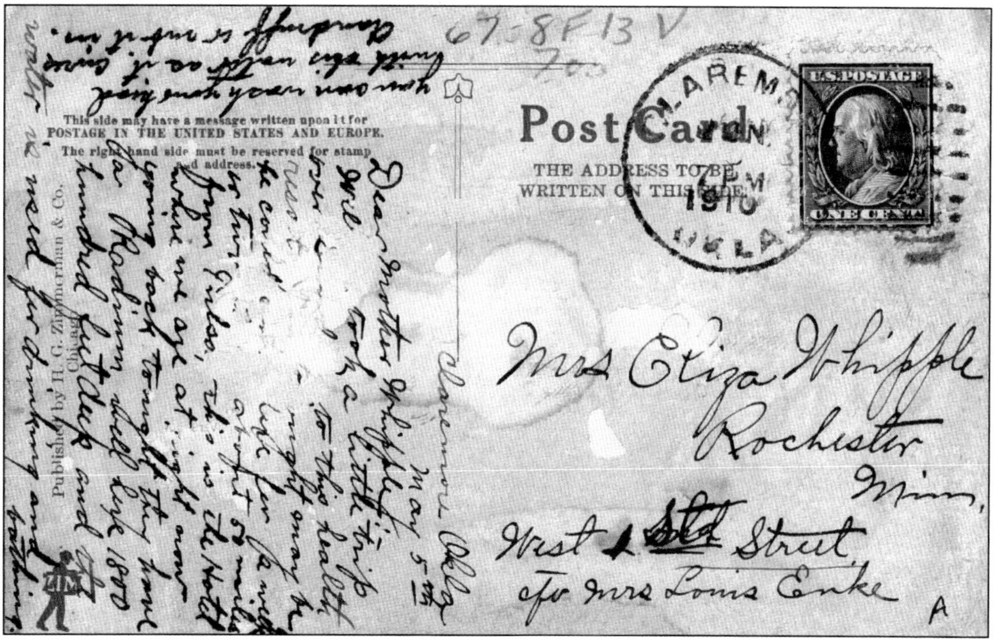


This postcard is dated May 5 and postmarked 1910 to Eliza Whipple in Rochester, Minnesota. "Dear Mother Whipple: Will took a little trip over Sunday to this health resort. I thought maybe he could have fun a week in town. It is about 50 miles from Tulsa. This is the Hotel [Bungalow Hotel] where we are at right now. Going back tonight. They have a Radium well here 1800 hundred feet deep and the water is used for drinking and bathing. You can wash your head this with this water as it cures dandruff so rub it in."

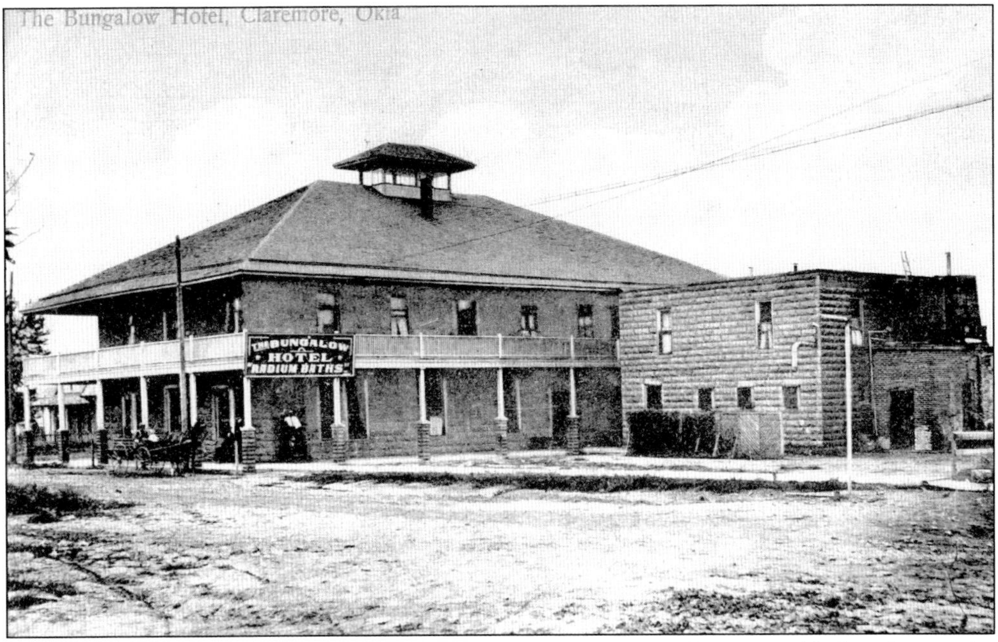


The Bungalow Hotel and Bath House is pictured above in 1910. The postcard below depicts the same bathhouse in 1944. The bathhouse was in existence as early as 1906. The Bungalow was located at 119 South Cherokee Avenue behind the present-day site of Ann's Cleaners.

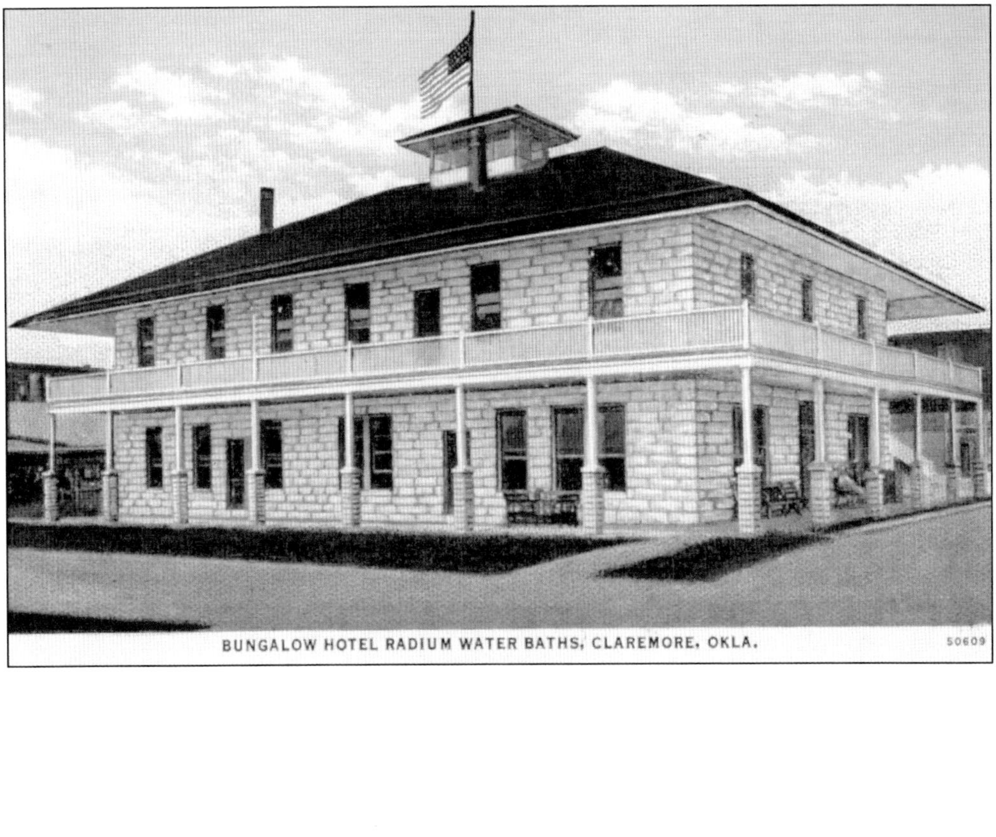

BUNGALOW HOTEL RADIUM WATER BATHS, CLAREMORE, OKLA. 50609

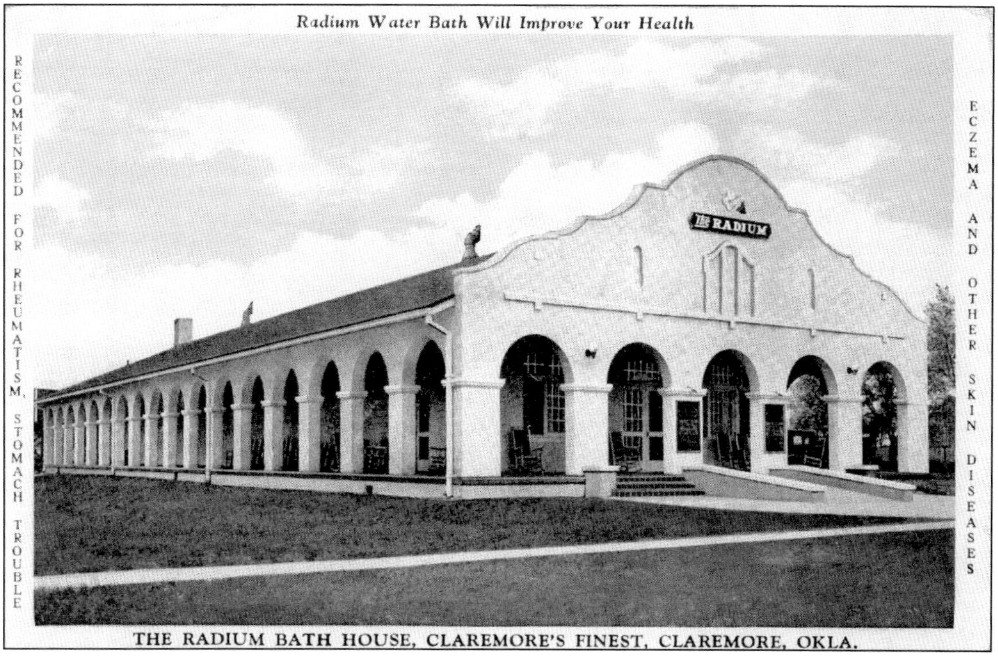


On July 29, 1924, ground was broken for the first community-sponsored bathhouse, the Radium. It was the fourth bathhouse in Claremore, and at a cost of $75,000, it was one of the nicer bathhouses. The Radium was located at 323 South Catalayah Street, now Lynn Riggs Boulevard. The bathhouse's last year of operation was 1956; Dr. Cecile E. Reed was director. In later years it was torn down, and the J. M. Davis Gun Museum was built at that location.

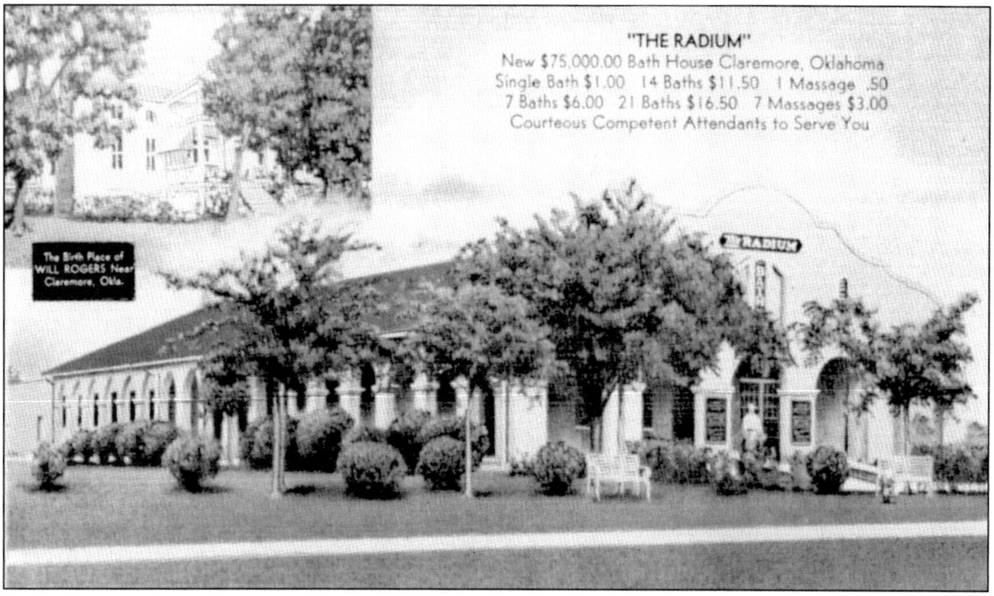

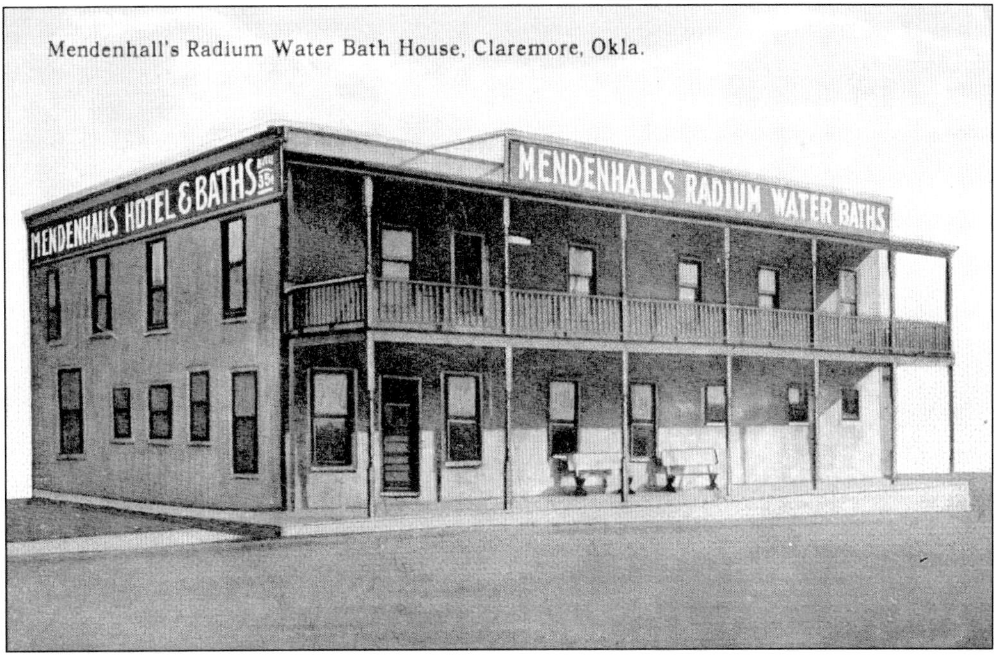


Mendenhall's Radium Water Baths was the built in 1905 by Watson James Mendenhall. It was built on G. W. Eaton's property where the original Radium Town well was located. It was later reconstructed and made into a two-story building, as seen here.

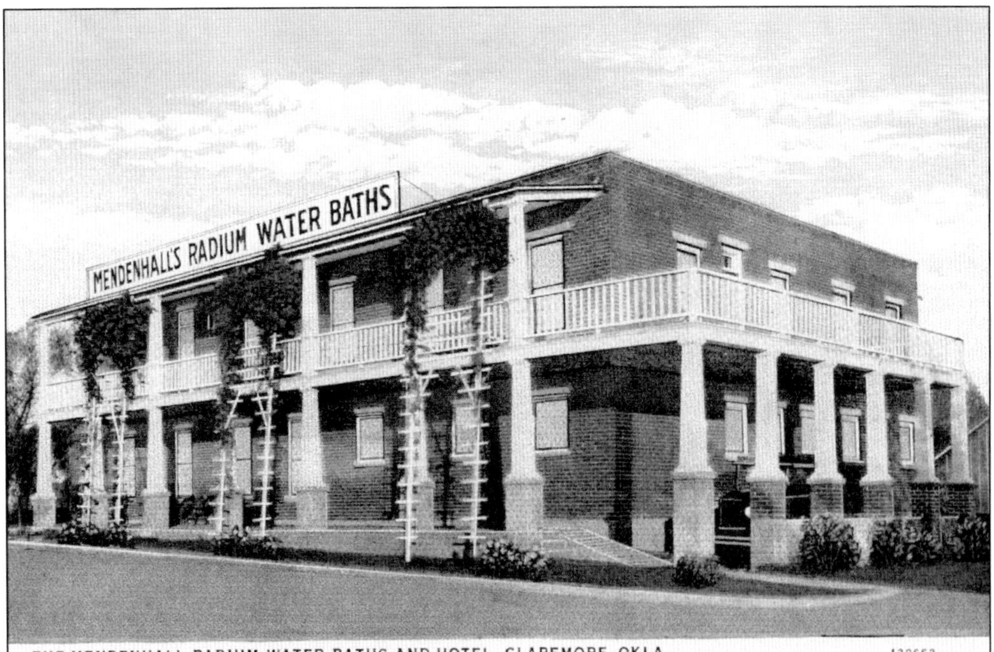


The Mendenhall was purchased by Bob and Patsy Keller. The business operated as Keller's Bath House until 1980. The building still exists at the corner of Seventh Street and Lavira Avenue in Radium Town and is used as apartments.

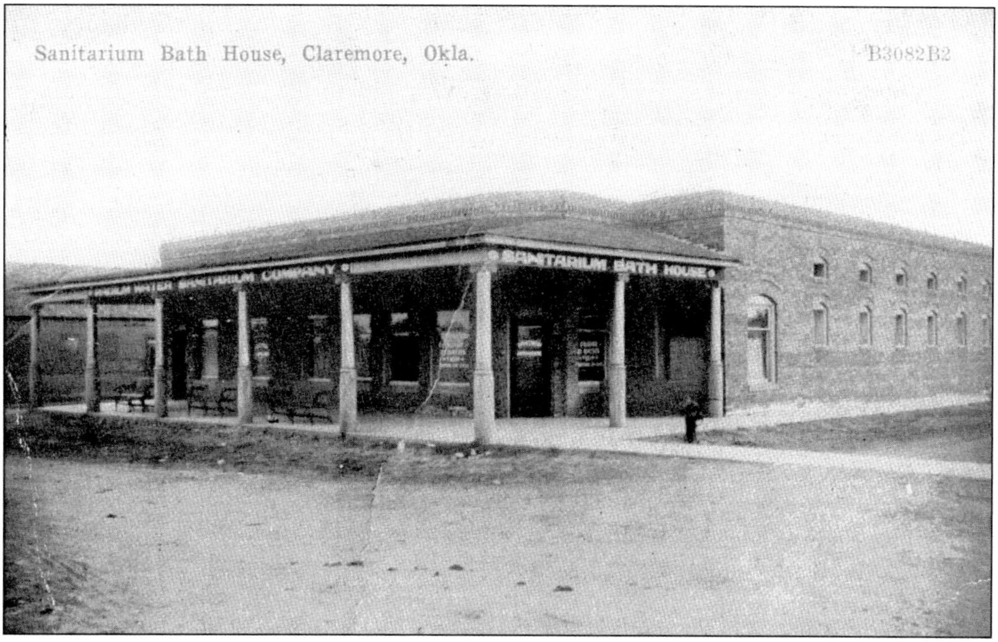


Due to confusion over the name radium water, the Sanitarium Bath House renamed the water mineral water. The Sanitarium radium water well was drilled in 1905, 200 feet from the original well. The Sanitarium was located in Radium Town at 601 East Ninth Street. Although today Claremore has enveloped Radium Town, during those days the Sanitarium was several miles from town and offered free taxi service from Claremore.

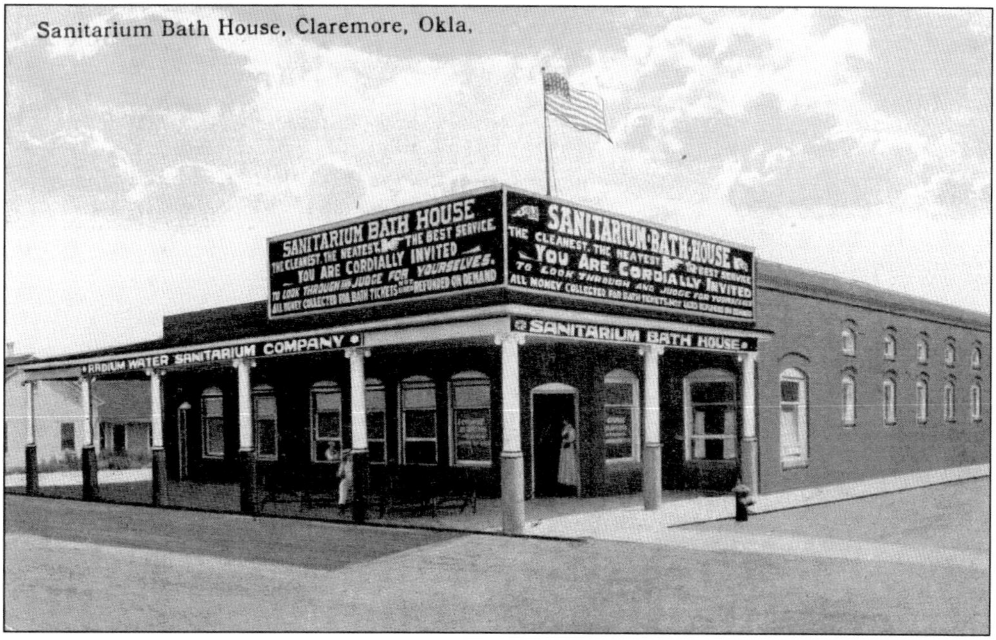


According to the marquee at the Sanitarium, it was "the cleanest, the neatest, [and offered] the best service. You are cordially invited to look through and judge for yourselves. All money collected for bath tickets not used refunded on demand." Note the lady standing in the doorway of the bathhouse.

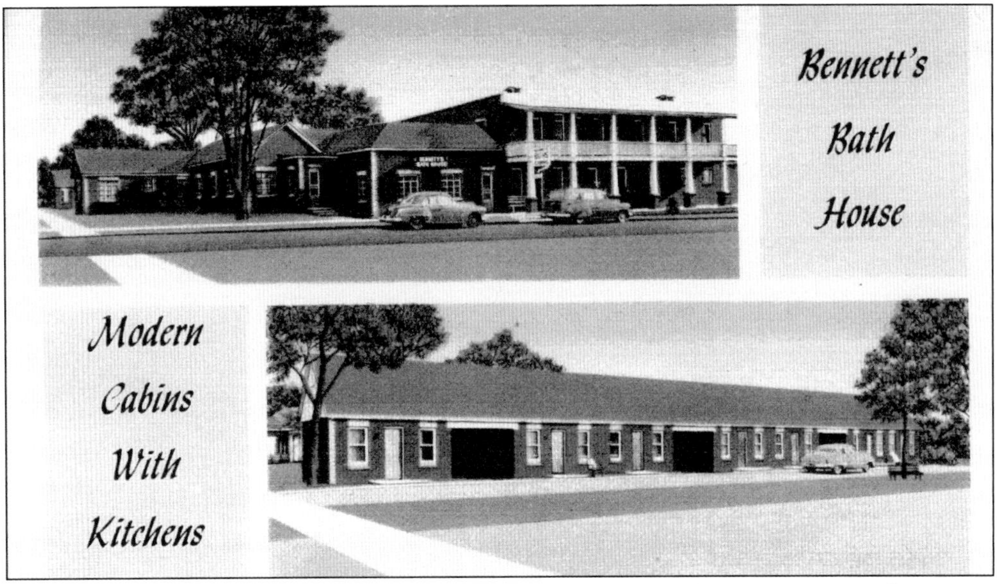


The Bennett family, John, Moses, and Minnie Mae, came to Claremore in 1928 hoping to find a cure for Minnie Mae's ailments. The Bennett brothers, John and Harold, purchased the Sanitarium Bath House. Then in 1945, they purchased the Mendenhall bathhouse, which was eventually sold to the Keller family. The Bennetts were in the mineral water business for over 44 years. Mrs. Bennett must have found her cure as she lived in Claremore until 1978.

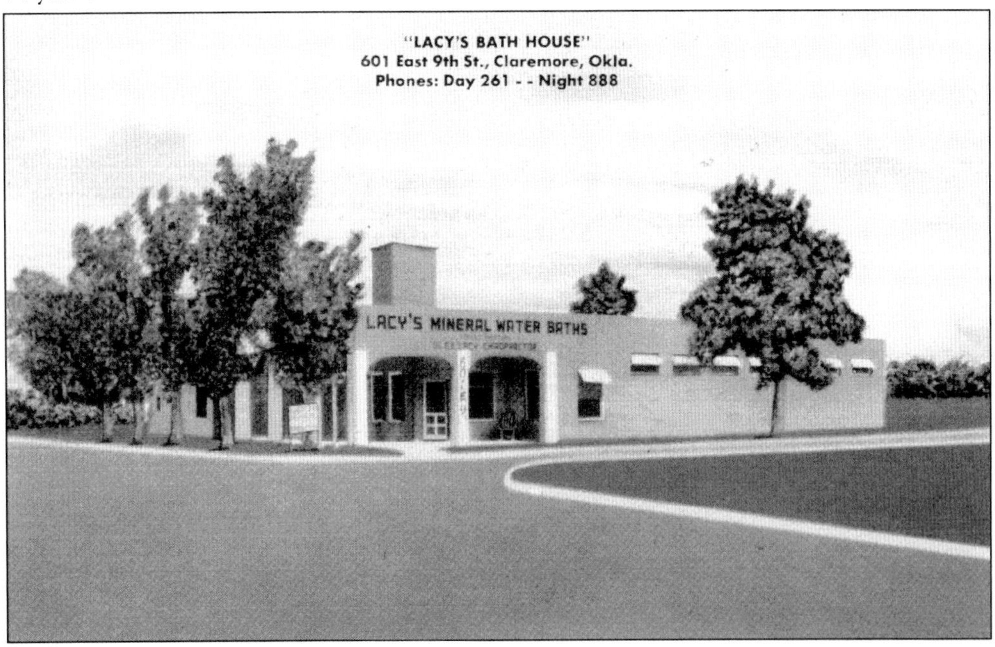


Lacy's Mineral Water Baths was owned and operated by Dr. E. E. Lacy. Lacy was also a chiropractor and practiced in this building until his death in 1991. Lacy's parents opened the bathhouse in 1948. The radium well was located in the middle of the lobby. Lacy was somewhat of a legend in Claremore and was notorious for having a messy office. One of his favorite sayings was "a clean desk is a sign of an empty mind." The building fell into disrepair and was eventually torn down in 1996.

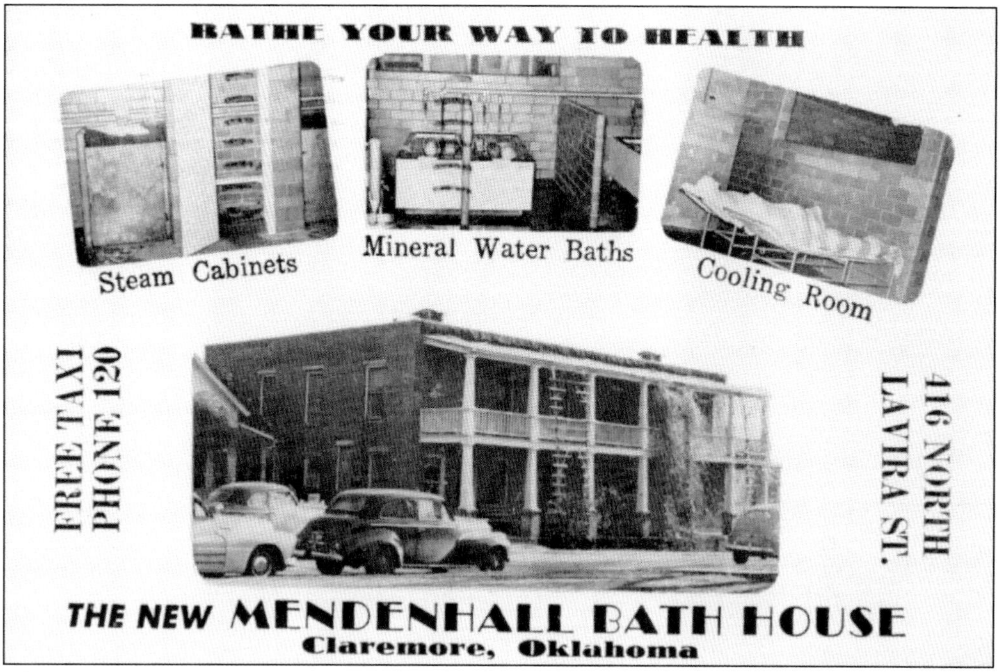


This postcard advertisement was distributed around 1949. At that time, the Mendenhall was under the direction of R. V. Bennett. Along with mineral water baths, it offered steam baths and a cooling room. It could be reached at telephone number 120.

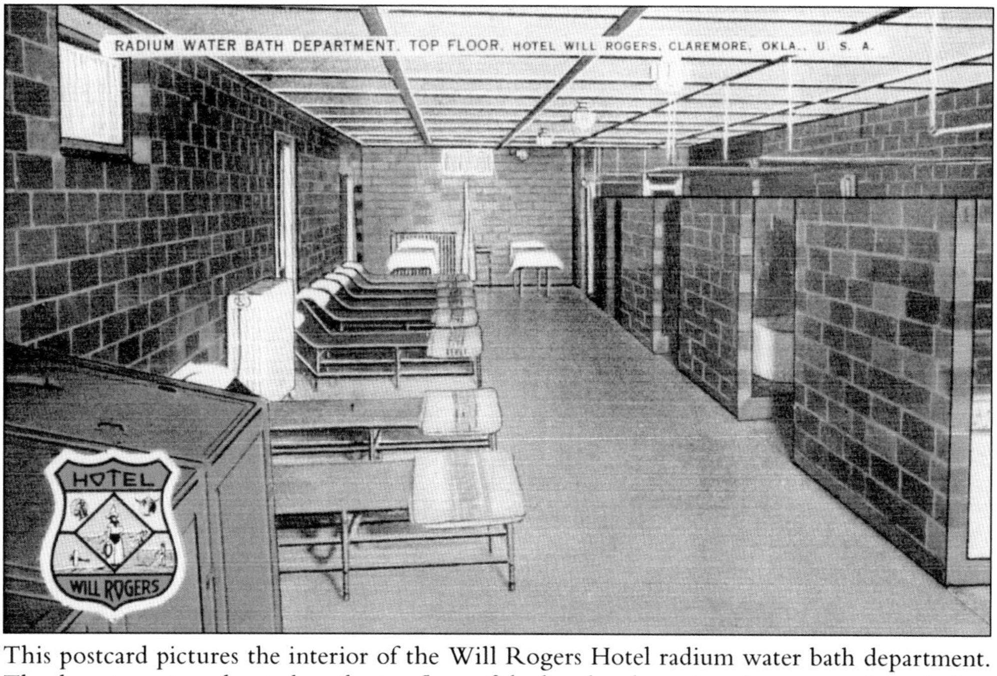


This postcard pictures the interior of the Will Rogers Hotel radium water bath department. The department was located on the top floor of the hotel and continued to operate into the late 1900s. Levi Harlin worked for the hotel as the operator of the bath department. In the early days, baths were priced at $1.50 and massages were $1.25. At times, 75 to 80 people came through the bathhouse daily.

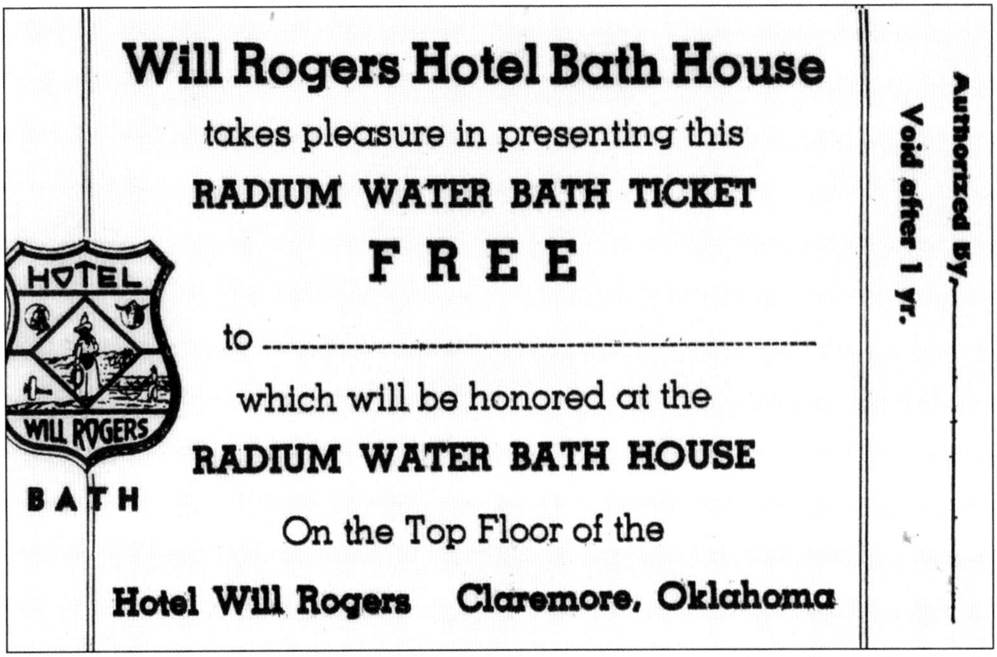
Will Rogers Hotel Bath House
takes pleasure in presenting this
RADIUM WATER BATH TICKET
FREE
to ..............................
which will be honored at the
RADIUM WATER BATH HOUSE
On the Top Floor of the
Hotel Will Rogers Claremore, Oklahoma
HOTEL
WILL ROGERS
BATH
Authorized By
Void after 1 yr.

Testimonial from a bath patron written on August 26, 1929, states, "After suffering for months with sciatic neuritis which had almost paralised my right leg, my doctor who had been treating me advised me to go to Claremore, OK, and try the baths. I came August 5th, 1929, on crutches. I could hardly get along without them, could not sit on a chair. After taking 7 baths I laid my crutches aside and walked from my room to the dining room without them. When I had taken 12 bathes I could walk fine without any crutches at all. Now at the end of 3 weeks I am feeling fine and am very thankful for what mineral water has done for me."

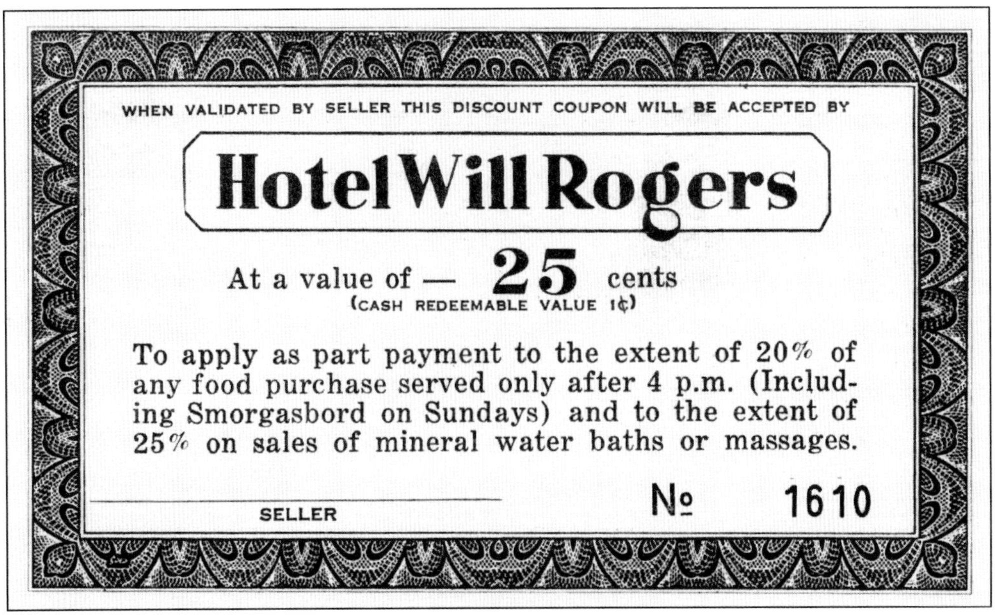
WHEN VALIDATED BY SELLER THIS DISCOUNT COUPON WILL BE ACCEPTED BY
Hotel Will Rogers
At a value of — 25 cents
(CASH REDEEMABLE VALUE 1¢)
To apply as part payment to the extent of 20% of any food purchase served only after 4 p.m. (Including Smorgasbord on Sundays) and to the extent of 25% on sales of mineral water baths or massages.
SELLER
№ 1610

Seen here is a coupon for a mineral water bath at the Will Rogers Hotel.

# *Four*

# Government, Churches, and Schools

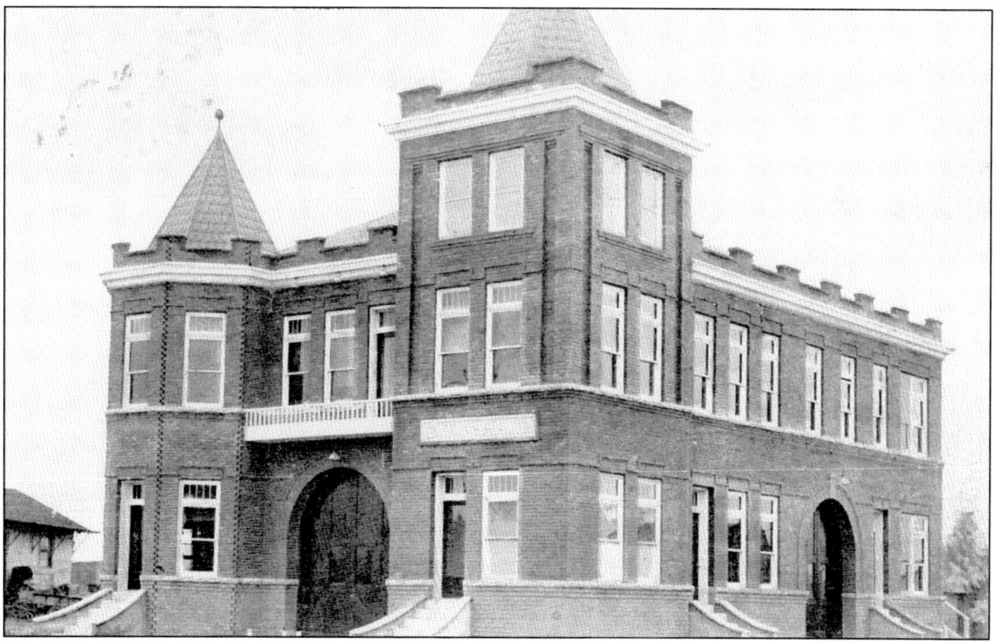

City officials moved into Claremore City Hall on November 21, 1911. The first floor of the building housed the police, judge, a private office, a courtroom, the fire chief's office, and the offices of the mayor and chief of police. The second floor contained sleeping quarters for the firemen as well as offices for the city superintendent, city clerk, city treasurer, and city surveyor and the council room. A six-cell jail was located in the basement. The building was torn down in 1963 to make room for a city hall/civic center complex.

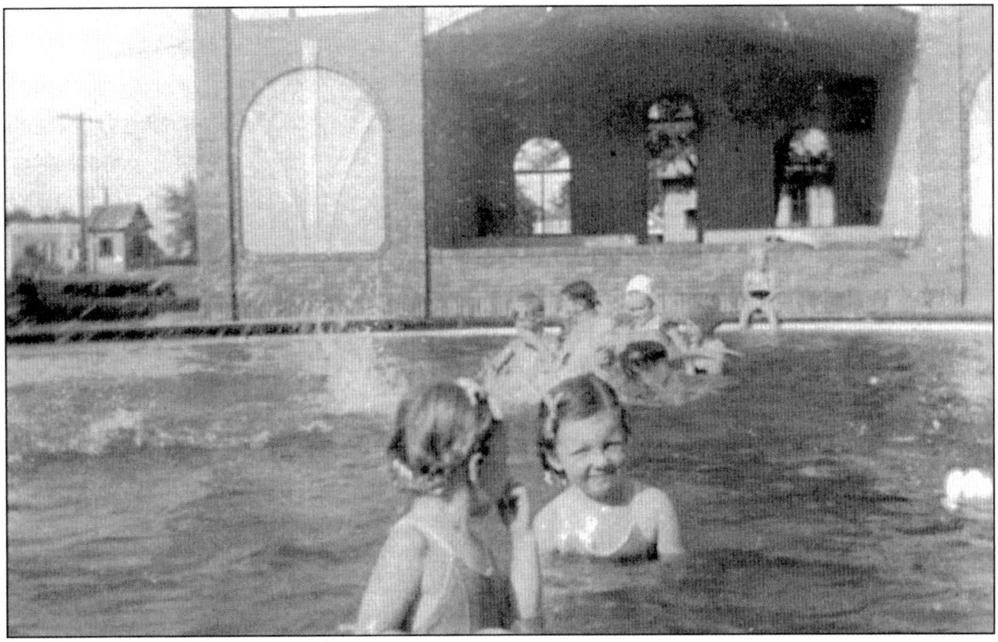


Claremore built a unique park just outside the city hall building. The park no longer exists but is seen in this rare park photograph from the 1930s. The park contained a large wading pool for children to cool off in the hot Oklahoma summers. It also housed an open-air amphitheater, seen here in the background, for band concerts. Tentlike monkey cages could also be found on the grounds.

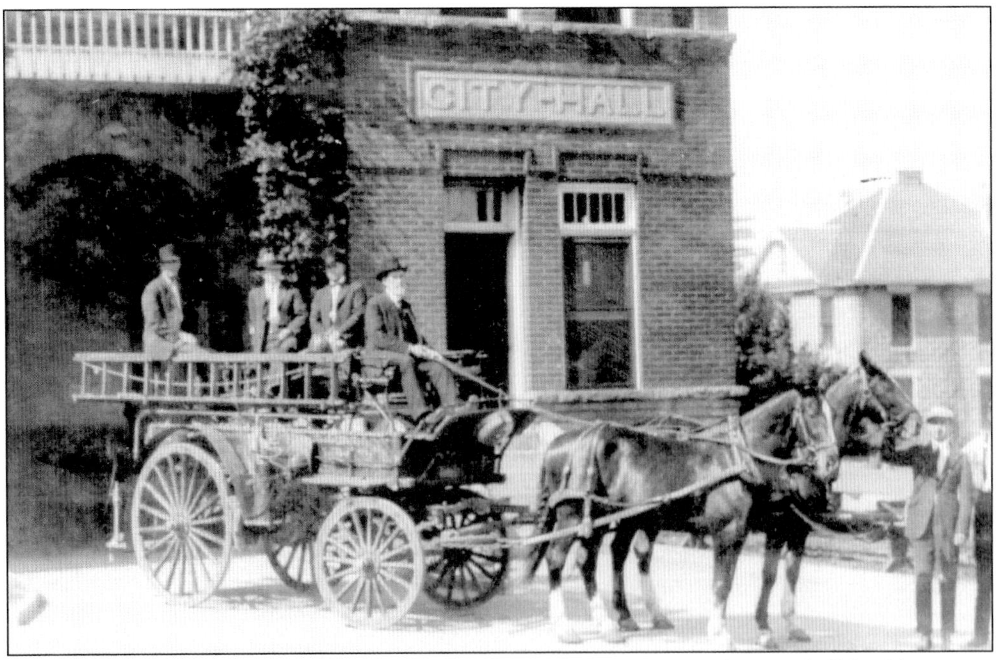


This early-day fire wagon and team of horses were once housed in the city hall building seen in the background. It was a wood-spoke wagon and carried buckets for hauling water to put out the fires.

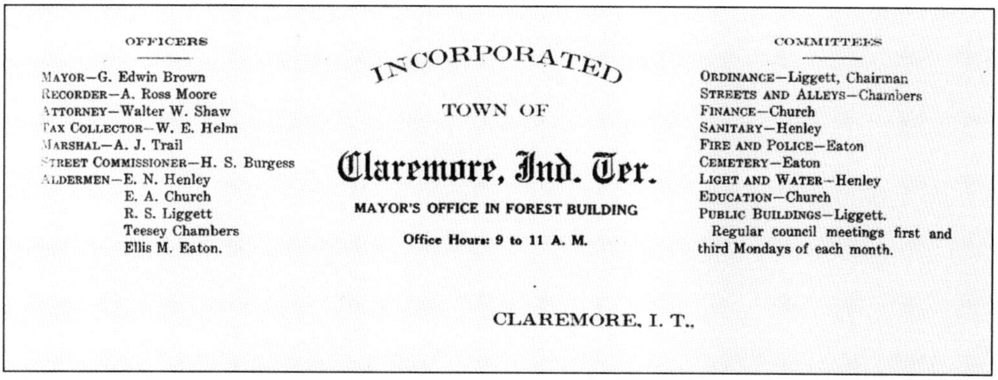

OFFICERS

MAYOR—G. Edwin Brown
RECORDER—A. Ross Moore
ATTORNEY—Walter W. Shaw
TAX COLLECTOR—W. E. Helm
MARSHAL—A. J. Trail
STREET COMMISSIONER—H. S. Burgess
ALDERMEN—E. N. Henley
E. A. Church
R. S. Liggett
Teesey Chambers
Ellis M. Eaton.

INCORPORATED

TOWN OF

Claremore, Ind. Ter.

MAYOR'S OFFICE IN FOREST BUILDING

Office Hours: 9 to 11 A. M.

COMMITTEES

ORDINANCE—Liggett, Chairman
STREETS AND ALLEYS—Chambers
FINANCE—Church
SANITARY—Henley
FIRE AND POLICE—Eaton
CEMETERY—Eaton
LIGHT AND WATER—Henley
EDUCATION—Church
PUBLIC BUILDINGS—Liggett.
Regular council meetings first and third Mondays of each month.

CLAREMORE, I. T.,

Claremore's first government offices were housed in the top floor of the Forest Building. The Forest Building is located next to the Eaton building on Main Street. The building still exists and is marked at the top with the name *Forest*. This rare copy of city letterhead is from Indian Territory. Many prominent citizens are listed on the paper.

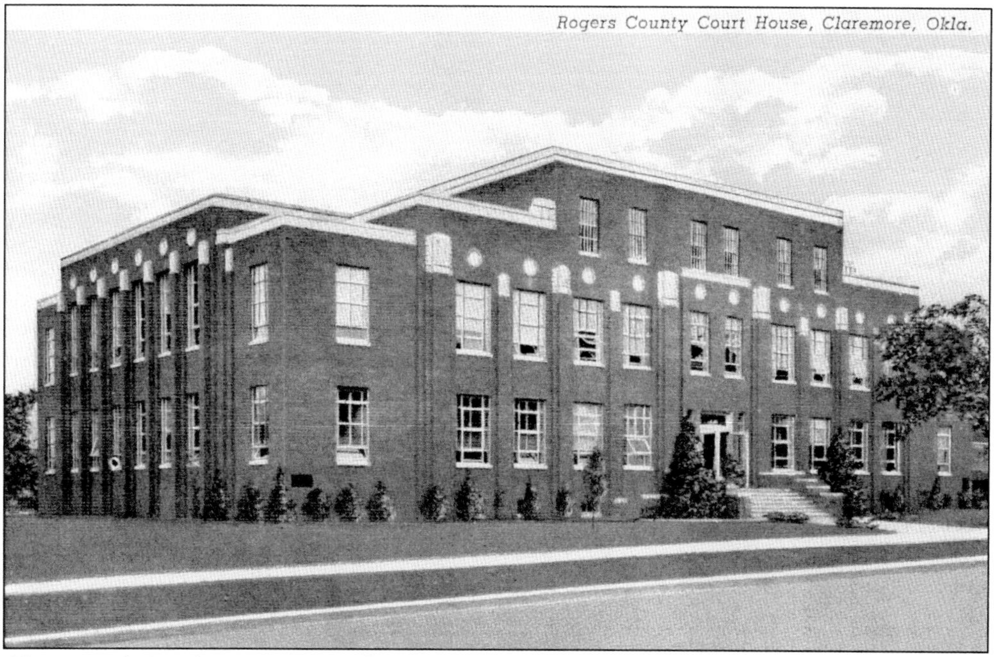


Claremore, being the county seat of Rogers County, dedicated the first courthouse on March 17, 1941. During the first 34 years after statehood, county officers had their offices in rooms on the second floor above business buildings. A building that originally housed an athletic center was purchased from John M. Bayless for the first Rogers County Courthouse.

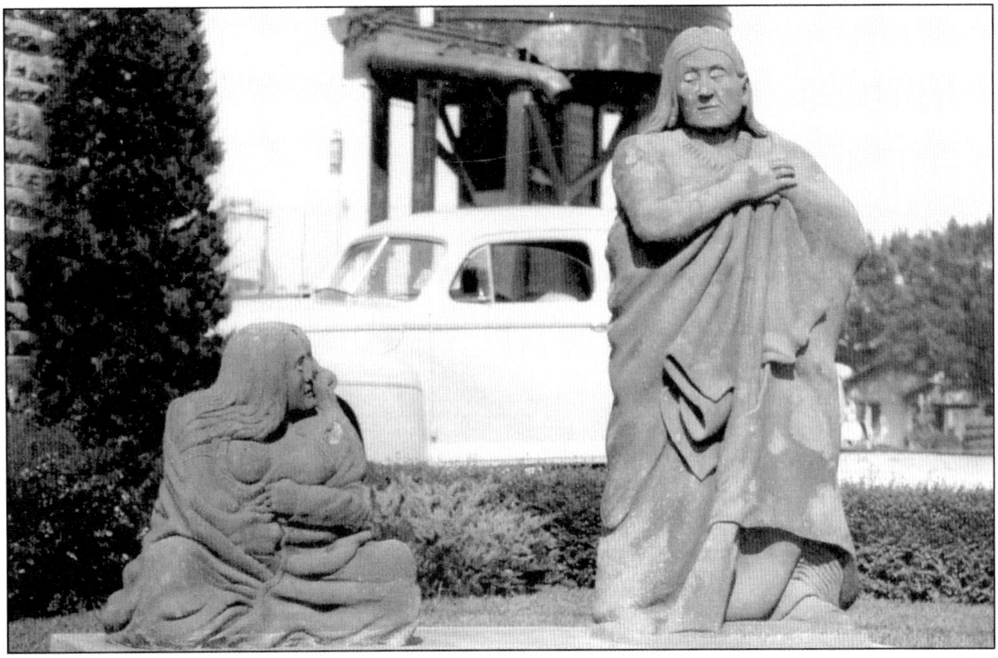

This statue sat in front of the highway patrol station in Claremore. The rock structure can be seen slightly in the background. It was located on the southwest corner of JM Davis Boulevard and Will Rogers Boulevard. The building still exists today as a private business. The statue originally belonged to Jim Parker and stood at Second Street and Choctaw Avenue before being moved to the patrol station. The statue was on loan and later removed and moved to Phoenix, Arizona, by the Parker family.

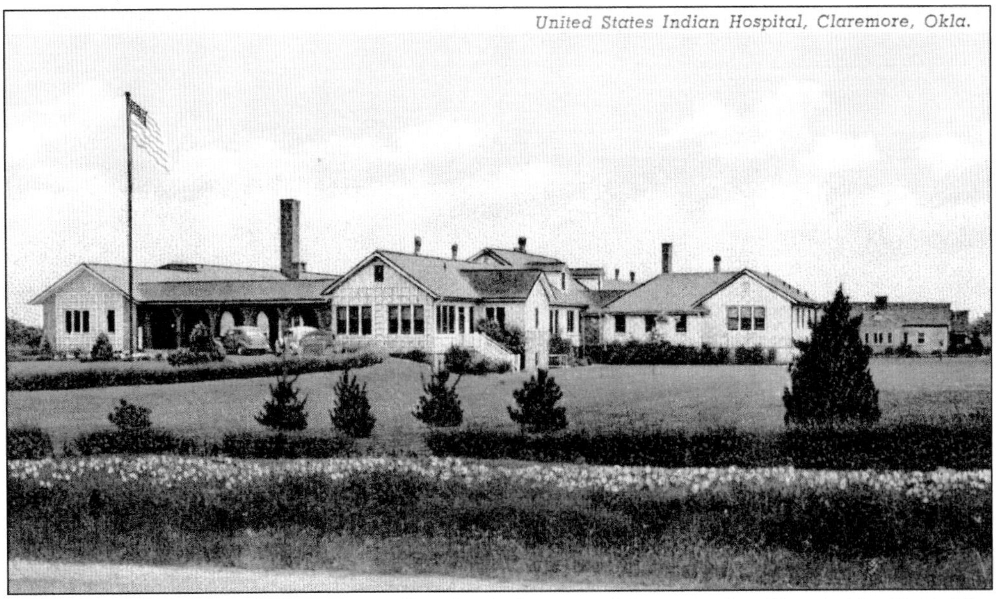


The United States Bureau of Indian Affairs built the United States Indian Hospital in 1942. The building above was used until 1976 when work began on a newer building. The new building was completed in 1977 and is still used today. The facility provides free medical aid to anyone who can provide a card proving Native American descent.

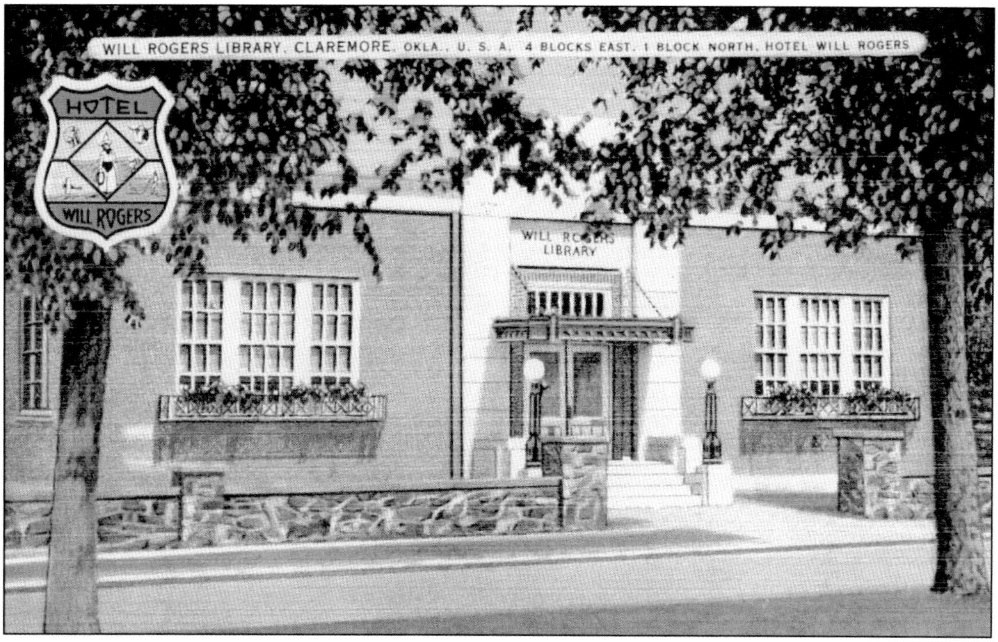


The original Will Rogers Library in Claremore was built as a result of a gift from Will Rogers. In making the donation, Rogers said, "Use this money for a good enterprise or give it to some old lady for a cow." Although Rogers objected to the library being named after him, when the structure was completed a year after his death, the city deemed it to be a fitting tribute to his generosity.

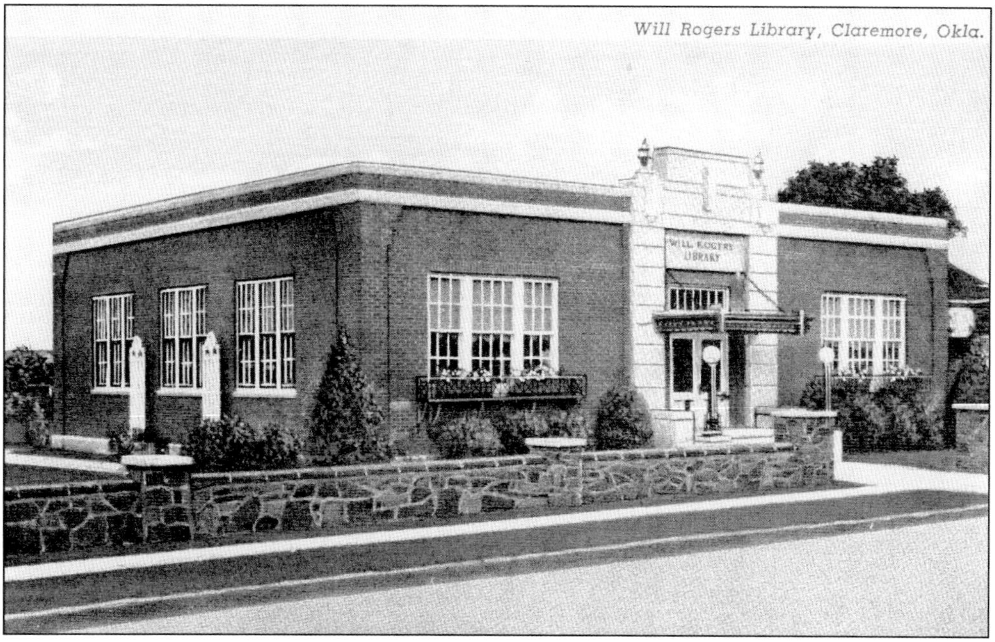


The Will Rogers Library was completed in 1936. It was built with material from the old Sequoyah Garage. It also contains the cornerstone from Claremore's first livery stable owned by Clem Rogers, father of Will Rogers. Today the building houses the fire administration offices as well as the Lynn Riggs Museum.

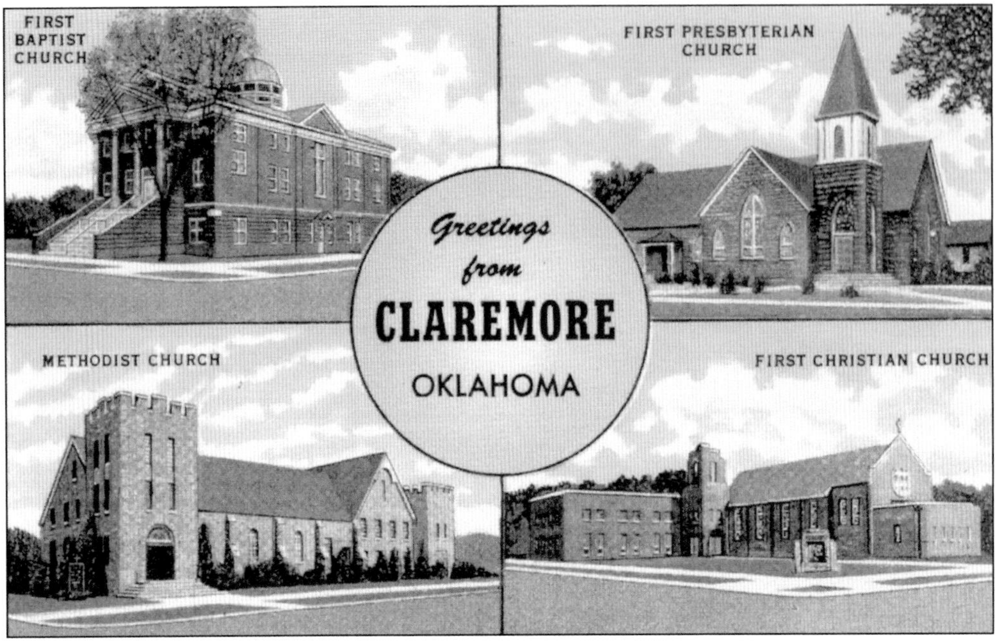


This postcard shows the four main churches in Claremore in the early 1900s: the First Baptist, First Presbyterian, Methodist, and First Christian Churches. Claremore lies right in the middle of the Bible Belt, and a church can be found on almost every corner now.

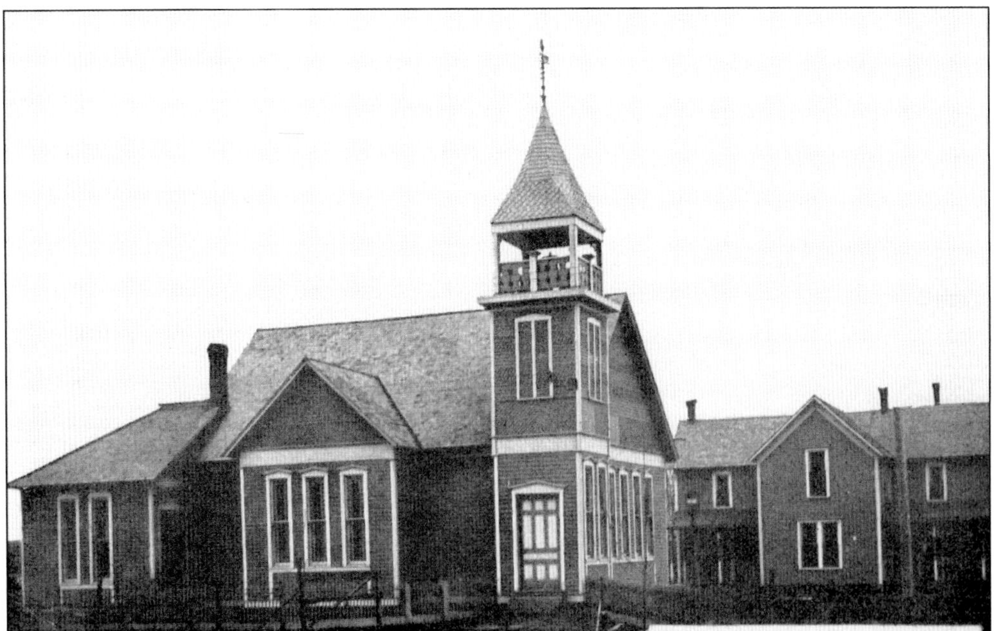


Mrs. F. A. Nielson donated half of a block of land in 1893 for the original First Baptist Church building. The other half of the same block of land was donated by F. A. Nielson for the Presbyterian church. The original First Baptist Church pictured here was a wood structure with a belfry.

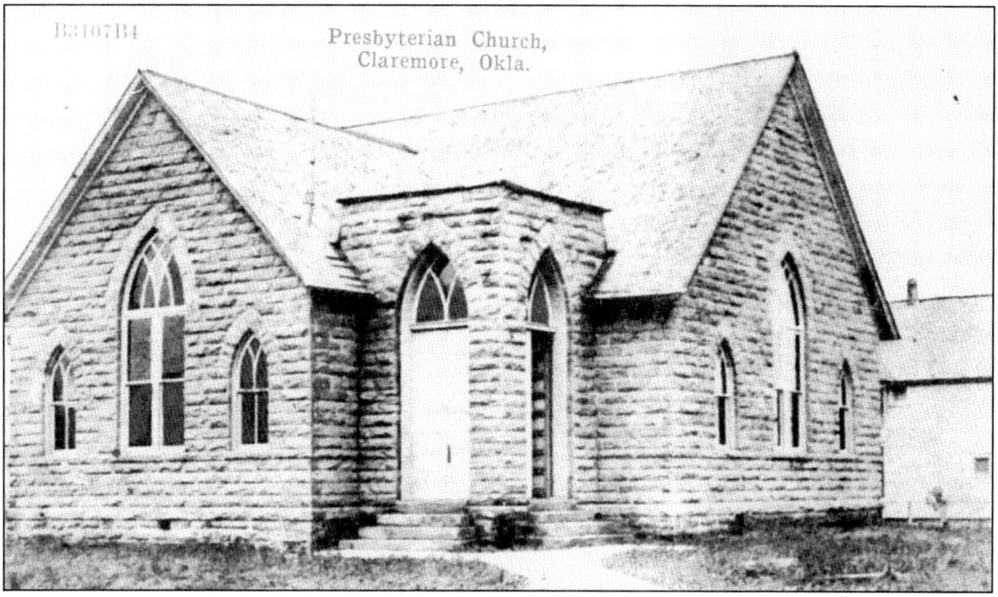


In 1889, the First Presbyterian Church was built at the corner of Second and Cherokee Streets. In 1893, there were four churches in Claremore. The Methodists, Episcopal South, and Presbyterians shared a building on alternate Sundays. The First Baptist Church had its own building. F. A. Nielson donated land at the corner of Fourth and Chickasaw Streets for the Presbyterian church. The church remains at this location today.

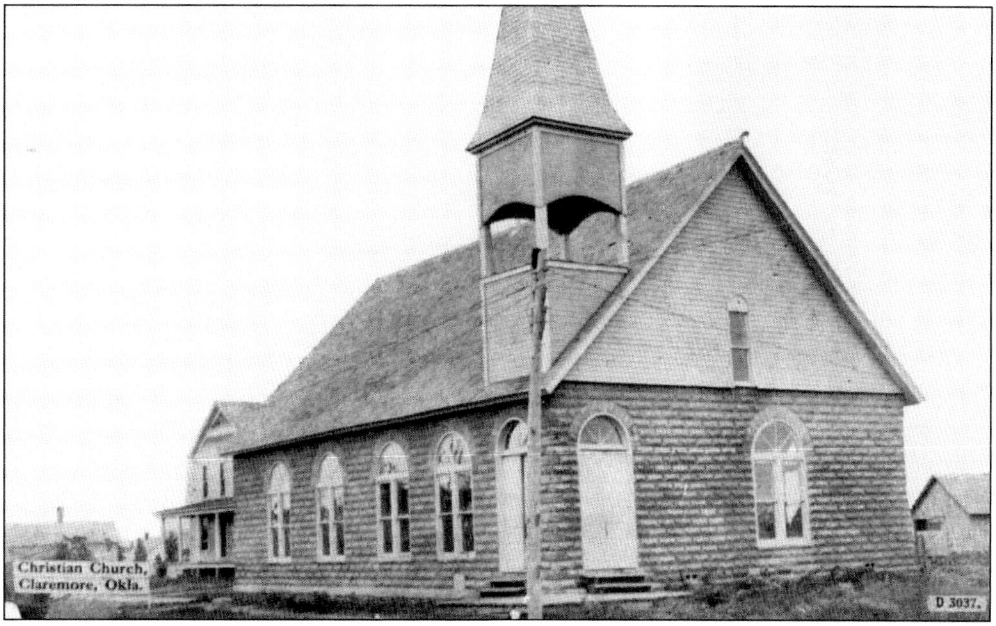


The First Christian Church has ties in Claremore, Indian Territory, dating back to 1894. However, its church structure, made of concrete block, was not built until 1907. It was a small building located at the corner of Sixth and Florence Streets. Baptisms were held at Allton Pond, north of Claremore. The first meeting in this building was held in November 1907. The building continued to serve its congregation until a newer building was built in 1947 at Fifth and Florence Streets.

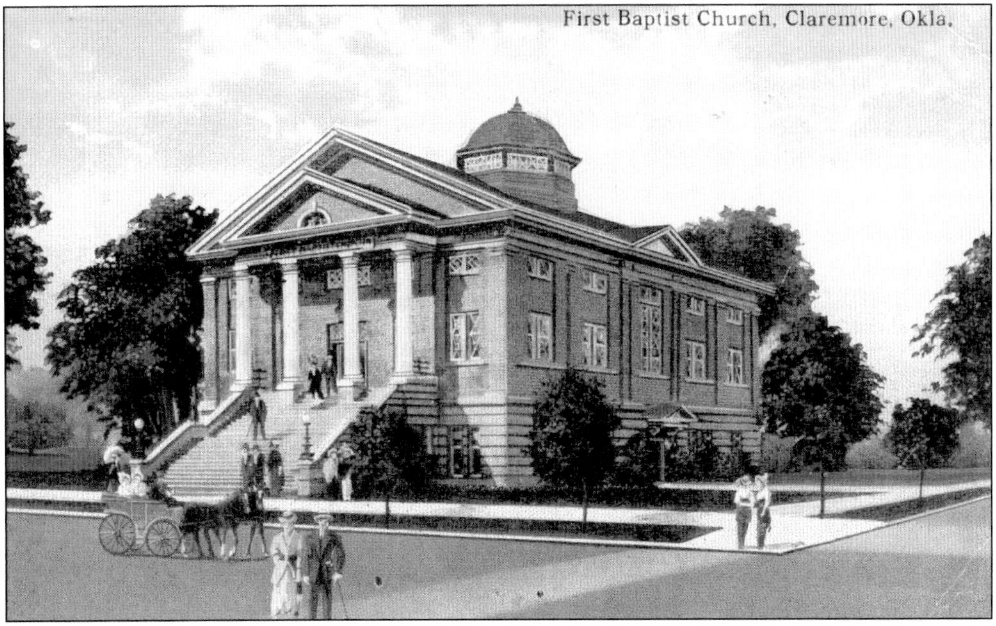


This postcard depicts a Sunday morning at First Baptist Church in 1916. Ground was broken for this new structure at the same location as the original on August 10, 1914. The dedication was in 1915. The brick building had beautiful stained-glass windows. The front steps and dome have been removed from the building, and major additions have been made; however, the main part of the building still stands.

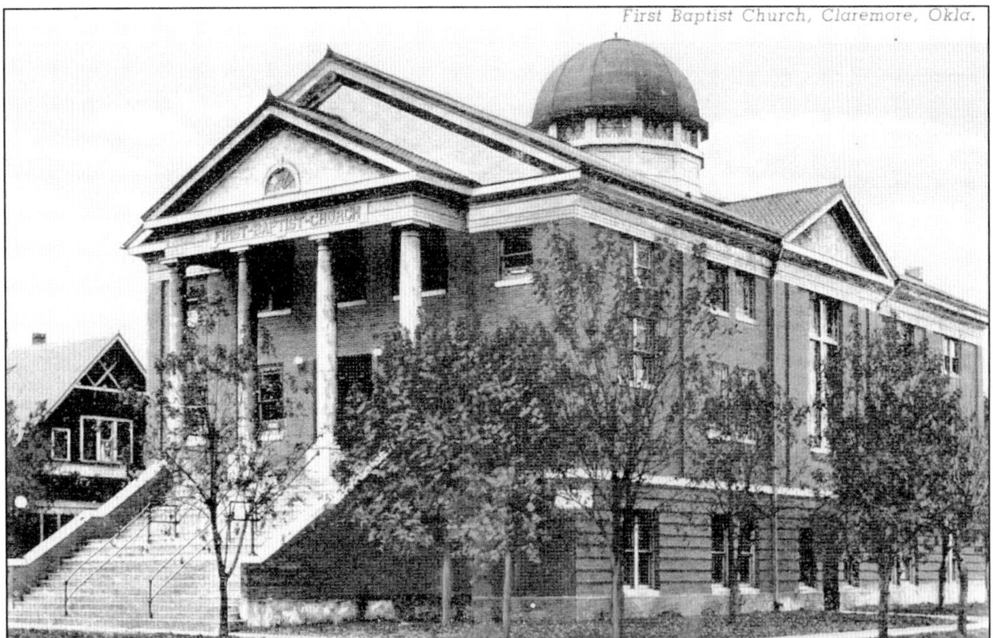


According to this postcard, First Baptist Church was also named Grace Temple and was known as the people's church. It was considered one of the handsomest church structures in the Southwest.

Early churches often could not afford baptisteries. Baptisms therefore took place in Dog Creek or area ponds. Sandra Dennis-Irwin is seen here being baptized in a rural farm pond by pastor George Maxwell.

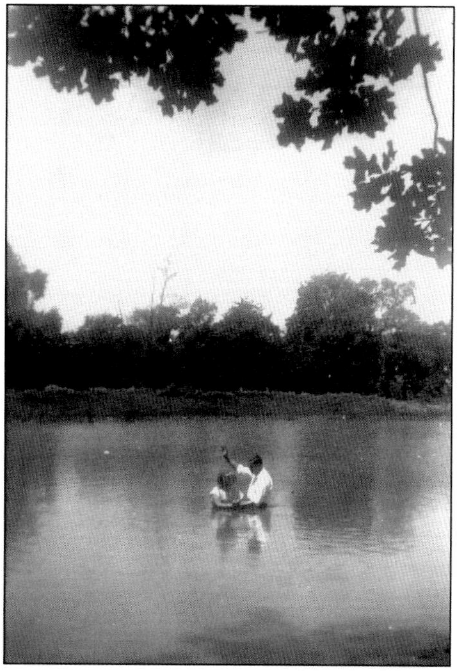

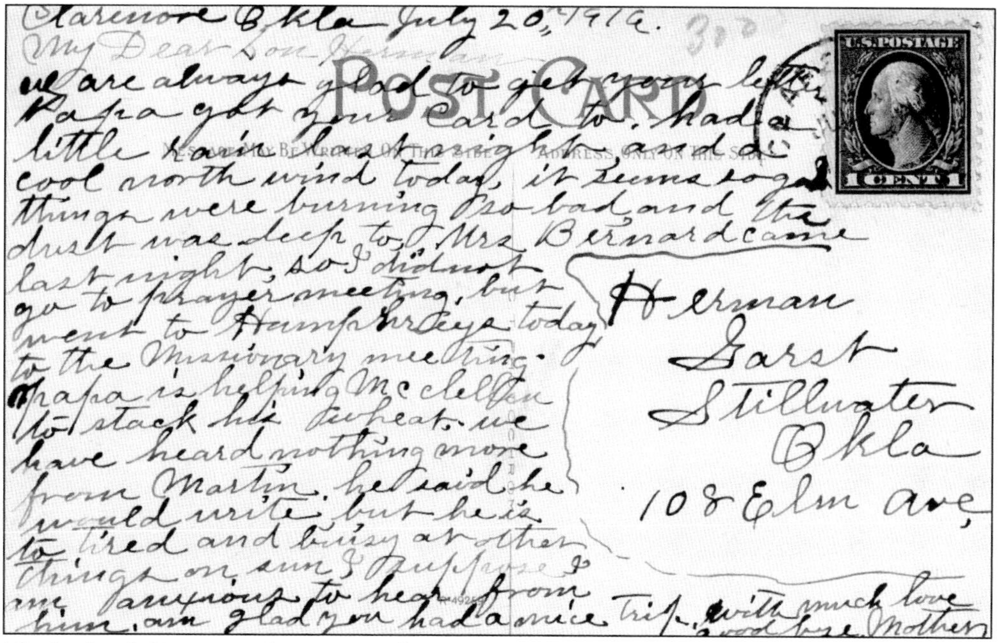


The back of this postcard, sent to Stillwater on July 20, 1919, reads, "My Dear Son Herman, We are always glad to get your letter. Papa got your card to. Had a little rain last night and a cool north wind today, it seems so good things were burning so bad and the dust was deep to. Mrs. Bernard came last night, so I did not go to prayer meeting, but went to Humphrey's today to the Missionary meeting. Papa is helping McClellan to stack his wheat. We heard nothing more from Martin. He said he would write but he is to tired and busy at other things. Oh son I suppose I am anxious to hear from him. Am glad you had a nice trip. With much love. Good bye, Mother."

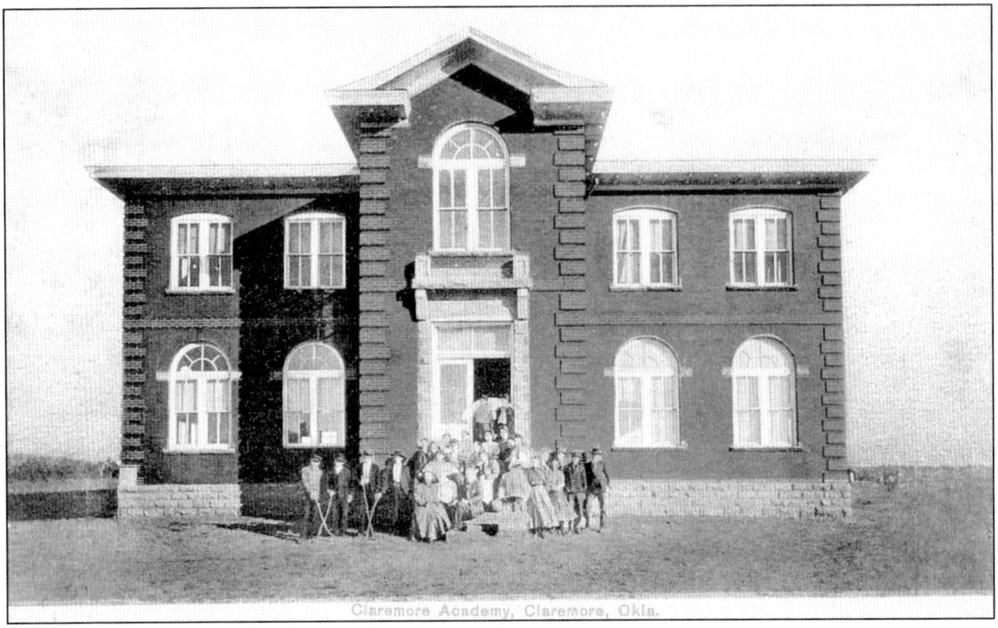


Claremore's Academy School was located on Academy Street, between Normal and Nome Avenues, overlooking Woodlawn Cemetery. The cemetery has now enveloped the land where the school once stood. It was built in 1905 by the Commercial Club. It was torn down between 1918 and 1940. It was one of only two schools in Claremore for a time, and both were subscription, or script, schools. Students could attend script schools for a small yearly fee.

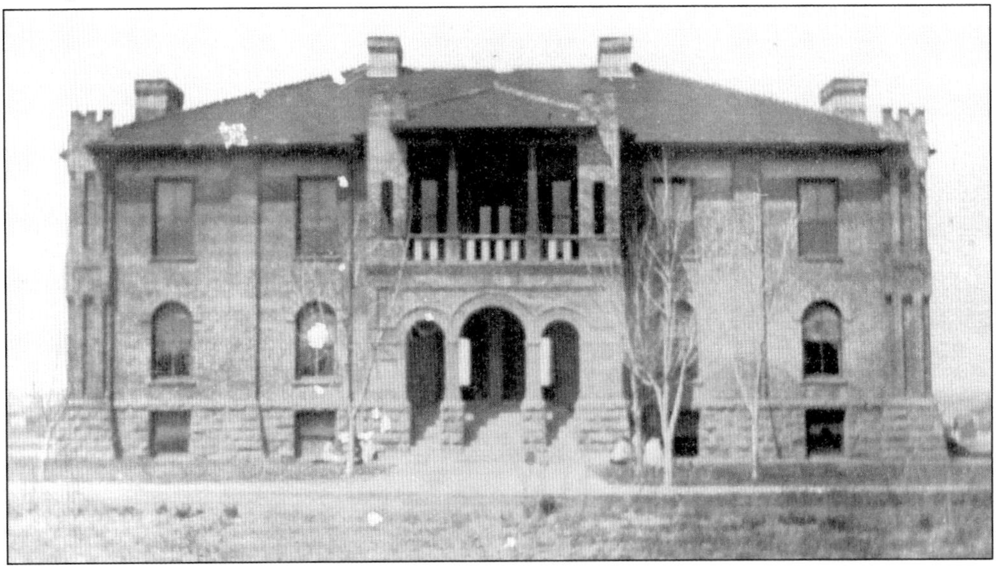

Claremont School was built in 1908 at Ninth Street and Wewoka Avenue. When students reached high school age, they attended Eastern University Preparatory School (EUPS). In 1909, the Claremont building was used for EUPS. The first year it enrolled 720 students. In 1910, a new building was built on "Prep Hill" for EUPS, the present site of Rogers State University. There was an argument in town over where to place the new building. Those in favor of the hill were called "hillbillies," and those in favor of the McClain place were called "prairie dogs." The hillbillies won out.

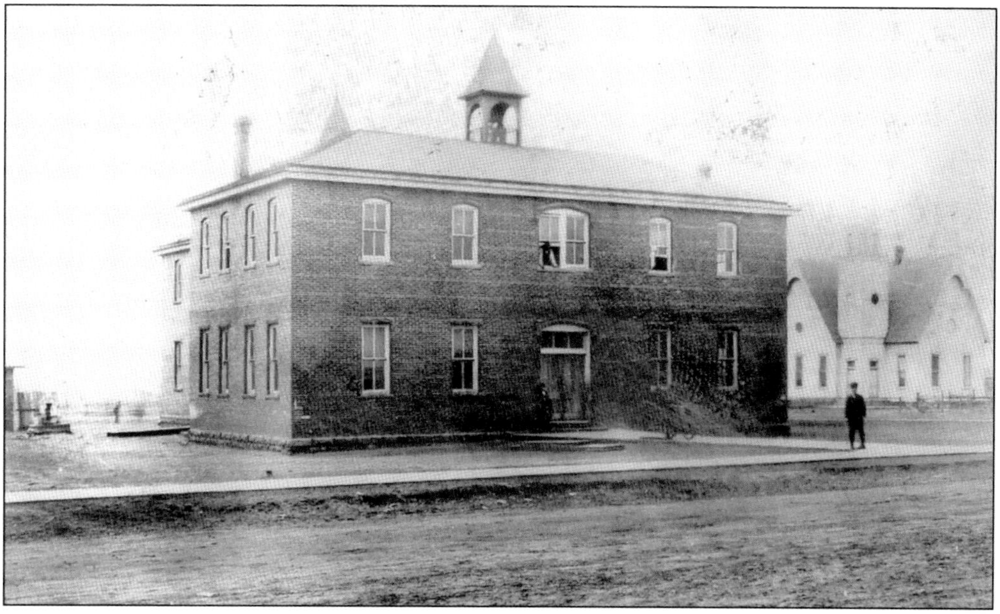

The Hiawatha School was built in 1906 at the corner of Fifth Street and Chickasaw Avenue. This two-story structure contained eight rooms. The Hiawatha was also a script school. The original building was torn down in 1955 to build a gymnasium.

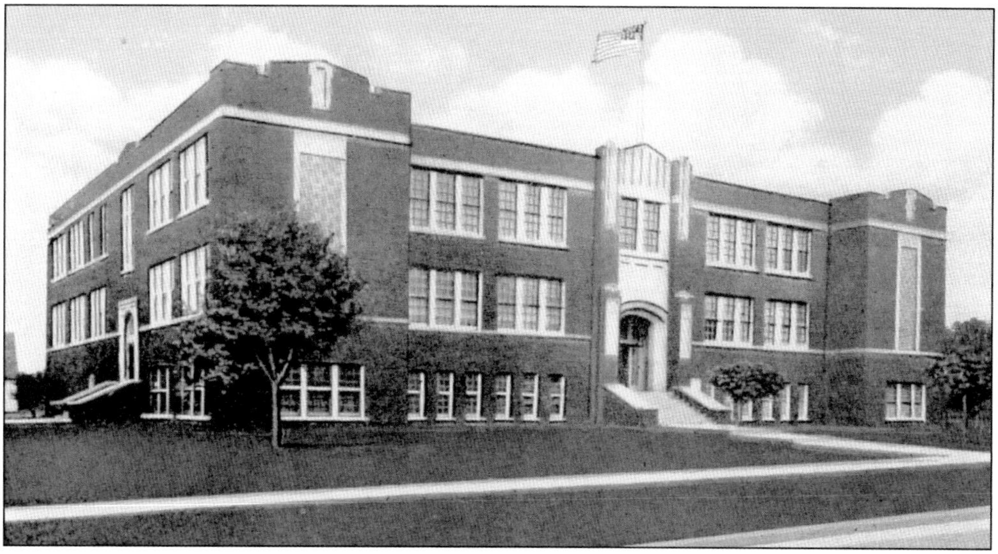

Claremore High School was constructed by the City of Claremore in 1914 at a cost of $20,000. It was located across the street from the Belvidere Mansion, at the northwest corner of Fourth and Chickasaw Streets. The four-story building served as the high school until a new building was constructed in 1973. It was then used as a junior high school for several years. The building still stands but is in a state of disrepair and is used for administration purposes only. The mascot for Claremore High School is the zebra. It seems there was a mix-up with the football uniforms. When the boys took the field for the first time in red and white stripes, a fan yelled, "They look like a bunch of zebras." The name stuck, and the colors remain red and white. The carriage house behind the Belvidere Mansion was later used as a candy store called the Sugar Shack. Teenagers of that era spent a lot of time after school at the Sugar Shack.

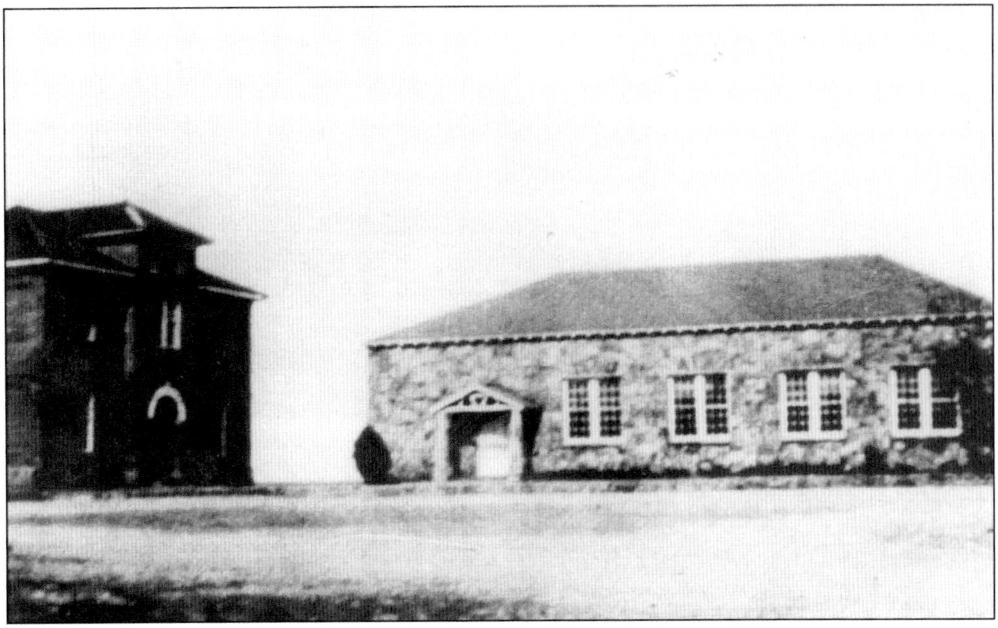

Sequoyah School is located just north of Claremore. The people of that area had a need for a school district without having to drive their children into Claremore. At the time it was built, nothing but prairie existed around it. The two-story building housed the elementary grades and a gymnasium. The classes were on the east and the gymnasium on the west. The other building housed the high school. These buildings burned; however, they have been replaced by newer, more modern buildings still used today.

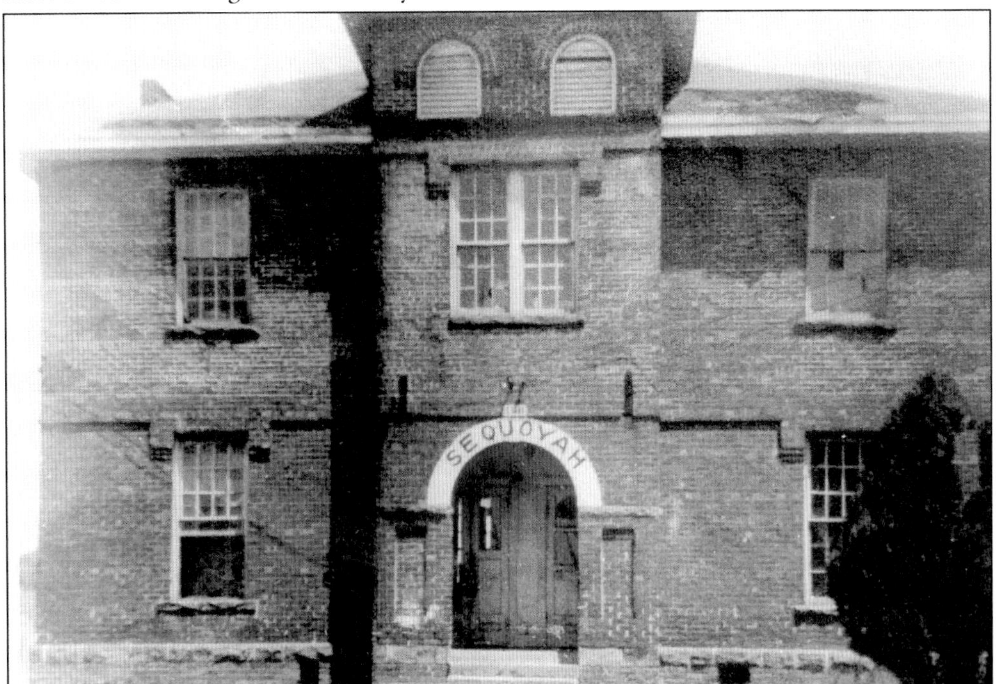

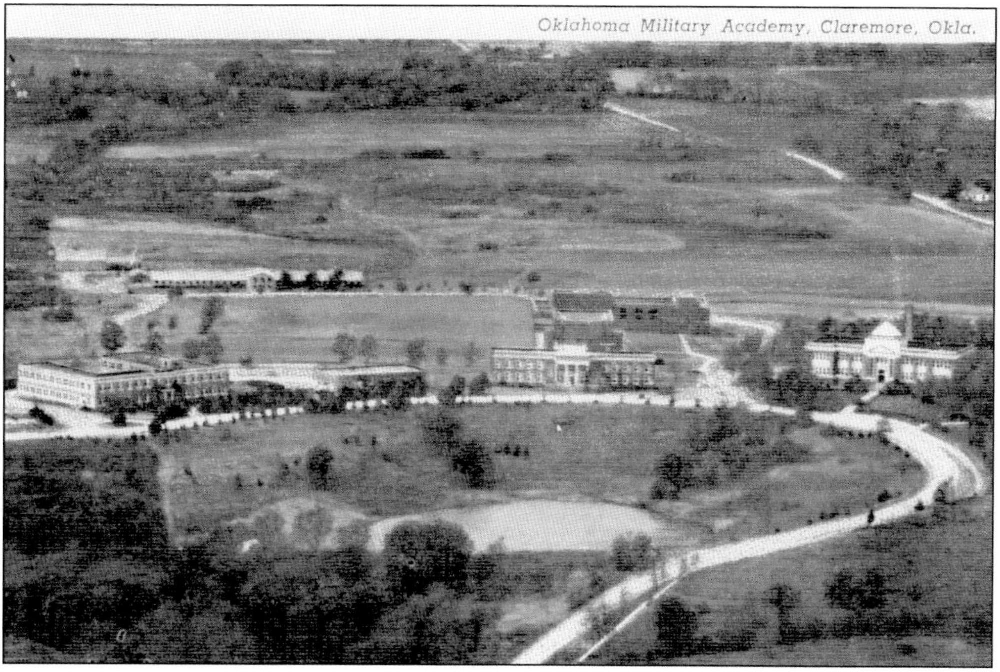


Oklahoma Military Academy began in 1919 on a hill overlooking Claremore. The academy was known as the "West Point of the Southwest," producing many leaders and war heroes. This aerial view was postmarked in 1950. The academy closed its doors on May 29, 1971. After several name changes, the growing campus is now home to Rogers State University.

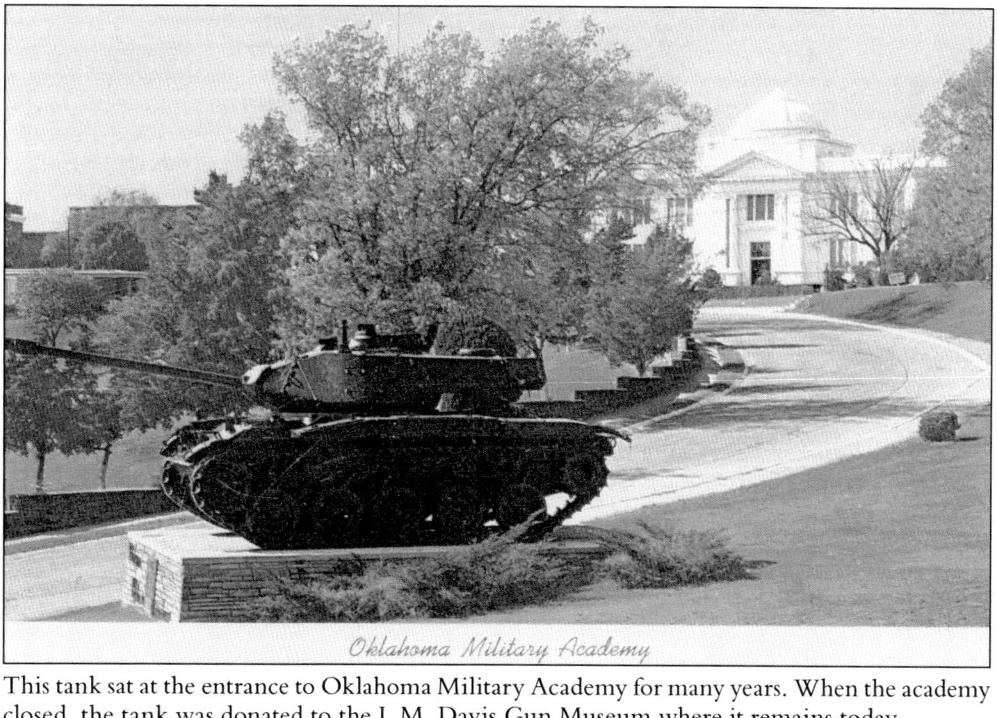


This tank sat at the entrance to Oklahoma Military Academy for many years. When the academy closed, the tank was donated to the J. M. Davis Gun Museum where it remains today.

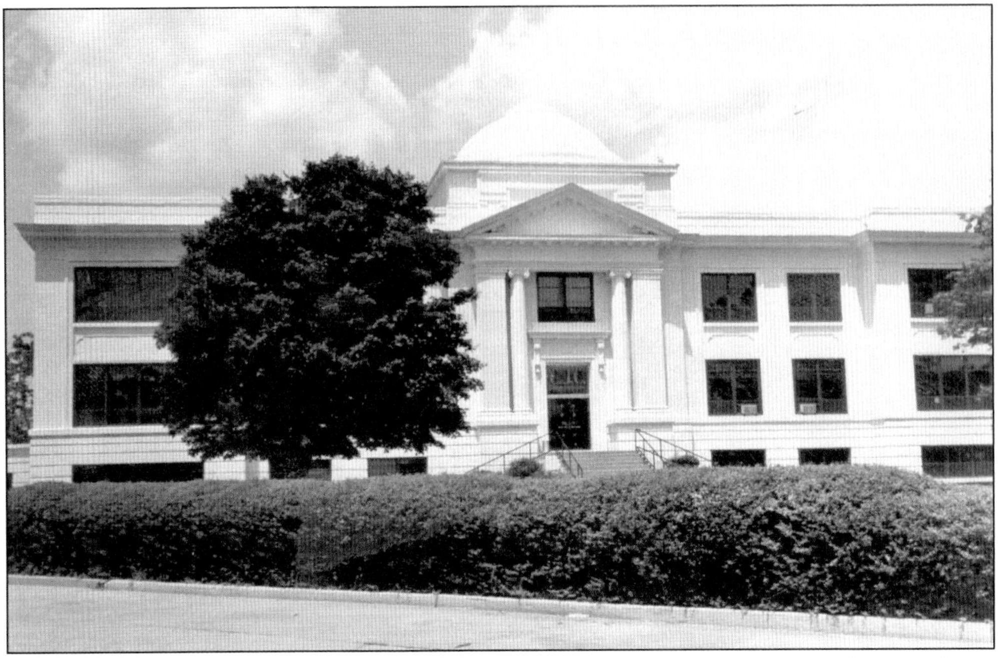

This white-domed building was originally built for Oklahoma Military Academy and was named Preparatory Hall. It now houses the administration offices for Rogers State University. It is situated at the top of the hill overlooking Claremore. The Main Street view looking west is reminiscent of looking at a capital building.

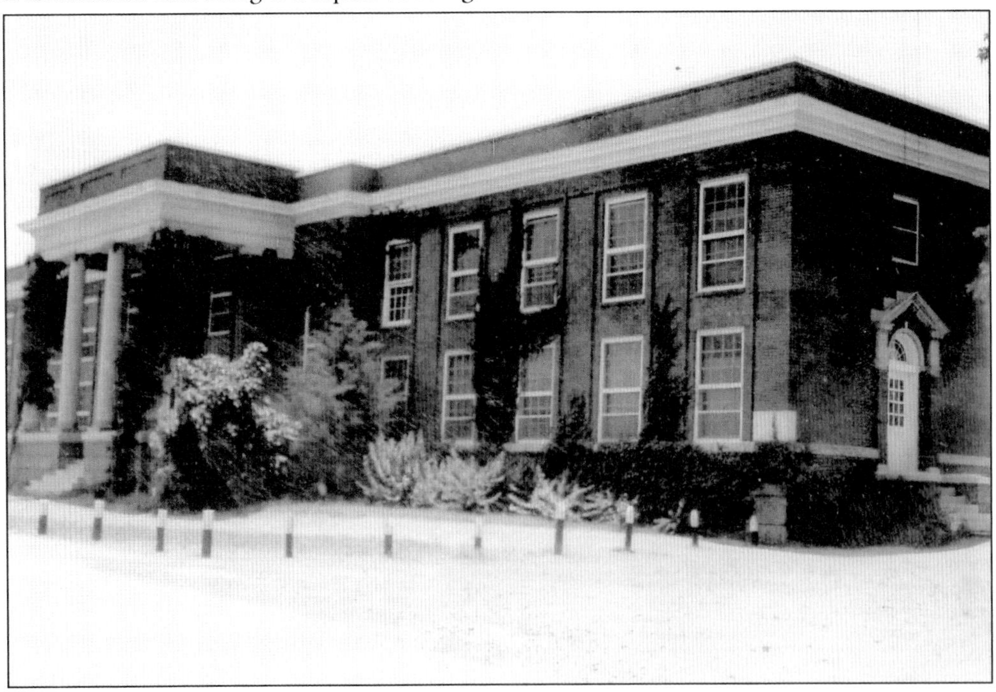

Oklahoma Military Academy named this building Meyer Barracks after the first Oklahoman killed in World War I, Maurice Meyer. This was the academy's first barracks as prior to it being built in 1920 the students stayed in tents.

*Five*

# Planes, Trains, and Automobiles

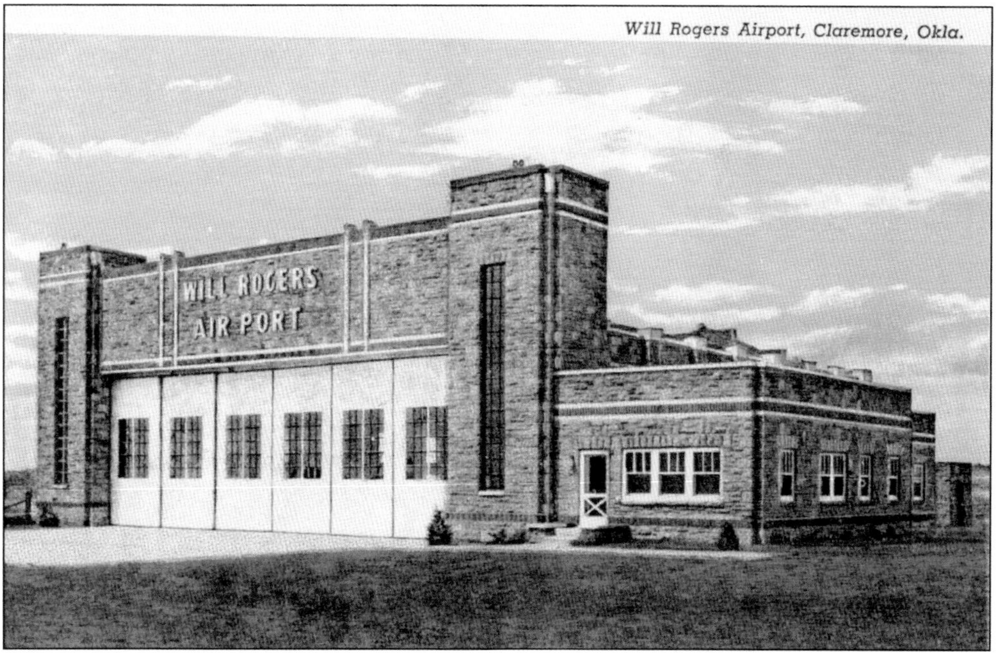


The Will Rogers Airport was dedicated on July 14, 1931, by Harold Gatty and Wiley Post. Will Rogers was the master of ceremonies. In Rogers's words, there were "30 acres of people present." The airport was built by the city in two weeks time in answer to Rogers's statement that he would "invite Gatty and Wiley to Claremore if it could be reached any other way than by parachute." Rogers made frequent stops here on his trips across the country. The airport was razed in 1980 to make way for Centrilift–Baker Hughes.

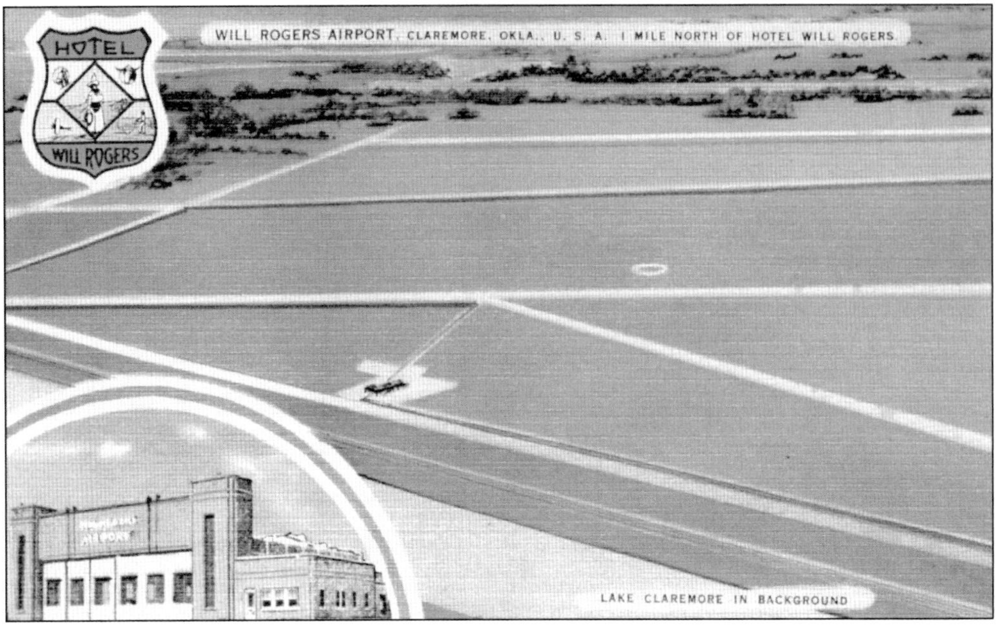


This aerial view of the Will Rogers Airport shows the airport's many runways. Claremore Lake can be seen in the background, and the road in the foreground is historic Route 66. The airport runways are now home to several private residences as well as Claremore High School and other area schools.

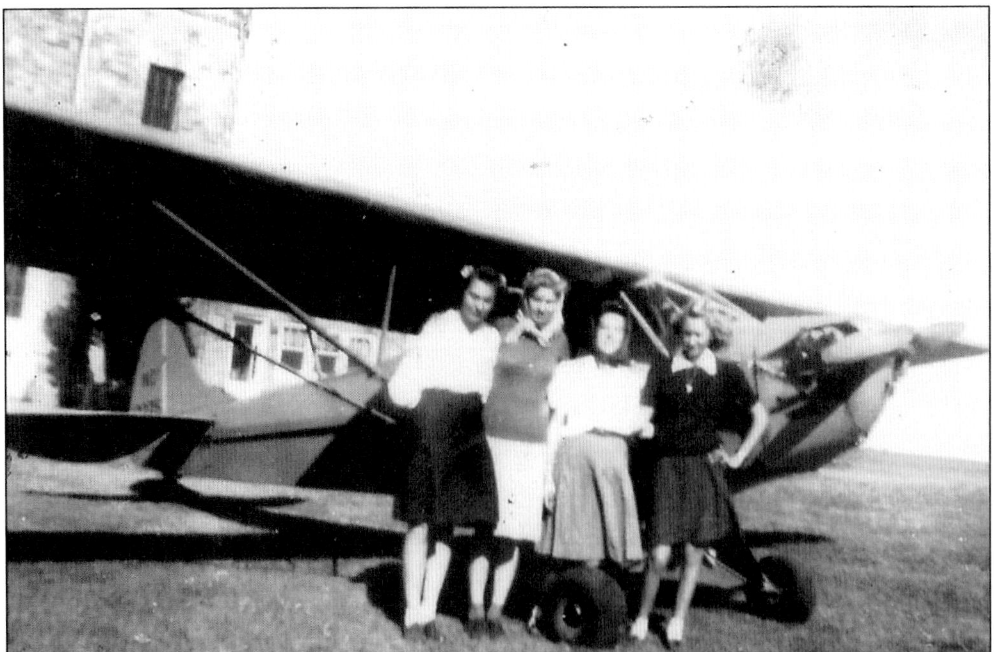

From left to right, Alma Ott Tabor, Imogene King Crutchfield, Doris Moore Vanaman, and Esther Dunlap Stark had been on a Sunday school outing at the totem pole and on the return trip decided to stop at the airport. This picture was taken in 1946–1947.

Will Rogers loved a fast horse, but he also had a passion for flying. Rogers is pictured here with the Ford Tri-Motor airplane. The Tri-Motor airplane was the first all-metal airplane in the world. Manufacturing the Tri-Motor airplane made Ford the world leader in the aviation industry.

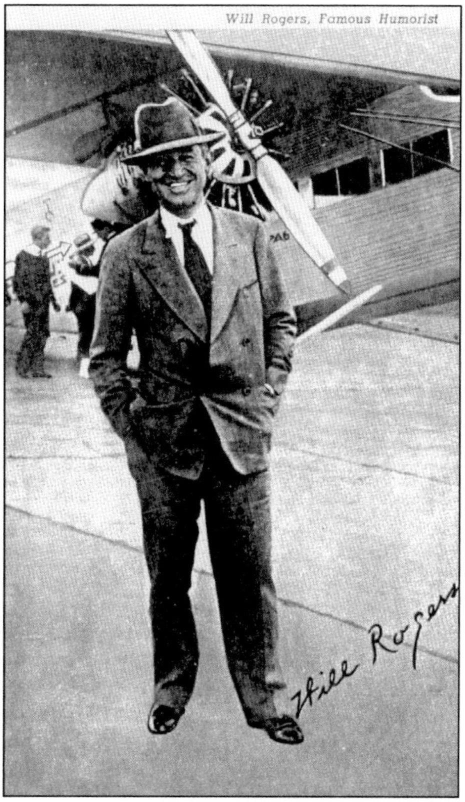


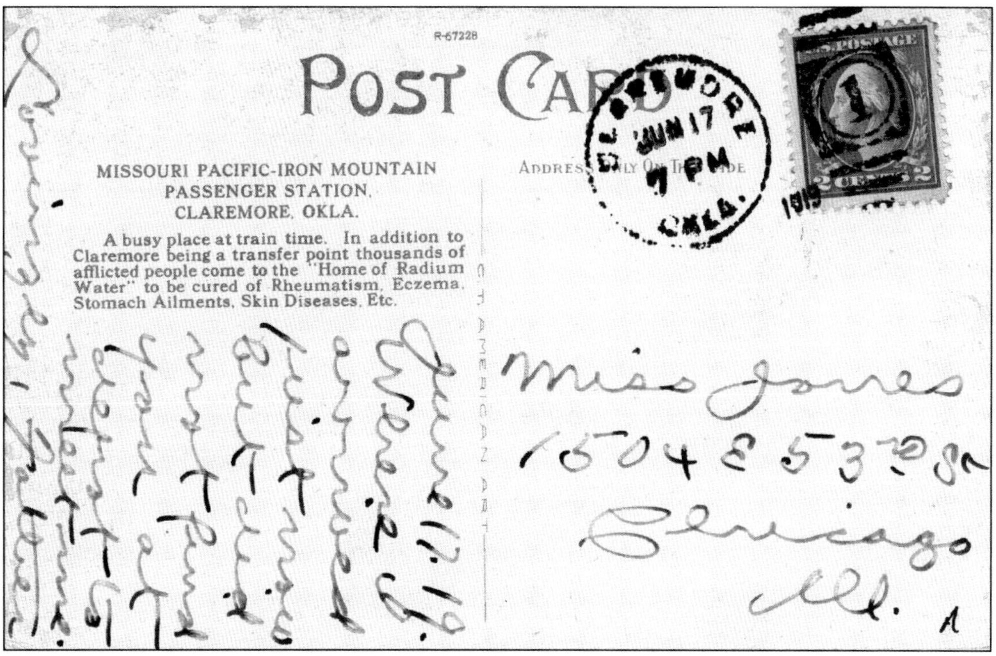


Written on the back of this postcard, postmarked June 17, 1919, is, "Where I arrived just now but did not find you at depot to meet me. Lovingly, Father." It is addressed to Miss Jones in Chicago, Illinois.

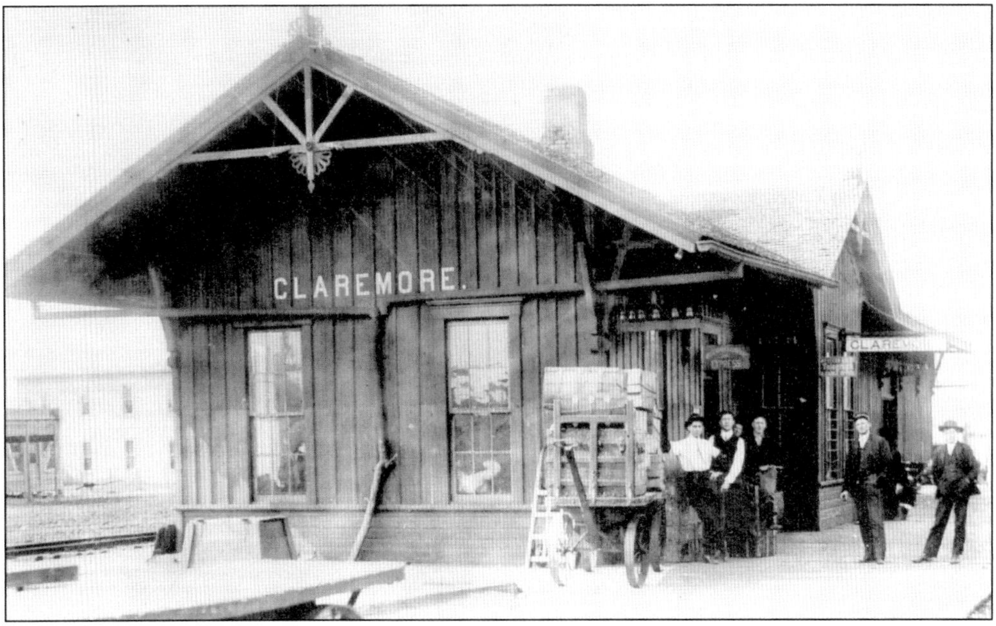


Claremore's future was drastically changed in 1882 when the St. Louis and San Francisco Railroad, better known as the Frisco Railroad, came roaring through town. The Frisco depot was built on the west side of Claremore. The railroad changed the face of Claremore, allowing area businessmen easier access for delivery of merchandise.

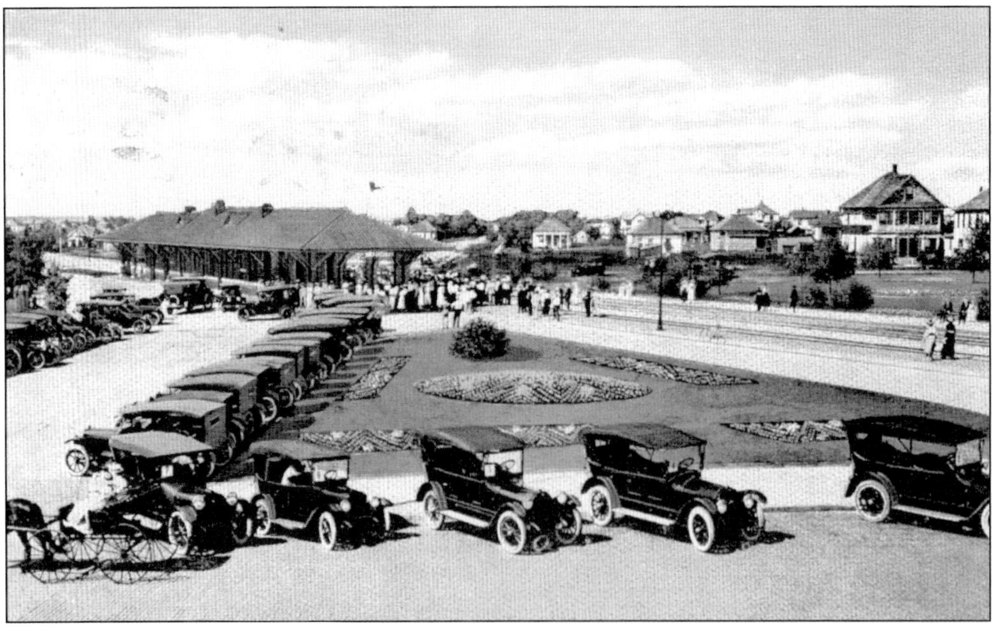

The Missouri Pacific and Iron Mountain train station was one of two passenger train stations operating in Claremore at the beginning of the 20th century. This particular station was located just behind the Belvidere Mansion near the present-day location of the Gazebo Park. These two railroads brought people from all over the nation to take healing radium baths. Although passenger trains no longer pass through Claremore and the depots have been destroyed, there is still an average of 100 trains per day passing through the town.

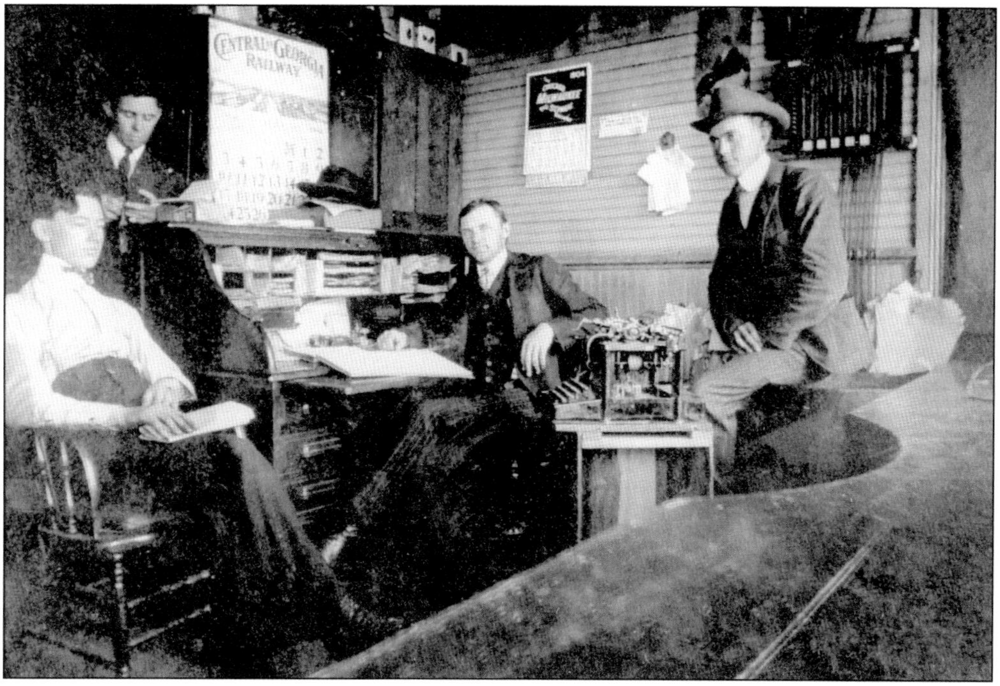


Pictured here is the interior of the Frisco Railroad station. The two calendars on the wall are turned to April 1904.

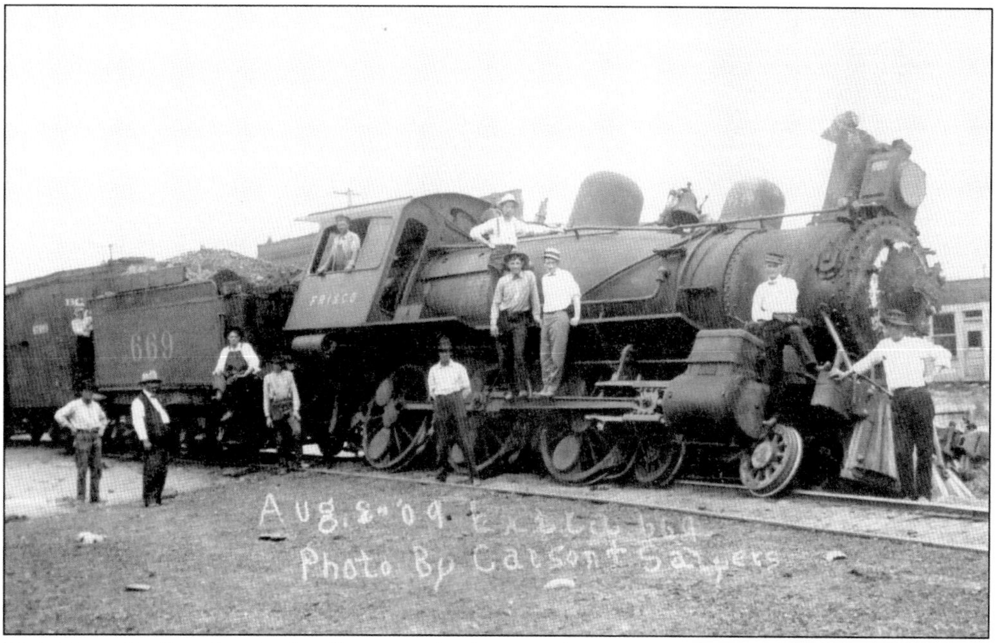


This Frisco Railroad train derailment took place in Claremore on August 8, 1909. Fortunately, judging by this picture, only the engine jumped the tracks.

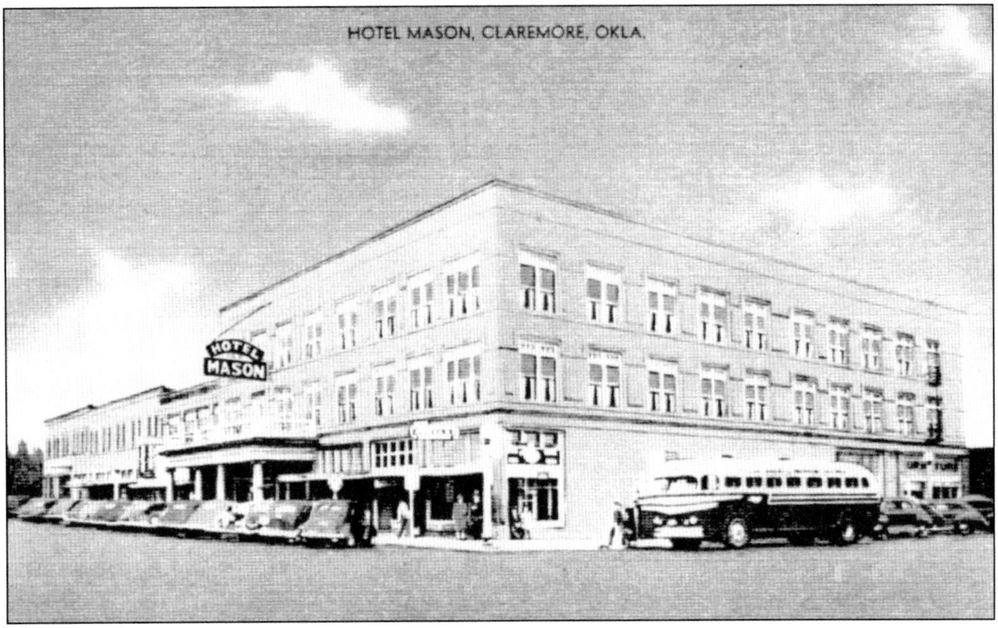


Claremore's bus depot was at one time located on Route 66 in the corner of the Mason Hotel building. Claremore was a routine stop along the bus route that continued on to Tulsa and farther points. The depot being at the hotel made it very convenient for weary passengers to spend the night or get a cup of coffee. Many young men caught this bus on their way to basic training after being drafted.

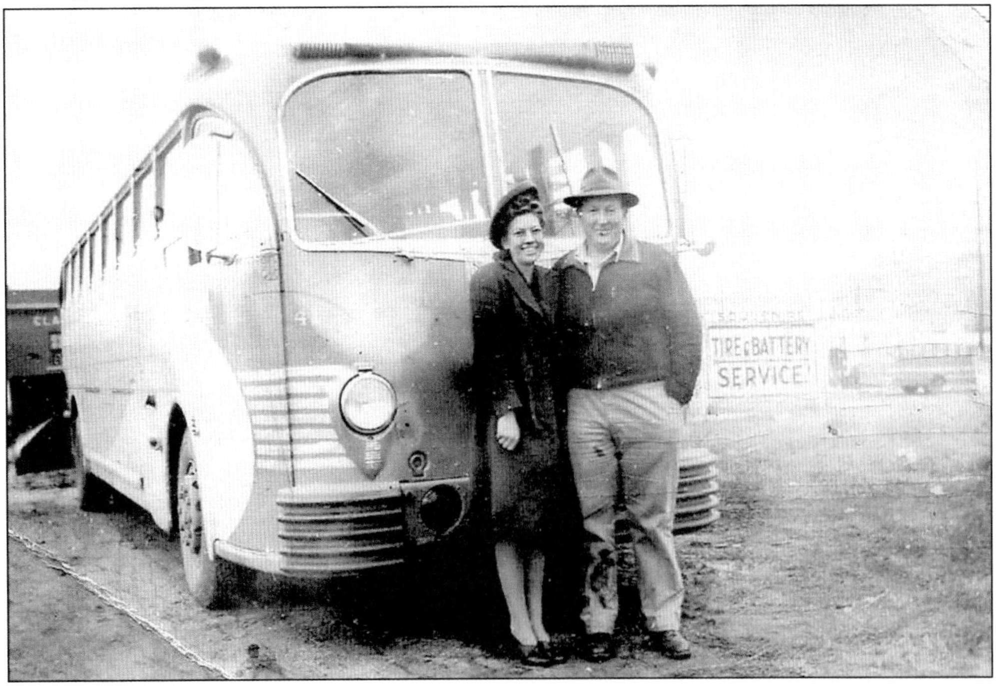


Lavell Dennis and Ella Mae Cheek-Dennis are waiting at the bus depot to depart on a short trip. The Frisco Railroad train station can be seen in the background as well as a tire and battery store. Ella Mae Cheek was born in Claremore and resides there still.

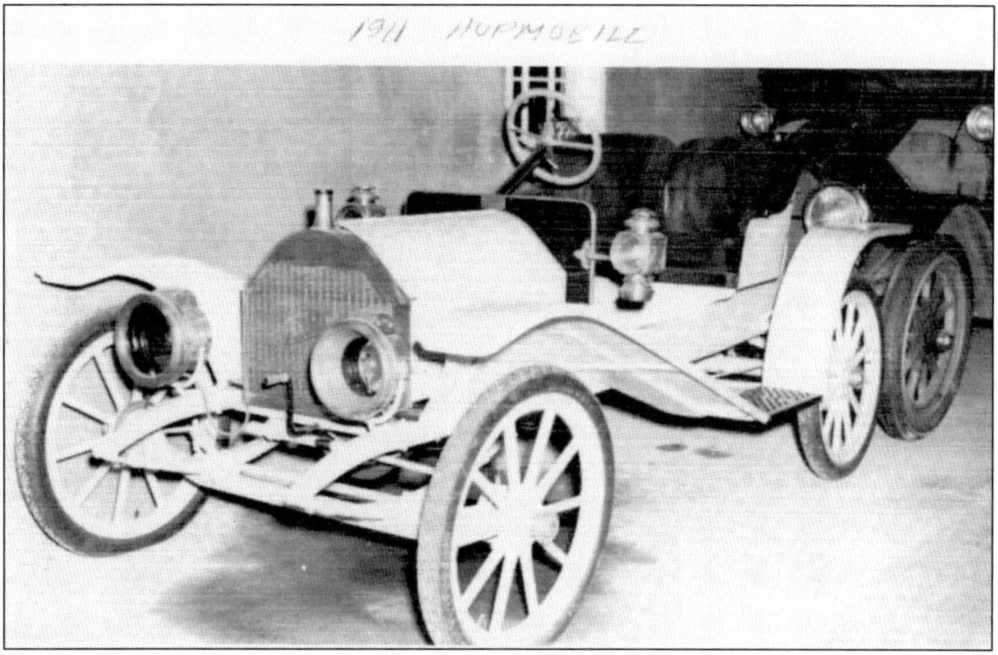


The Hupmobile was a common form of transportation in Claremore after the invention of the automobile. A 1918 issue of the *Claremore Messenger* reported, "Dr. A. M. Arnold, a native of Kentucky, and a lover of fine horses, came to Oklahoma and after several years has caught the Oklahoma spirit. Last week he went to Muskogee and bought one of those nice Hupmobile touring cars. Nothing like the Oklahoma spirit when it once gets a hold."

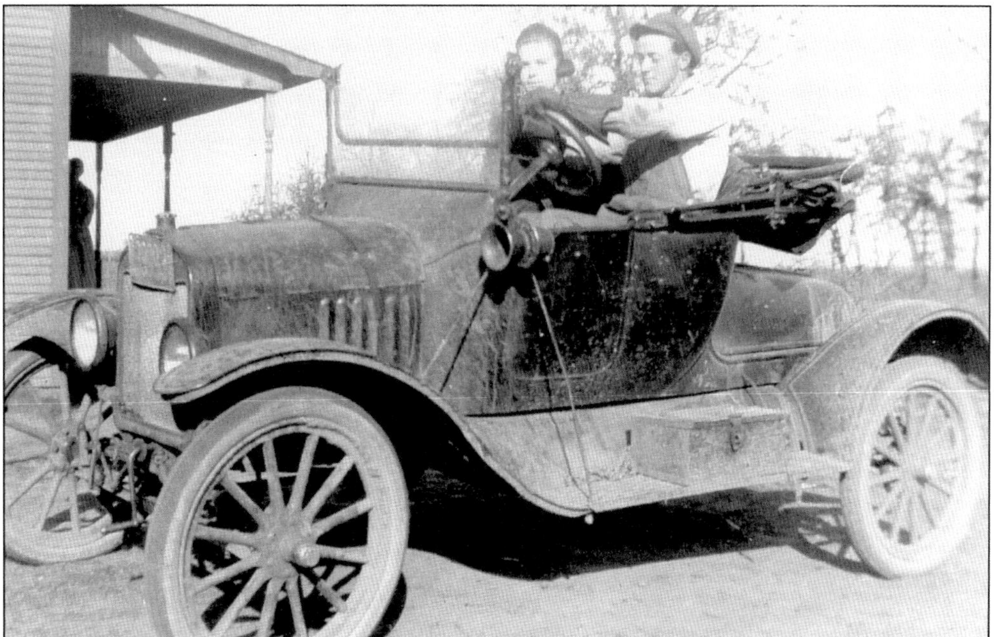

Carl Cooper and Elza Cheek-Cooper are out for a leisurely Sunday drive in their Model T in the early 1920s. The wheels had wood spokes, and the tool chest sat on the running board. The Coopers lived and farmed north of Claremore.

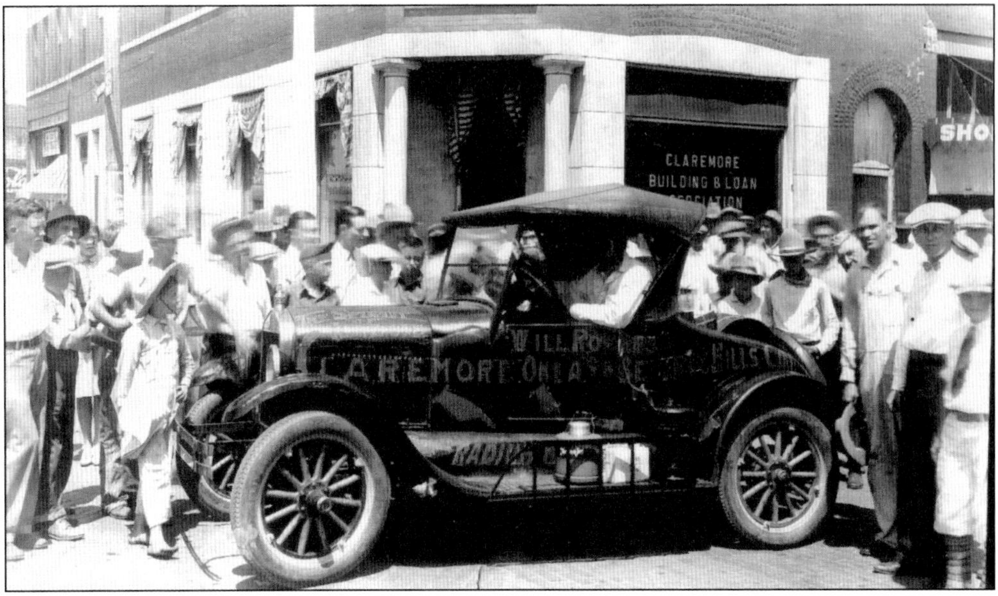


This Ford car made a nonstop drive from Claremore to Will Rogers's Beverly Hills, California, home. Driving the car is Bob Klaher with Jude Hutchins. The group shown here gathered to see them off from the corner of Will Rogers and Lynn Riggs Boulevards. The building in the background was once the First National Bank.

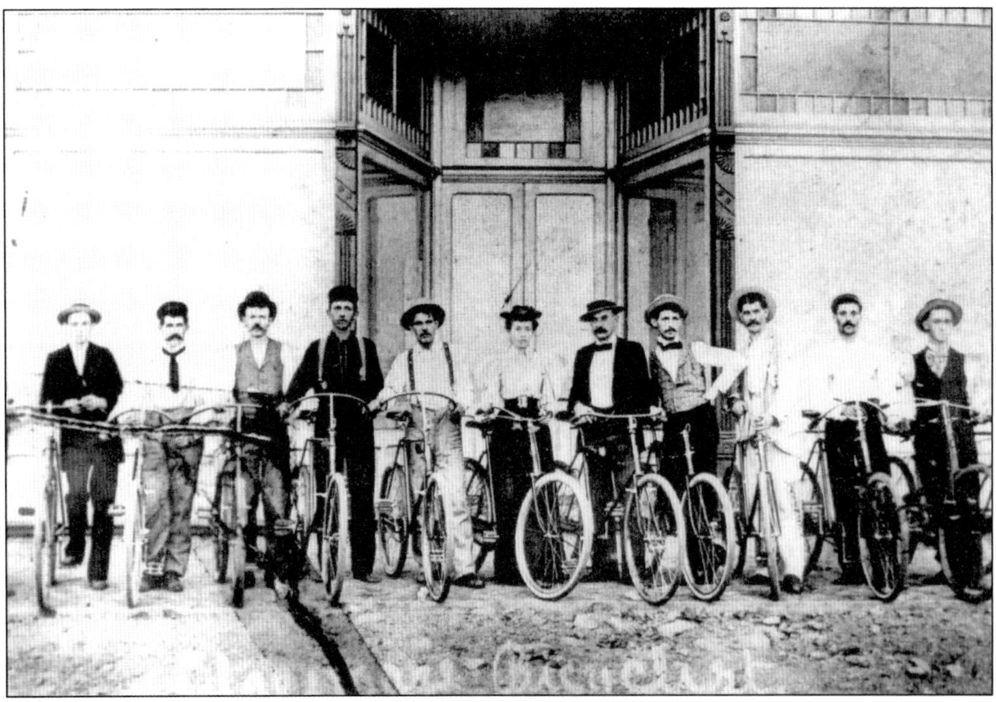

The Claremore Bicyclist Club poses in front of F. A. Nielson's store in 1909. At one time, Claremore had 13 bicycles and no automobiles. Note the lone woman in the center of the photograph.

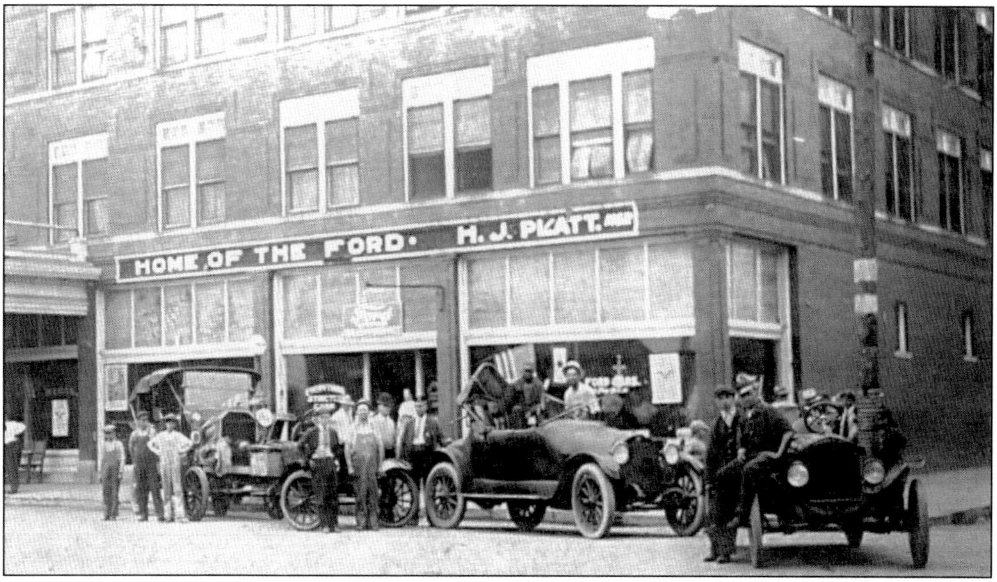


H. J. Platt owned one of the first car dealerships in Claremore, known to be in business as early as 1918. Platt sold and serviced Ford automobiles. His business was located in the corner of the Mason Hotel building where Walker's Department Store was once located.

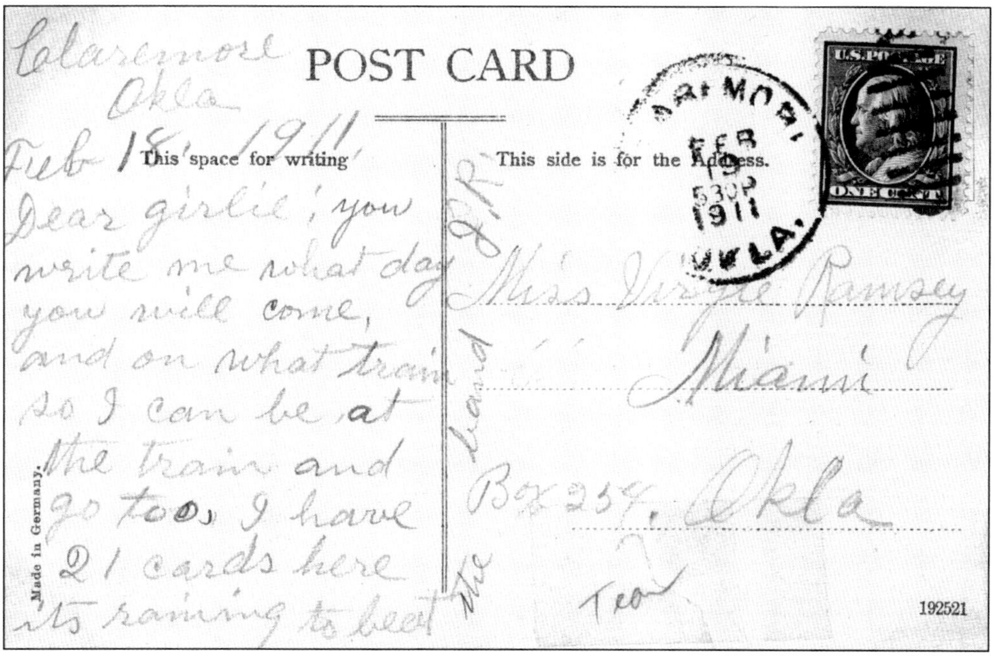


The back of this postcard, postmarked February 19, 1911, says, "Dear girlie: you write me what day you will come, and on what train so I can be at the train and go too, I have 21 cards here. Its raining to beat the band. J. R."

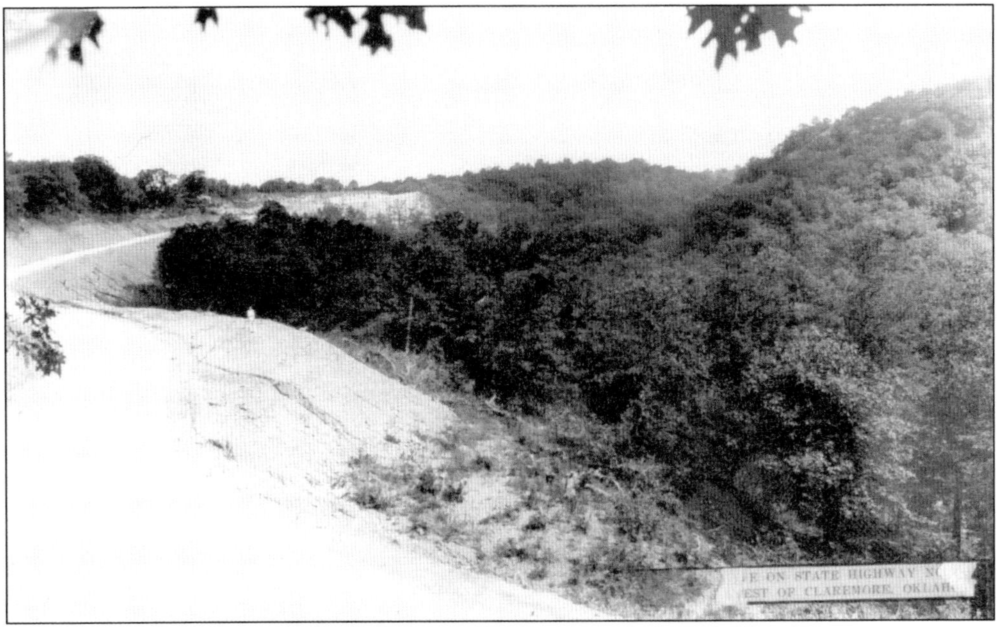

This view is of Keatonville Hill along Highway 20 just west of Claremore. Natural springs dotted the hillside. Many weary travelers would stop for a cool refreshing drink before continuing their journey.

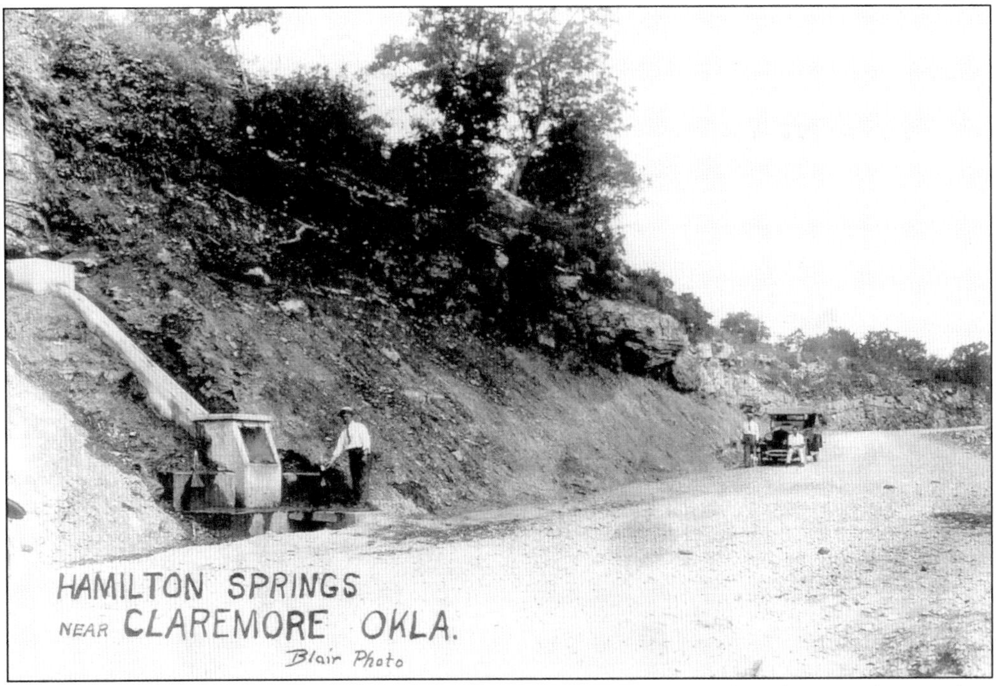


Hamilton Springs was one of the springs located on Keatonville Hill. This photograph was taken by Blair Studio. Owner of the studio, John Blair, was the great-uncle of Ralph Bridwell.

# Six

# Entertainment

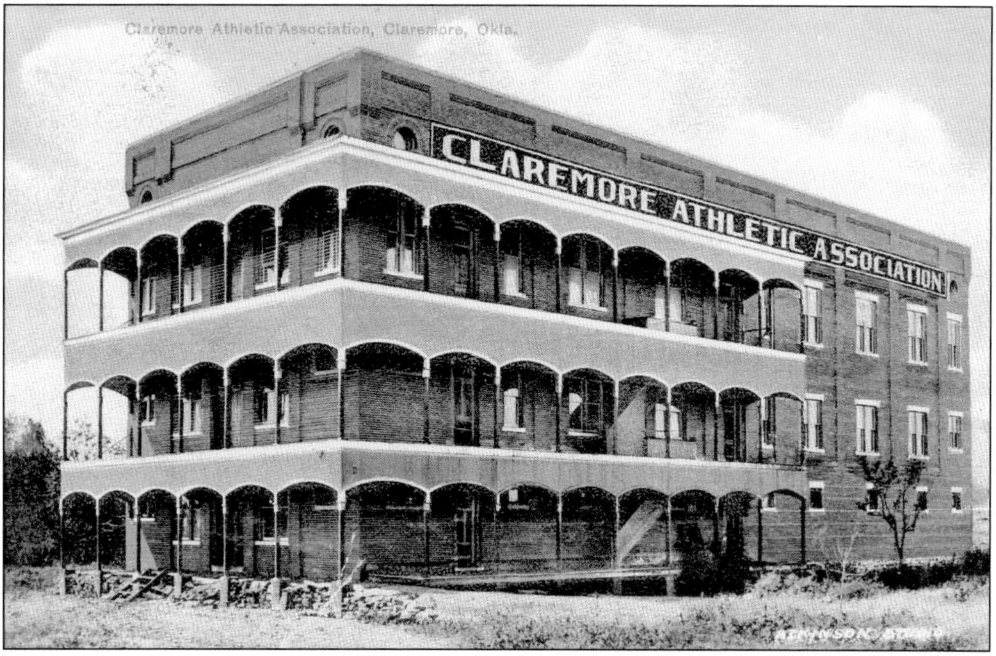


The Claremore Athletic Association was built between 1901 and 1909 by John M. Bayless. The building had three floors; it was 50 by 140 feet with 10-foot verandas on the east and north sides. It was built at a cost of $10,000 and contained private and public radium baths plus 50 guest rooms. The first floor contained a large swimming pool complete with trapezes. The second floor housed bowling alleys and other amusements. The third floor was designed for a summer theater and skating rink. It was known as the largest entertainment complex this side of Chicago. It was located on the present-day site of the Rogers County Courthouse.

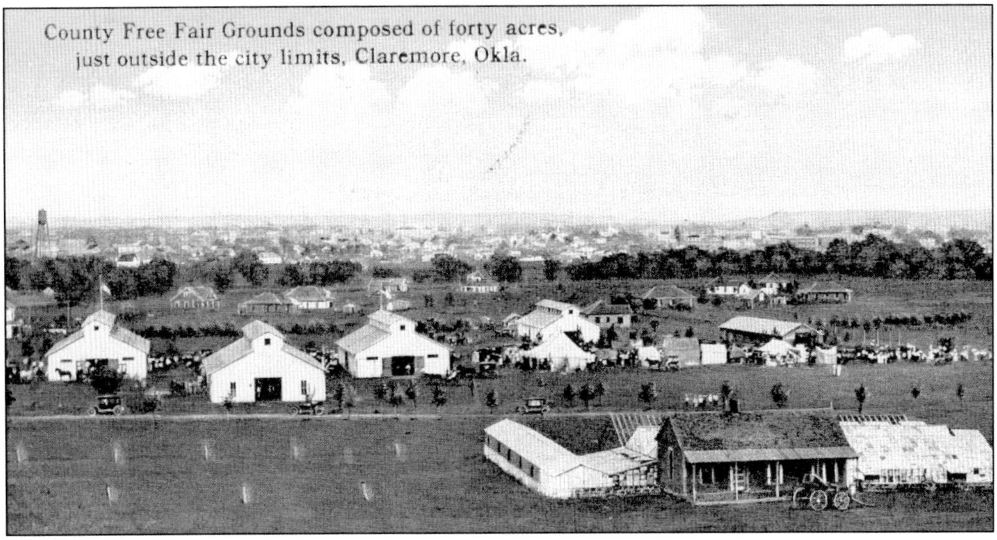


Claremore is host to the annual Rogers County Free Fair. The early-day fair pictured here encompassed 40 acres. The fair brought farmers and ranchers from all over the county to show their prized livestock and crops.

# ROGERS CO. FREE FAIR

## September 17 - 20 1918

**Bigger and better than ever.**

**Big tent provided for cattle.**

**Park benches for your comfort.**

**Prepare your exhibit now and show what you are doing to help feed the world.**

**Call at any bank, or write the secretary for premium list.**

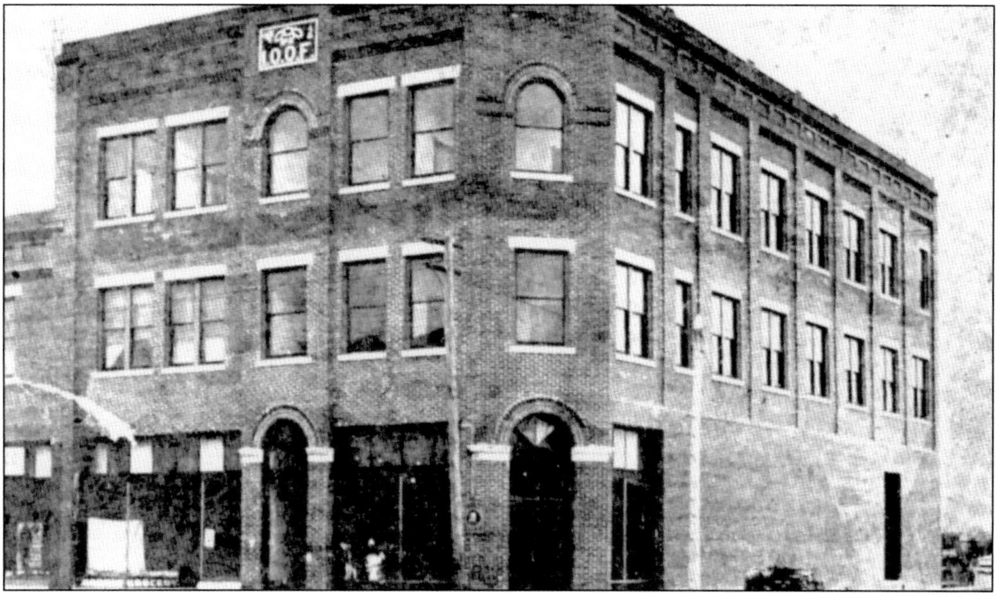


The Odd Fellows hall was located on the southeast corner of Will Rogers Boulevard and Lynn Riggs Boulevard, on the present site of RCB Bank. The Grand Lodge of the Indian Territory held its first meeting in 1893. Claremore began its lodge also in 1893 and was the 17th charter lodge. W. S. Jackson was the Claremore representative to the Grand Lodge of the Indian Territory. The Odd Fellows organization has its roots in 17th-century England. At that time, it was odd to find people who organized to give aid to those in need. Those who belonged to such an organization were called Odd Fellows.

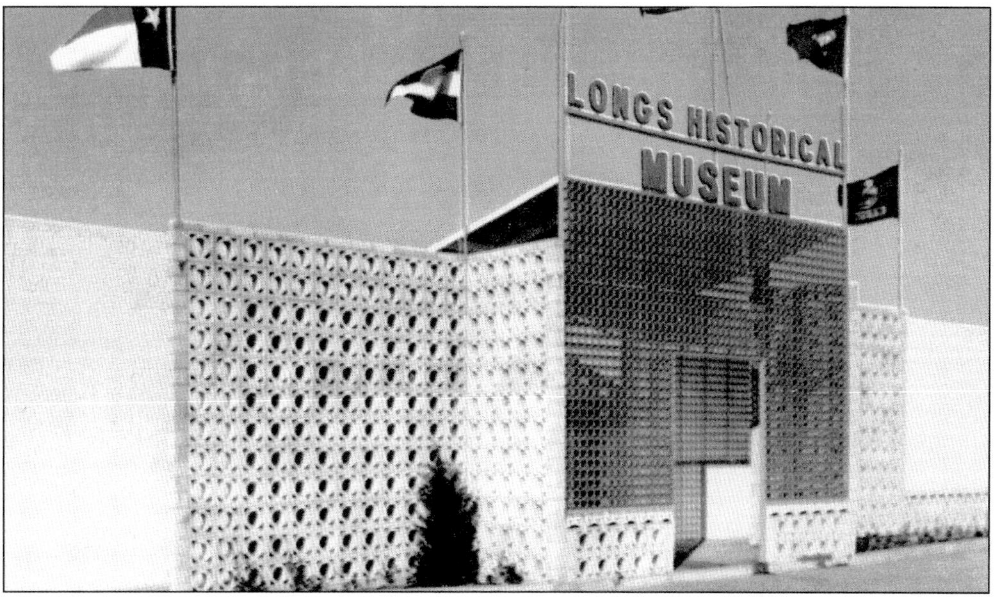


Long's Historical Museum contained over 50,000 items of historical importance from all over the world, dating back to the 17th century. The museum was located at the present site of Reasor's Grocery Store and was owned by C. C. Long. Adjacent to the museum was Long's Motel and Copp's Restaurant. A swimming pool was located behind the motel. The museum was closed in the 1970s. After Long's death, his son Jack moved the museum to Florida.

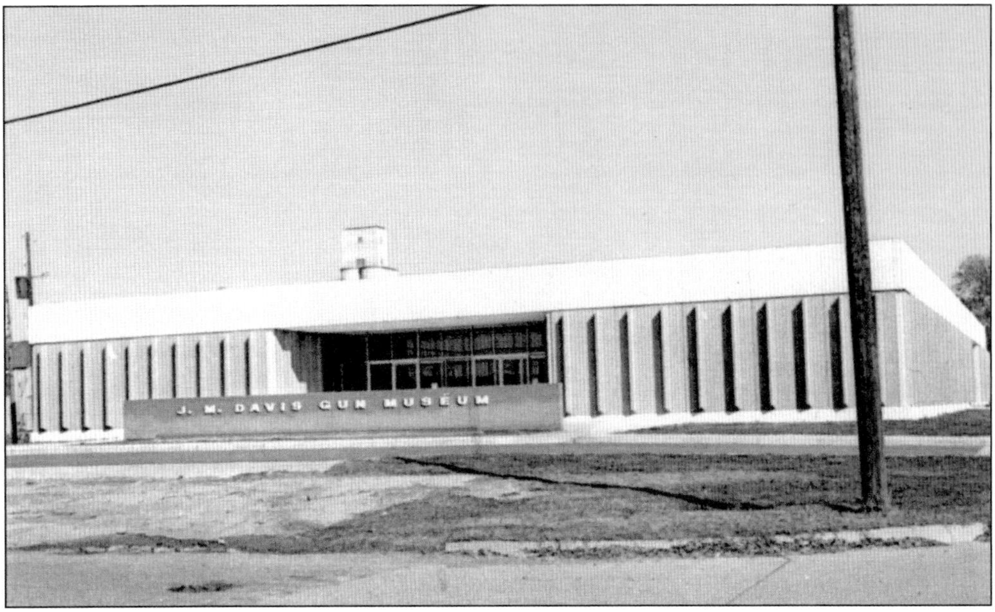


The J. M. Davis Gun Museum was built in 1969. It houses the world's largest private gun collection. Owner of the collection, J. M. Davis is buried on the property. The collection houses over 50,000 artifacts, 13,400 of which are guns. It is open daily, and admission is by donation only.

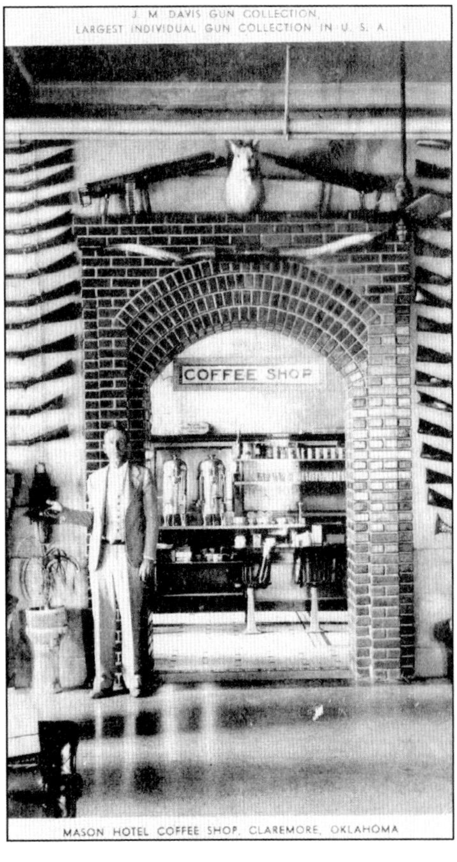


This was the entrance to the Mason Hotel coffee shop. The guns that line the walls are now housed at the J. M. Davis Gun Museum. In honor of Oklahoma's centennial celebration, the museum is set to open a new display that will be an exact replica of the lobby of the Mason Hotel.

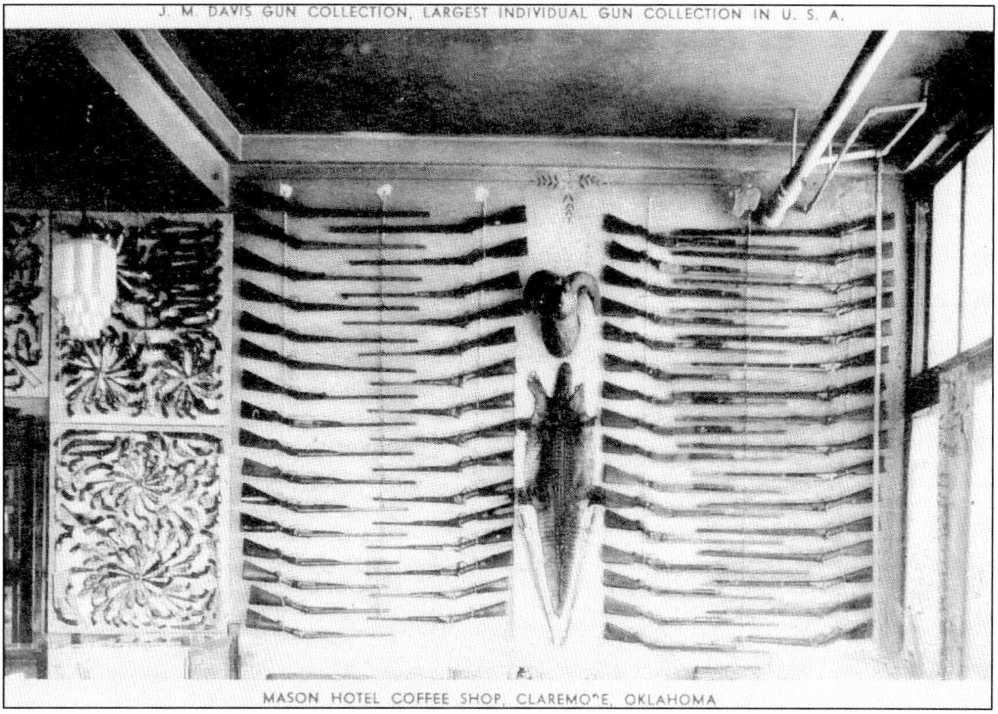


Pictured here are a few of the 13,400 guns currently on display at the J. M. Davis Gun Museum. The guns range from those owned by lawmen to outlaws and mobsters. The museum also contains a large display of actual hangmen's nooses and wanted posters.

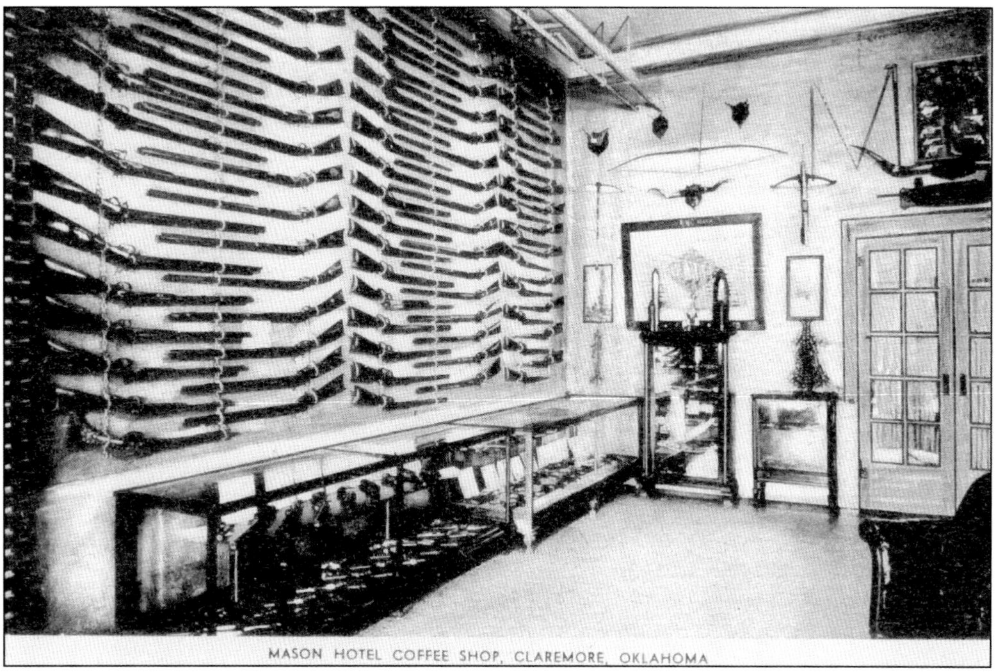

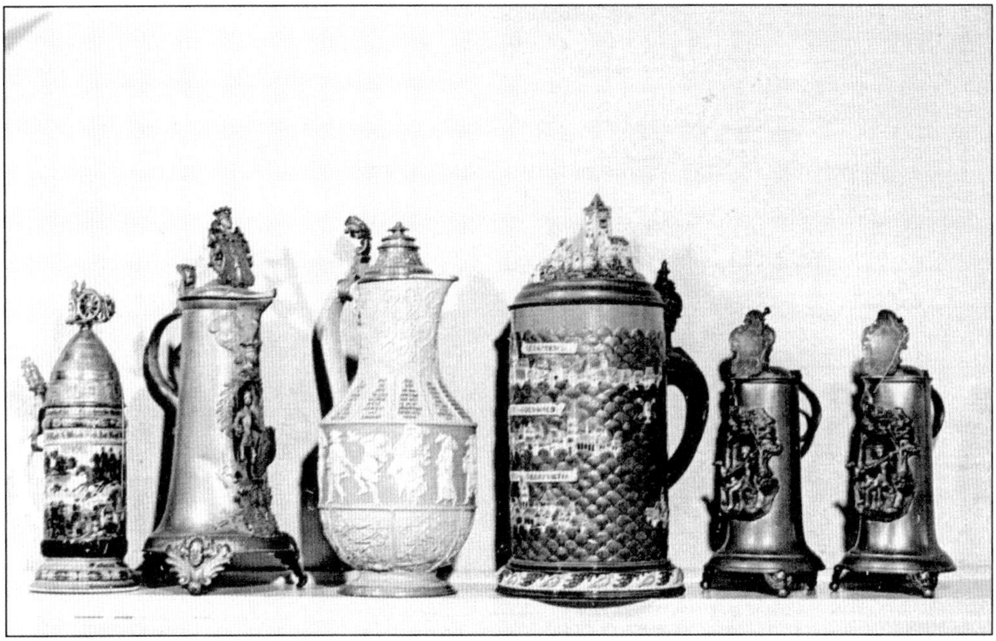

The gun museum also houses a collection of antique beer steins owned by J. M. Davis. The collection numbers 1,500 and includes Meissen pieces, Mettlach, and Franco-Prussian regimentals. The steins range in size from a half ounce to six gallons.

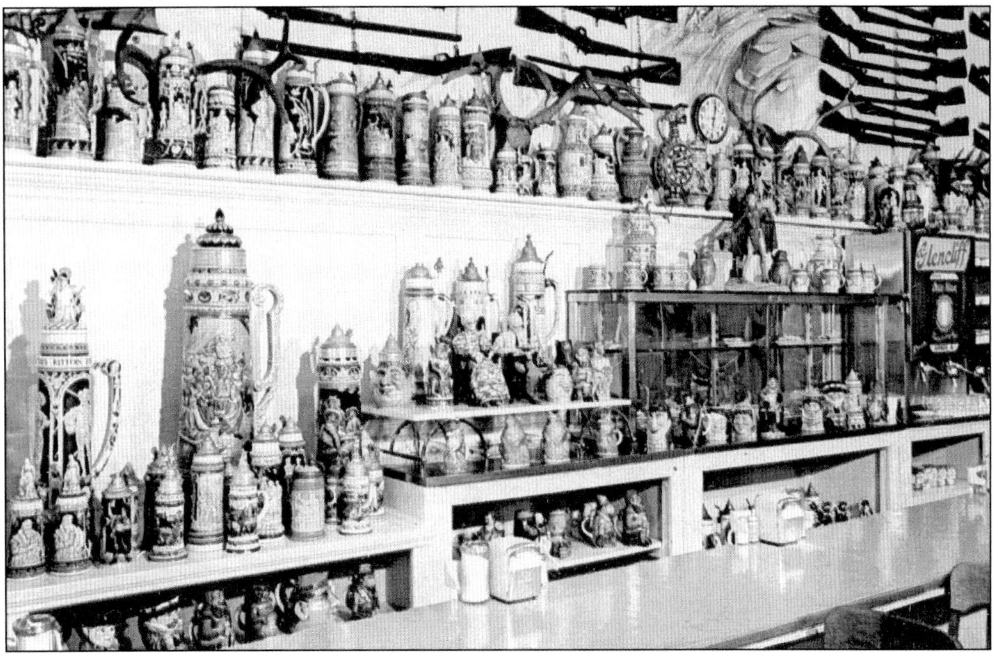

Aerial View of Will Rogers Memorial Museum and Tomb, Claremore, Oklahoma

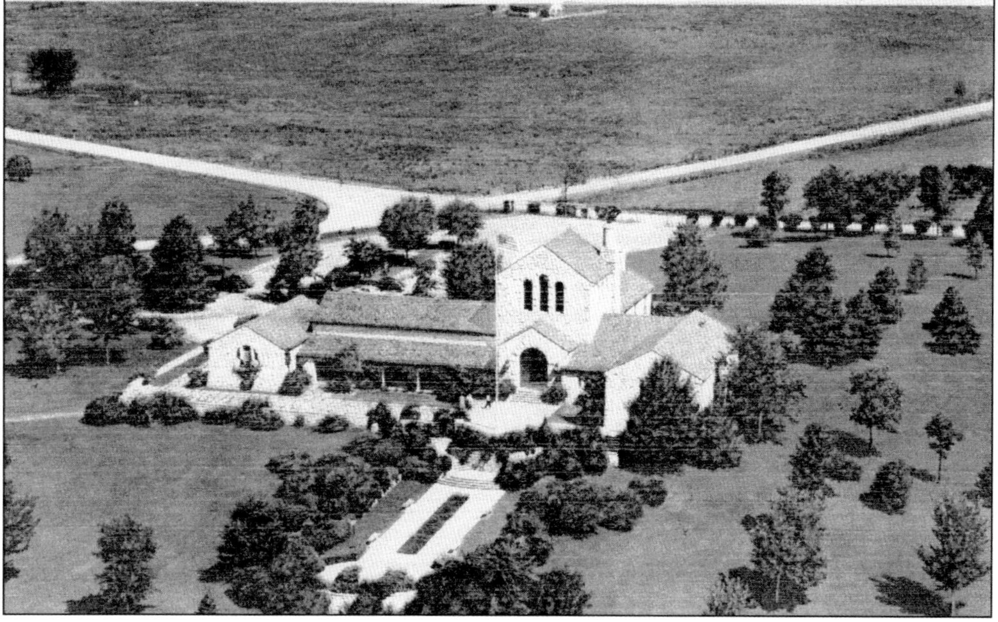

The Will Rogers Memorial was built by the people of the state of Oklahoma to pay tribute to their native son. It was dedicated on November 4, 1938, on what would have been Rogers's 59th birthday. It was built in the same Spanish style as the Rogers home in California. The rock used in the building was quarried near Claremore. Admission to the memorial is free to the public, although donations are accepted. It sits on a hilltop overlooking Claremore on land purchased by Rogers for his home.

Will Rogers Tomb and Garden, Claremore, Okla.

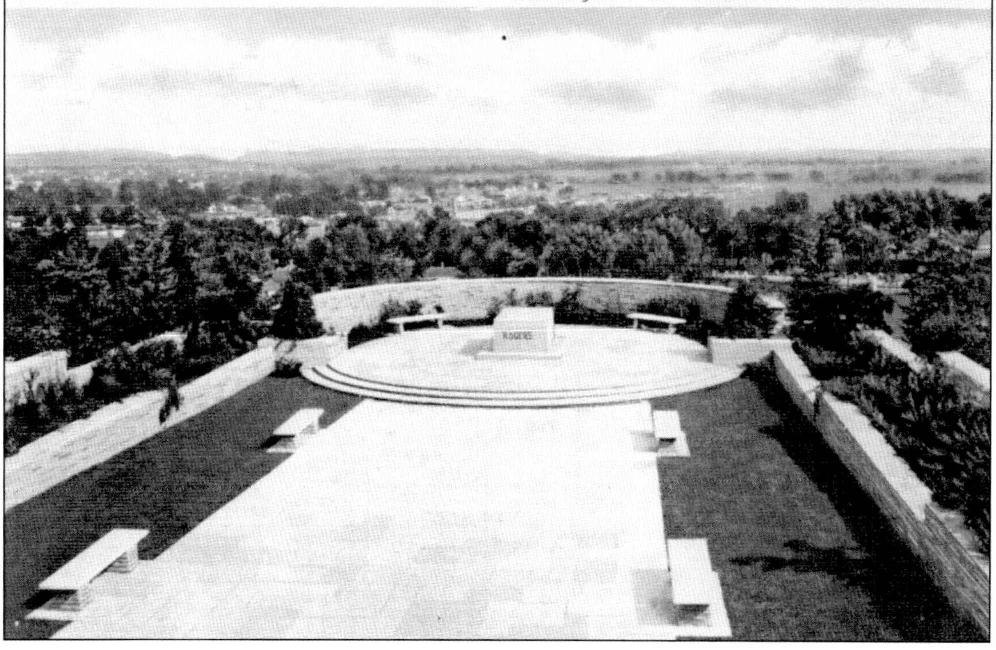

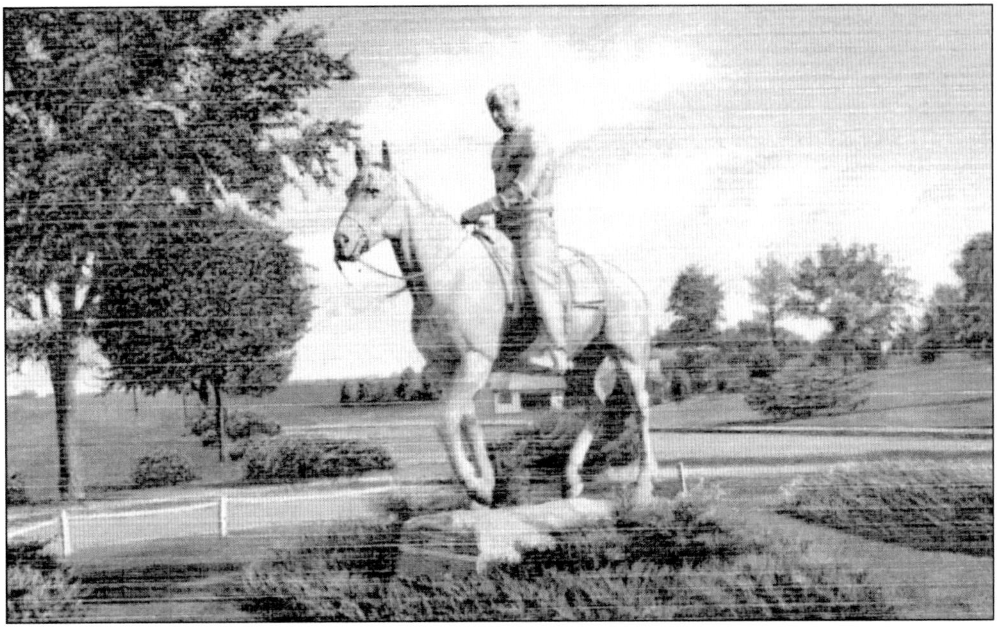

This statue of Will Rogers sitting on his horse Soapsuds once stood at the entrance to the Will Rogers Memorial. The statue now stands at the back of the memorial, just behind the Rogers family burial site. One of Rogers's life lessons from his father, Clem Rogers, was that a man needed to learn to "sit his own horse." In other words, a man should take care of his responsibilities, make his own way, and take responsibility for his own actions.

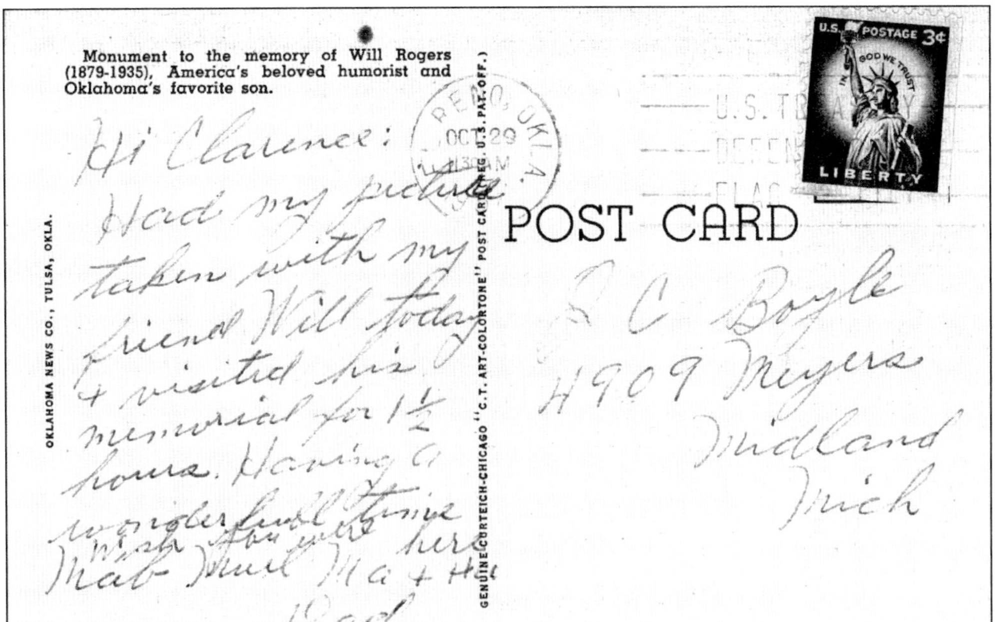


The back of this postcard reads, "Hi Clarence: Had my picture taken with my friend Will today & visited his memorial for 1½ hours. Having a wonderful time. Wish you were here . . . Ma & Dad."

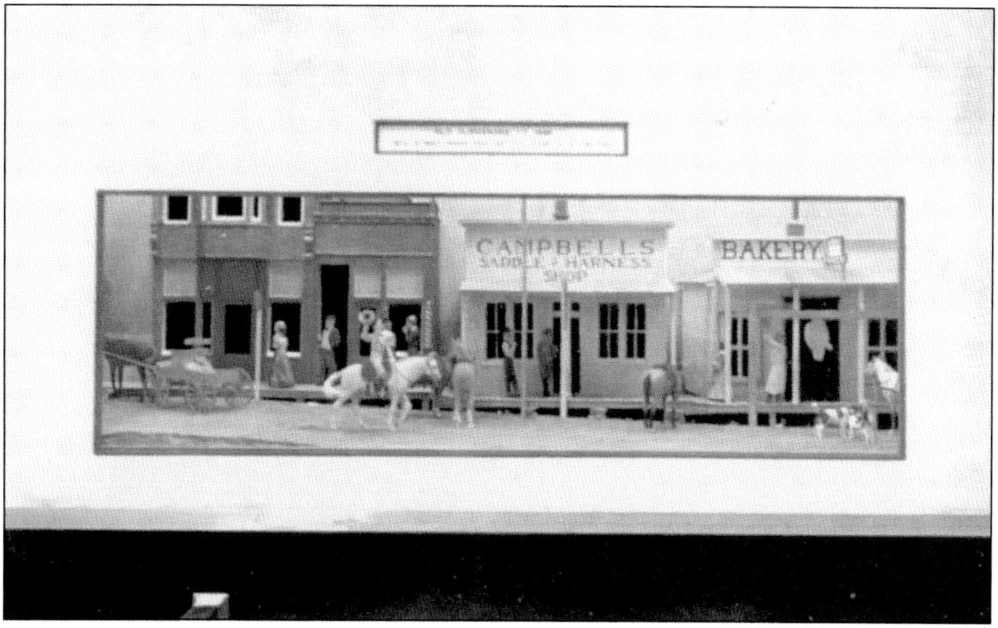


This diorama of Claremore, Indian Territory, was once located in the Will Rogers Memorial. It depicts Claremore in 1895. These buildings were located on Main Street. The building on the left was the City Drug Store, and Campbell's Saddle and Harness Shop is next to it. At one time the memorial contained an entire room of dioramas.

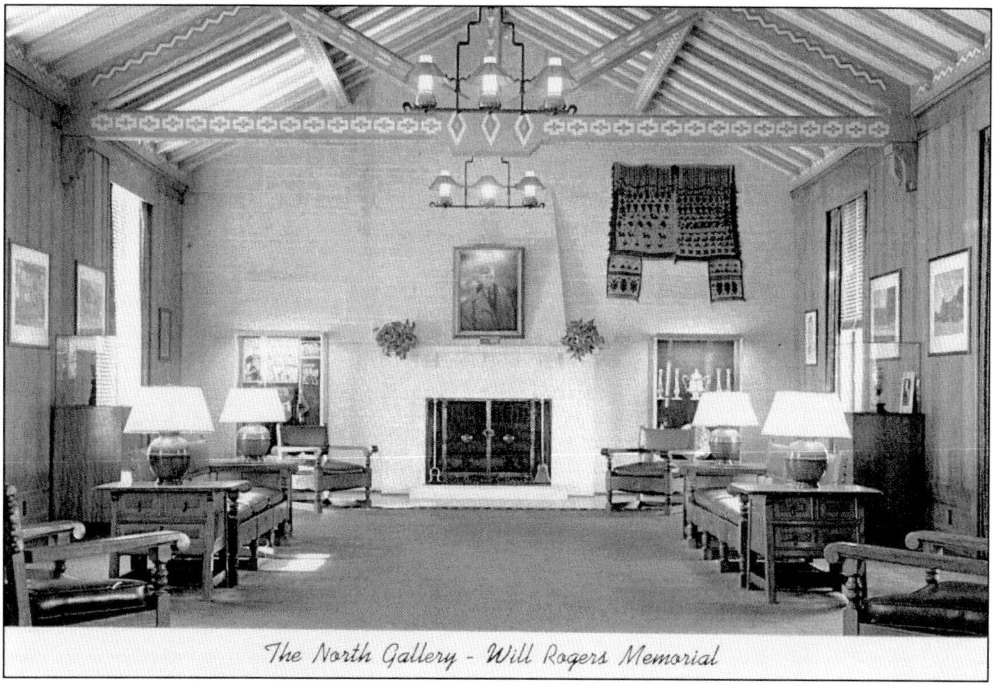


Seen here is one of the many exhibits in the Will Rogers Memorial. The room was in the style of Rogers's ranch home in California. It contained trophies and other keepsakes. This exhibit no longer exists as such, although the items are still housed at the memorial. Exhibits are sometimes changed in an effort to offer returning visitors something new.

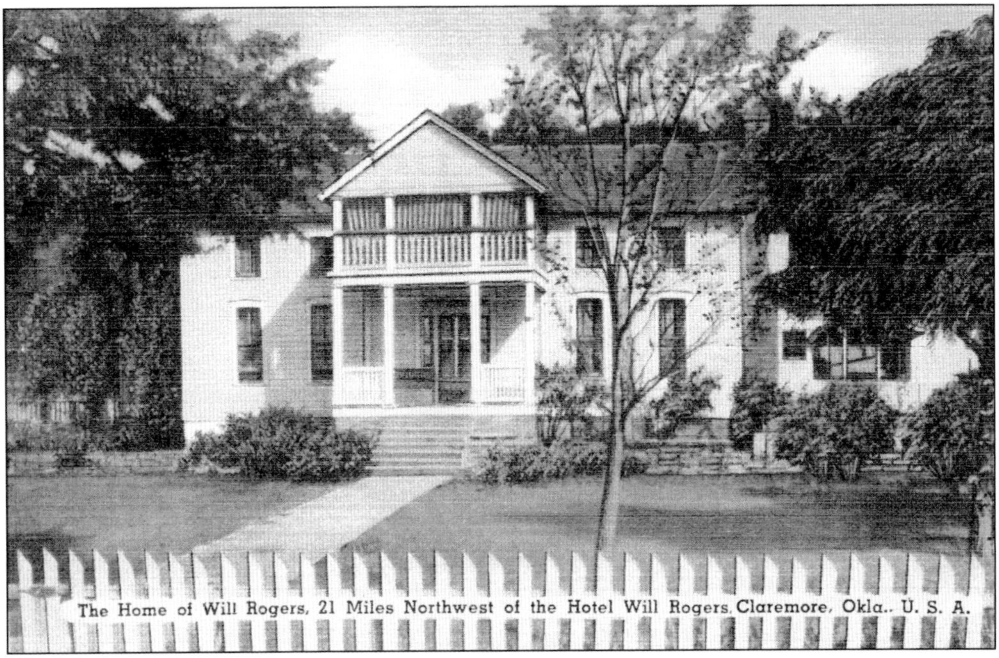


Will Rogers was born in this home in 1879, just 12 miles northwest of Claremore in Oolagah. Will's father, Clem Rogers, eventually moved into Claremore. Although Will never owned a home in Claremore, he had a room in his father's home for his frequent trips home. It was for this reason that Will called Claremore his hometown.

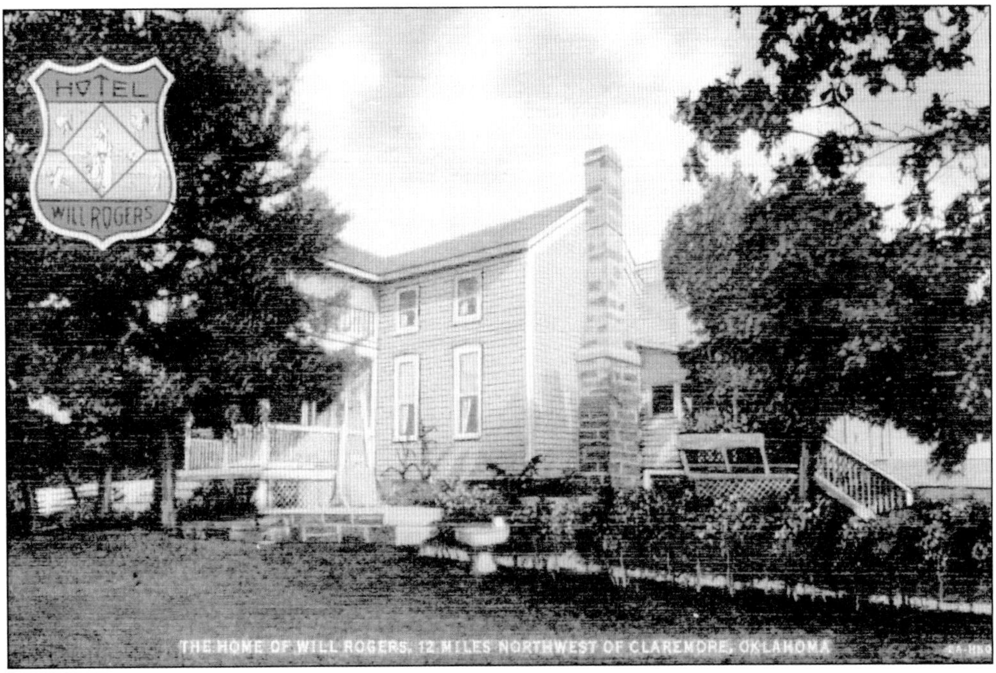

The Yale Theatre was located on Missouri Street on the same site as the old livery stable. The Yale was known to be in existence as early as 1918. During the early years, it provided vaudeville acts as well as motion pictures. The Yale closed in the mid-1970s.

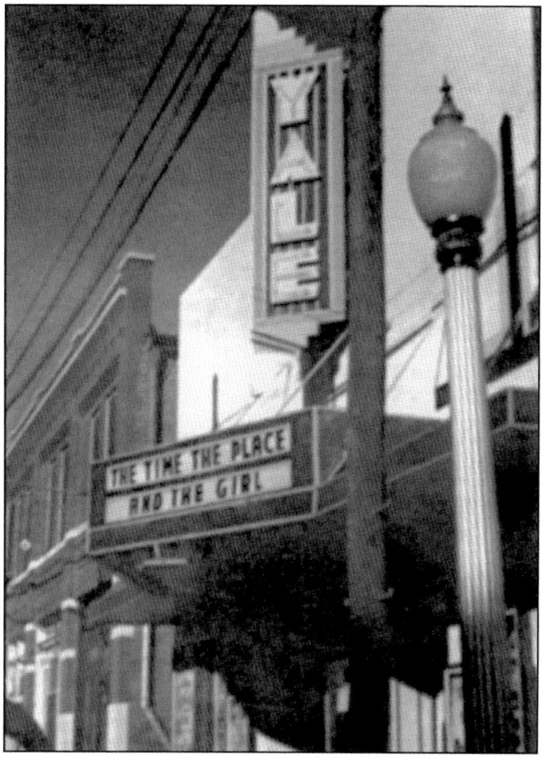


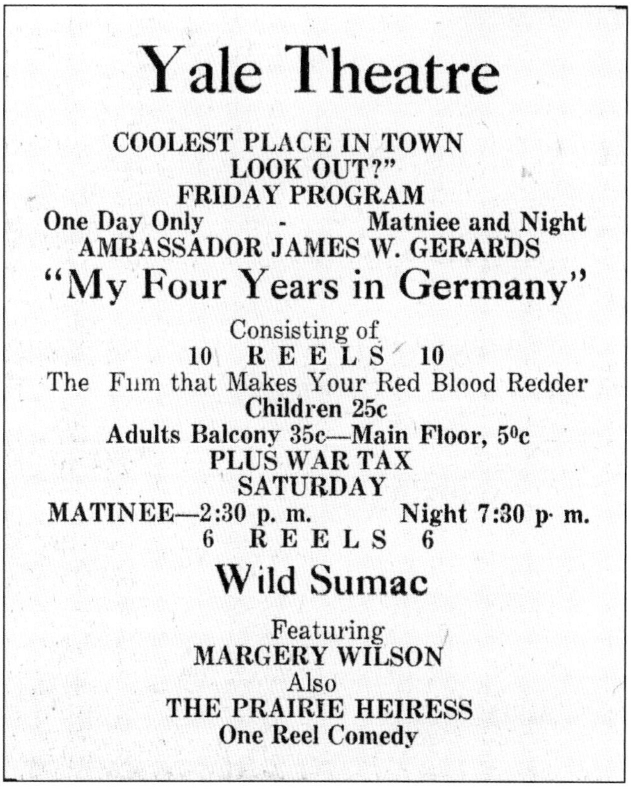

# Yale Theatre

COOLEST PLACE IN TOWN
LOOK OUT?"
FRIDAY PROGRAM
One Day Only - Matniee and Night
AMBASSADOR JAMES W. GERARDS

## "My Four Years in Germany"

Consisting of
10 R E E L S 10
The Fim that Makes Your Red Blood Redder
Children 25c
Adults Balcony 35c—Main Floor, 5$^{0}$c
PLUS WAR TAX
SATURDAY
MATINEE—2:30 p. m. Night 7:30 p. m.
6 R E E L S 6

## Wild Sumac

Featuring
MARGERY WILSON
Also
THE PRAIRIE HEIRESS
One Reel Comedy

This advertisement for the Yale was taken from a 1918 issue of the *Claremore Messenger.* The theater had a balcony, and those seats were priced at 35¢. During this time period, there was also a "war tax" added to the ticket prices.

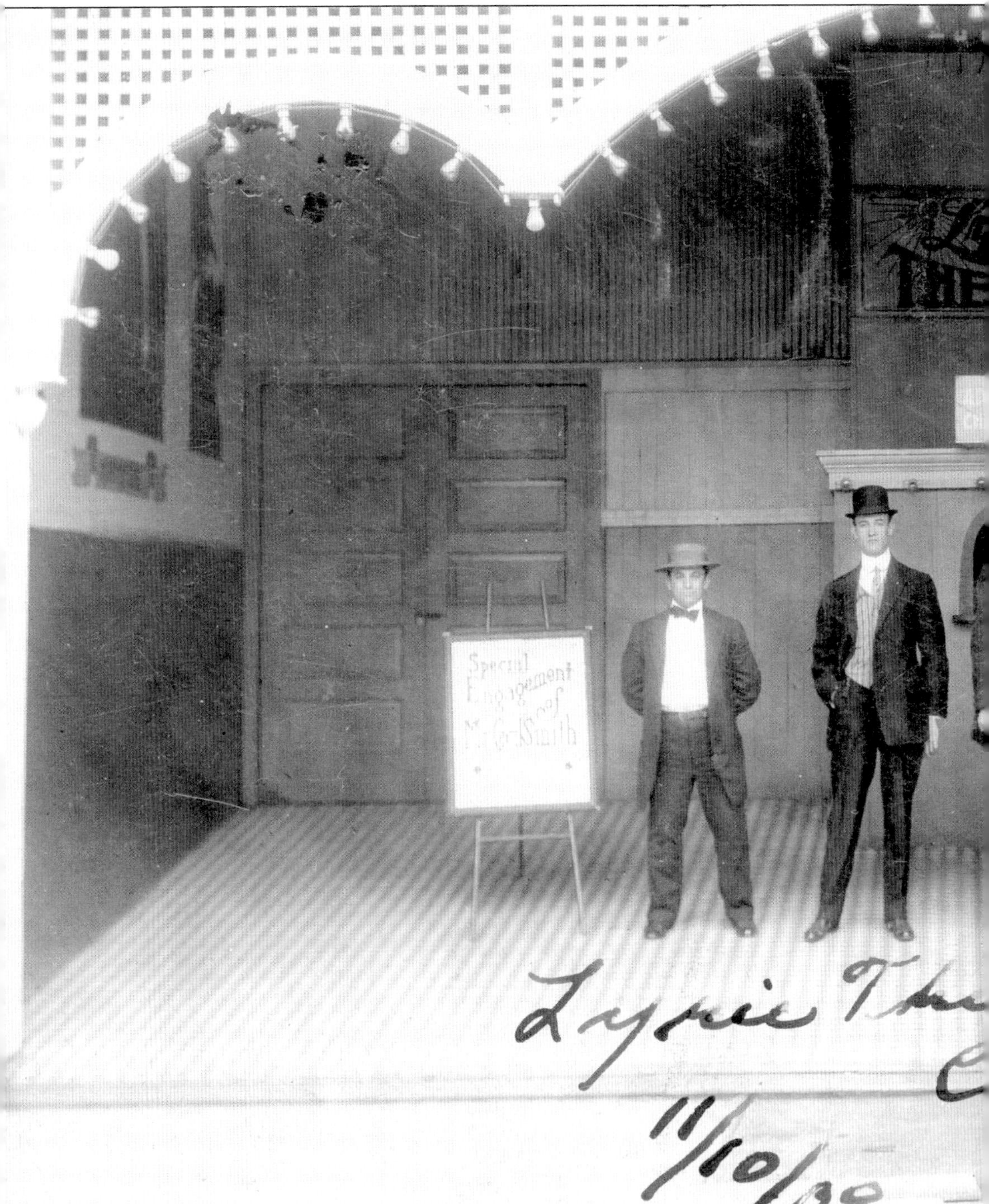


The Lyric Theatre may have been Claremore's first theater. The photograph for this postcard was taken on November 10, 1909. The theater is believed to have been located at 404 West Will Rogers Boulevard. Ticket prices were 10¢ for adults and 5¢ for children. The small chalkboard on the left says, "Special Engagement of Mr. Cecil Smith." The board on the right, advertising

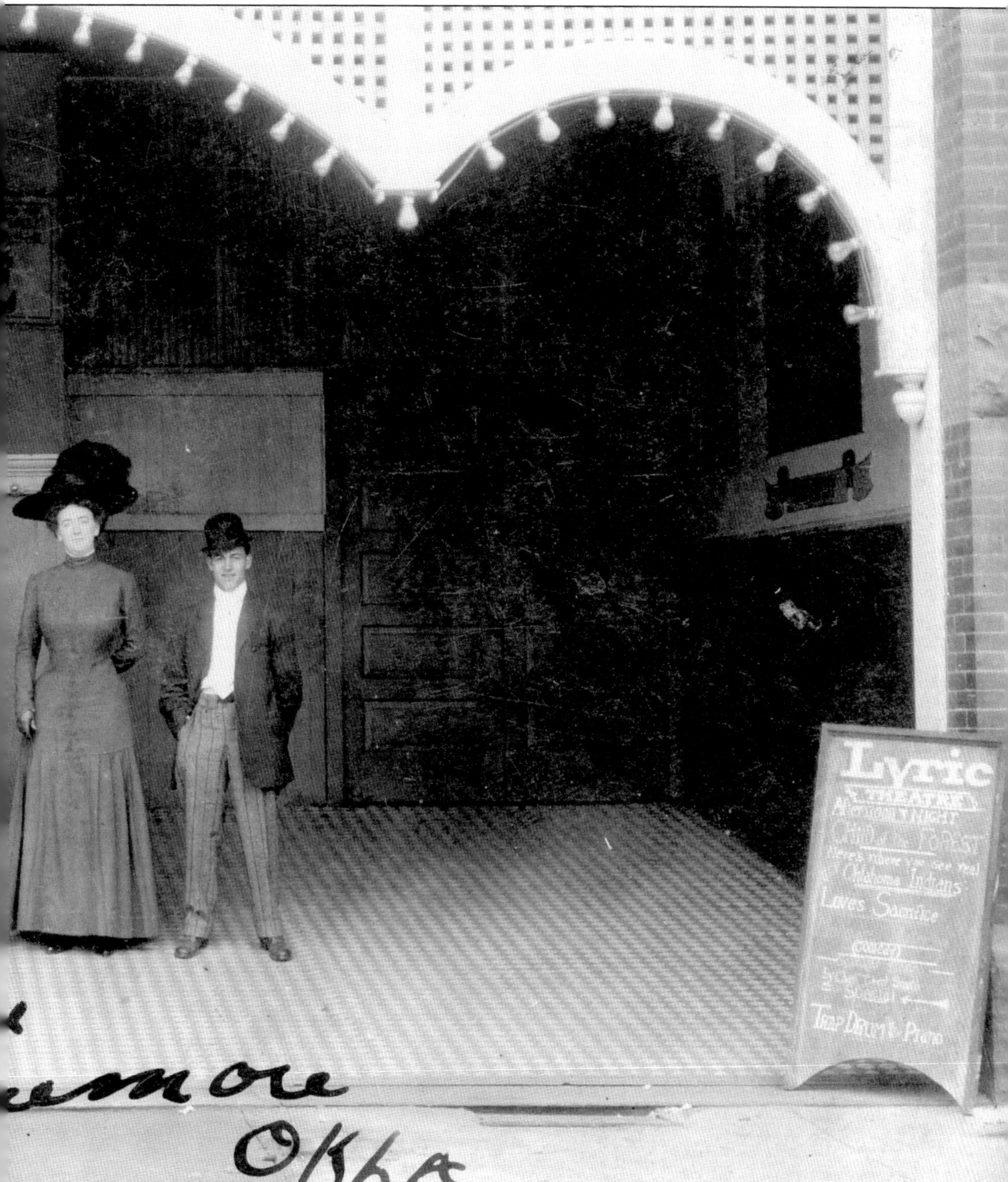


afternoon and night at the Lyric Theatre, reads, "Child of the Forest . . . see real Oklahoma Indians, Loves Sacrifice . . . Trap Drum & Piano." Note the tiled entry. The theater brought in vaudeville acts and also showed motion pictures. It was known to be in existence as late as 1918.

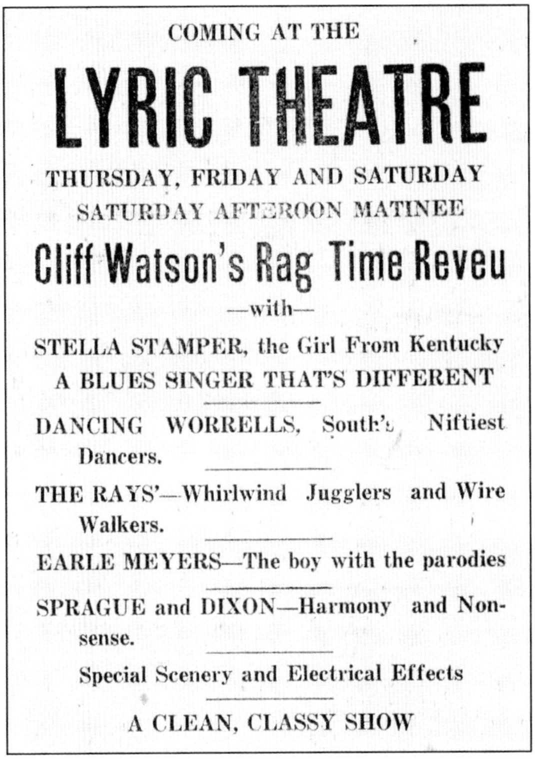


Cliff Watson's *Rag Time Reveu* was playing the Lyric Theatre in 1918. According to its advertisement, it was a clean and classy show.

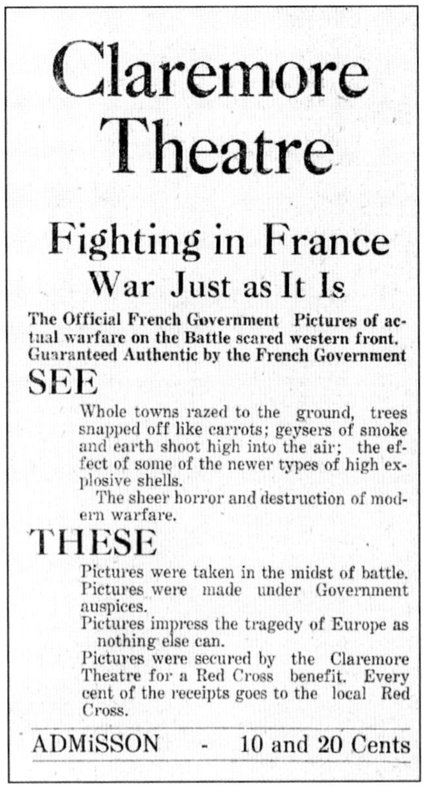


According to the *Claremore Messenger*, the Claremore Theatre was in business as early as 1918.

Not much is known about the Electric Theatre. This advertisement was found in a 1918 *Claremore Messenger* newspaper. The newspaper also ran a story about the Electric, stating it was the only theater in town that only showed motion pictures.

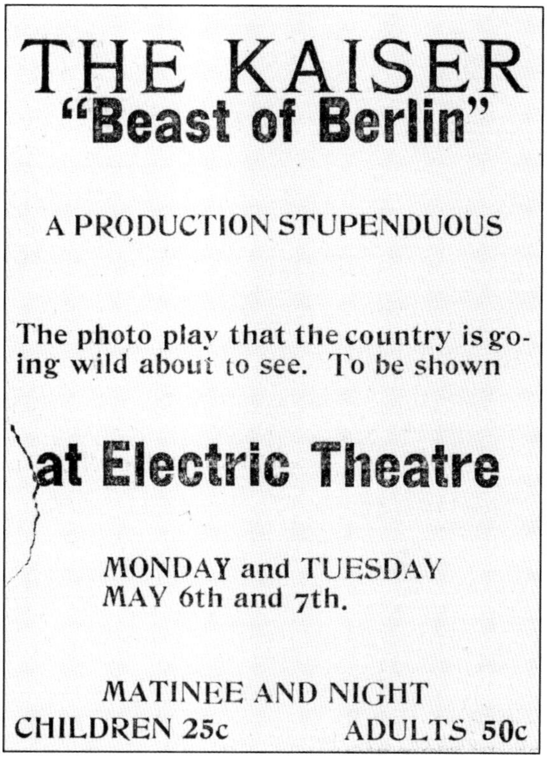


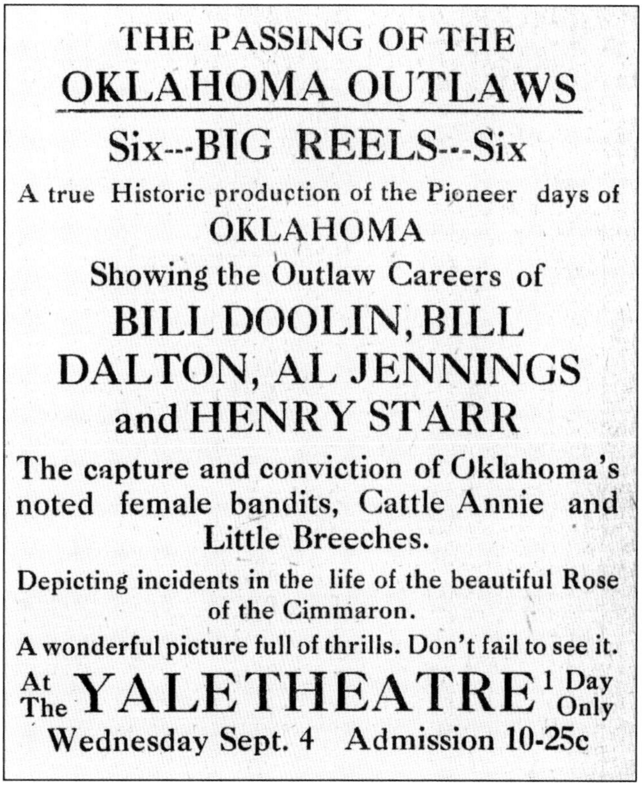


On September 4, 1918, *The Passing of the Oklahoma Outlaws*, a true historic picture of Oklahoma pioneer days, was playing at the Yale Theatre.

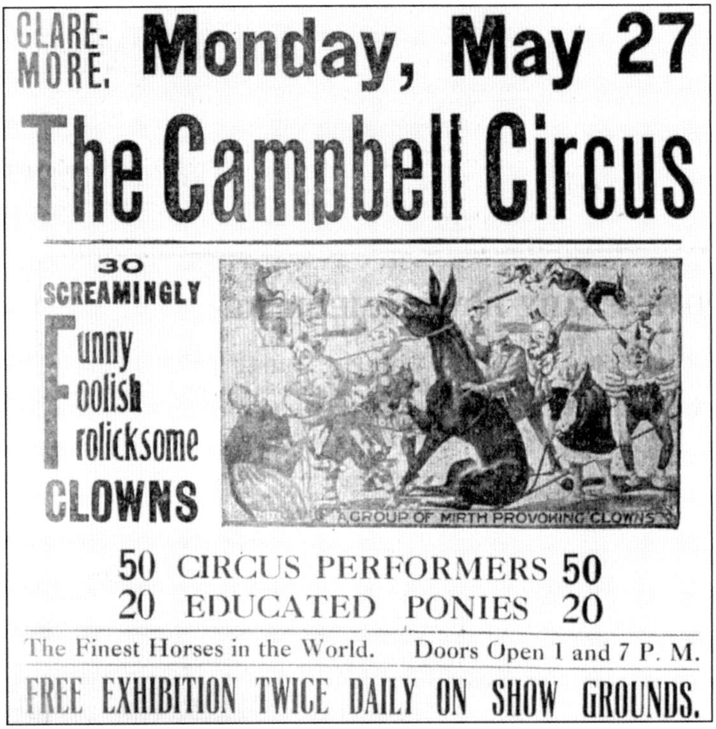


The Campbell Circus came to town on Monday, May 27, 1918. The circus was composed of 50 performers and 20 "educated" ponies.

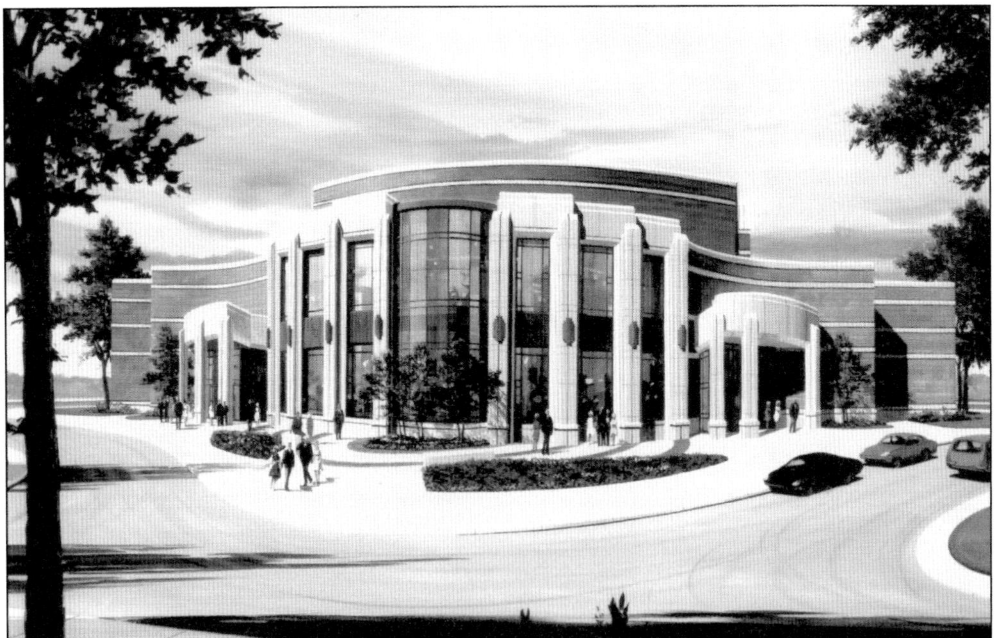

Due largely to the generosity of Frank and Ludmilla Robson, Claremore may once again become the entertainment mecca it once was. The Claremore Performing Arts Center was completed in 2006 and was built with donations from Frank and Ludmilla Robson. The $13 million facility seats 1,100 people and hosts attractions throughout the year. It also houses the fine arts departments for Claremore High School.

*Seven*

# Outdoor Life

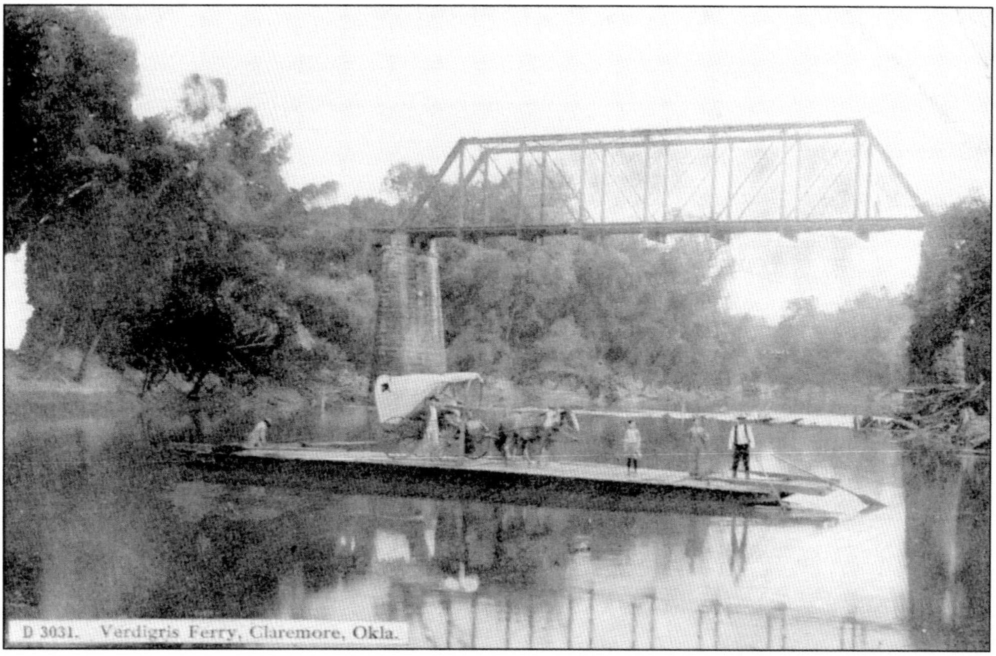


The Verdigris River separates Claremore from Catoosa and Tulsa. In the early 1900s, the only way to cross the river was on horseback. In 1908, the industrious Wofford brothers built the ferry pictured here. Jim Wofford, his wife, Bessie, and daughter Clara are shown at the front of the ferry. The ferry operated on the river on the Keatonville Hill cutoff road until 1914 when a horse bridge was built. The bridge shown in the postcard is the Frisco Railroad bridge.

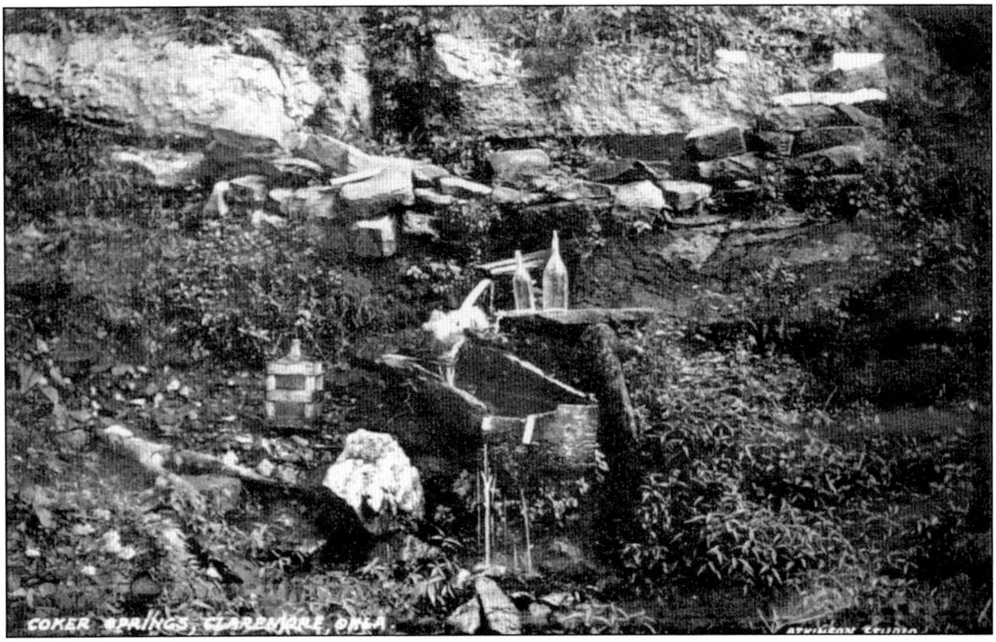


Coker Springs is believed to have been southeast of Claremore on the Verdigris River. Around 1864, Dempsey Coker settled near this spring, becoming its namesake. Coker was a Baptist preacher and was the first person to settle the area in several years.

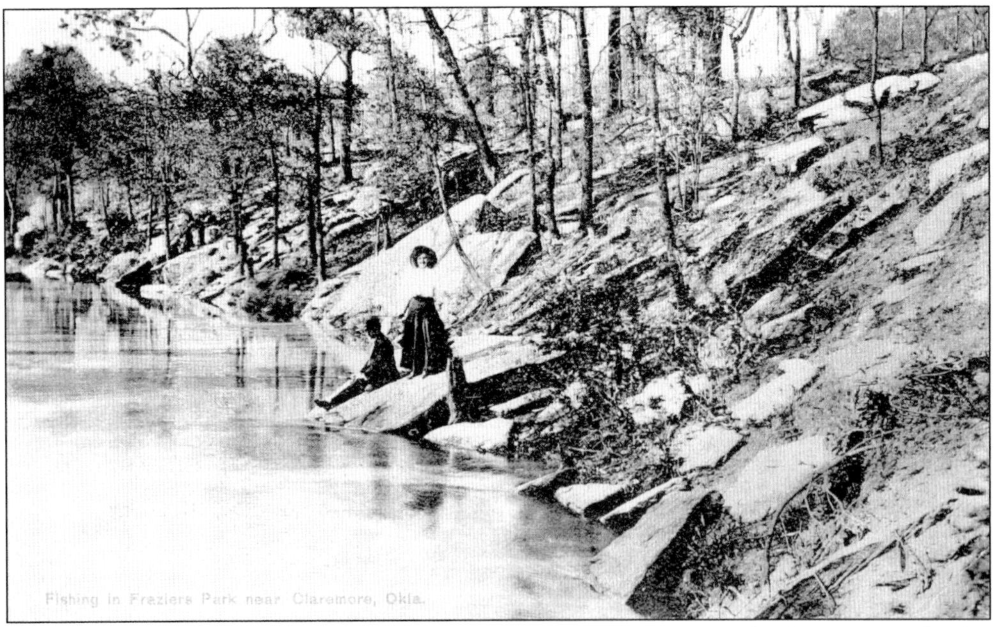


Fraziers Park has all but been erased from Claremore's history. Evidently it was early-day Claremore as no one has been able to recall the park. It is possible that the area existed near the Claremore Lake area before the dam was built.

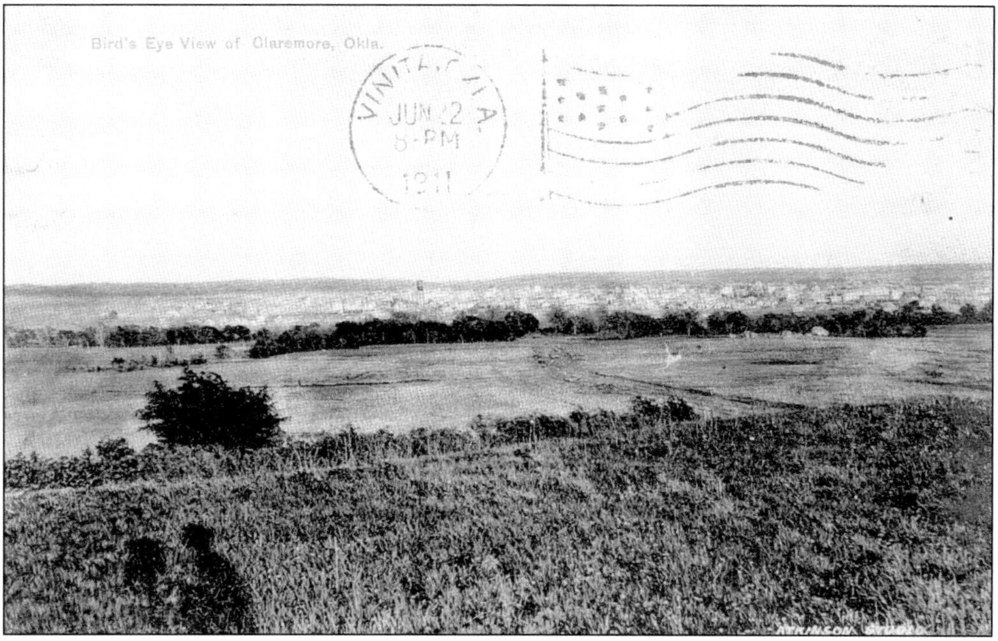


This bird's-eye view was taken from a hill overlooking Claremore prior to 1911. It is believed to have been taken from what is commonly known as Talbert Hill on the west side of the city. Notice the shadow of the photographer and his camera in the foreground of the postcard.

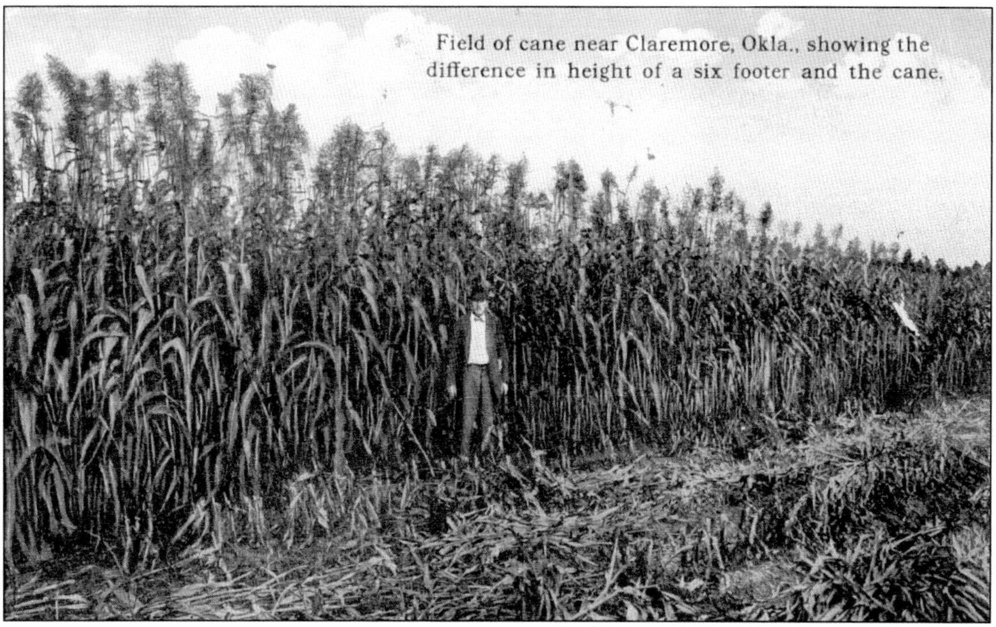


Besides oil and ranching, Claremore also has an agricultural history. It is located in what at one time was known as the richest agricultural district of Oklahoma. This postcard shows a large sugarcane field. In comparison to the 6-foot man in the picture, the cane appears to be about 11 or 12 feet.

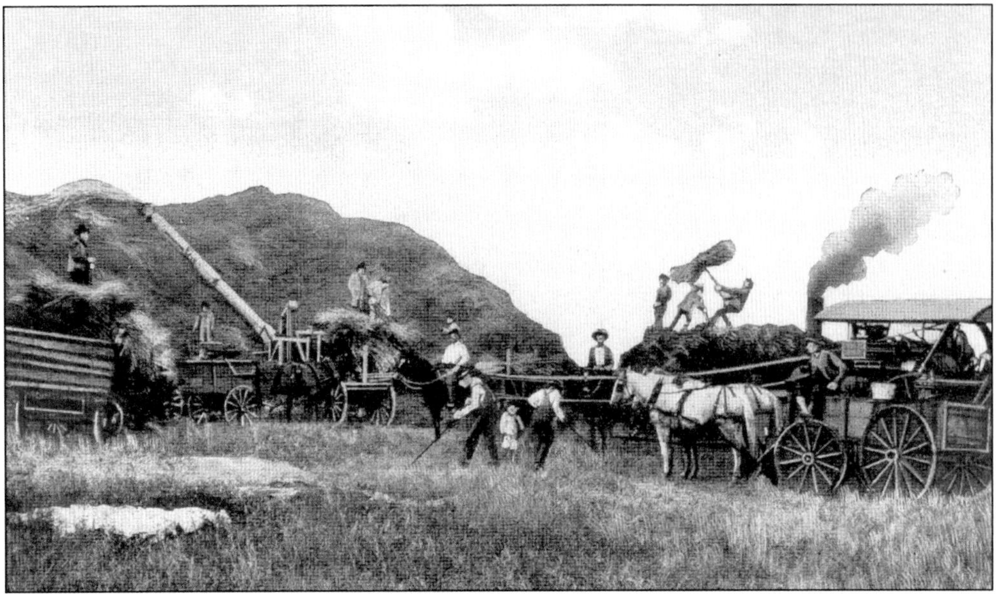

When the wheat was ready to be harvested, things came to a halt around Claremore. Newspapers advertised that all billiard parlors, amusement facilities, and so on were to be closed until the crops were harvested. The notices were placed by court order and under penalty of the law.

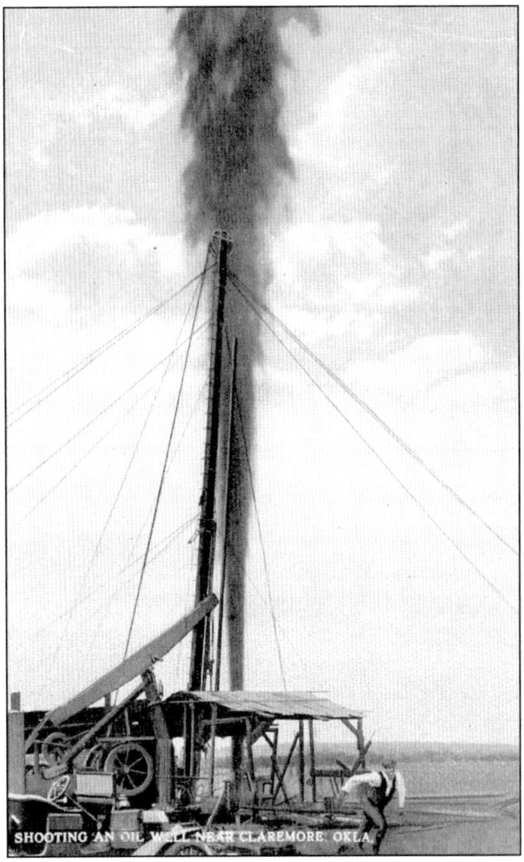


In the early 1900s, some of the largest oil and gas fields west of the Mississippi River were within just a few miles of Claremore. The reverse side of this postcard accurately predicted that Claremore had a great future as a manufacturing center. Today the city is home to many manufactures, including Centrilift–Baker Hughes, an oil field services company.

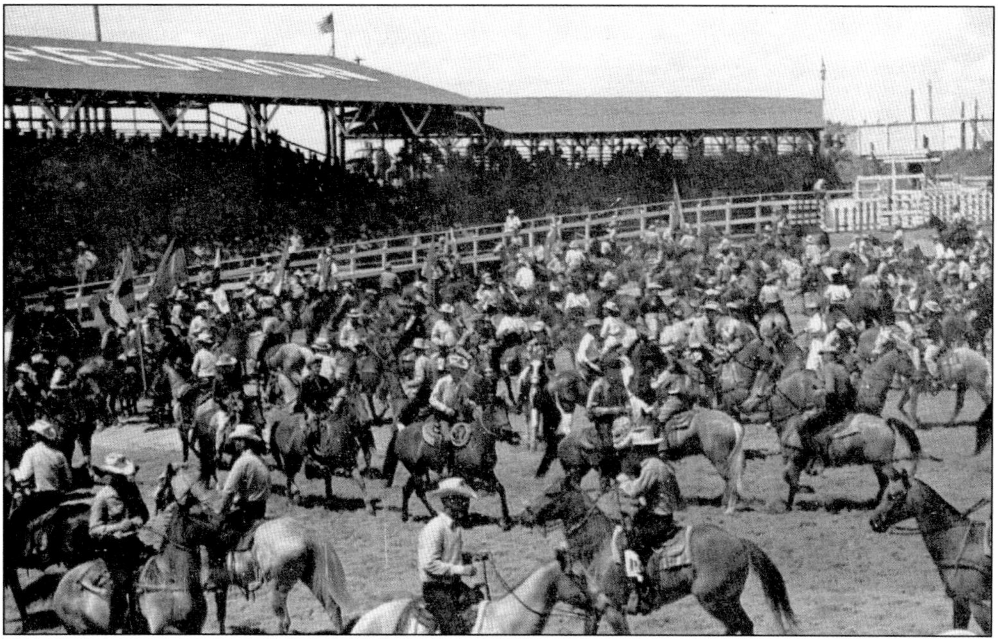

Rodeos are a main event in Claremore. The Will Rogers Rodeo is held every year and brings a large crowd of people to town. The Lipe family also holds a rodeo.

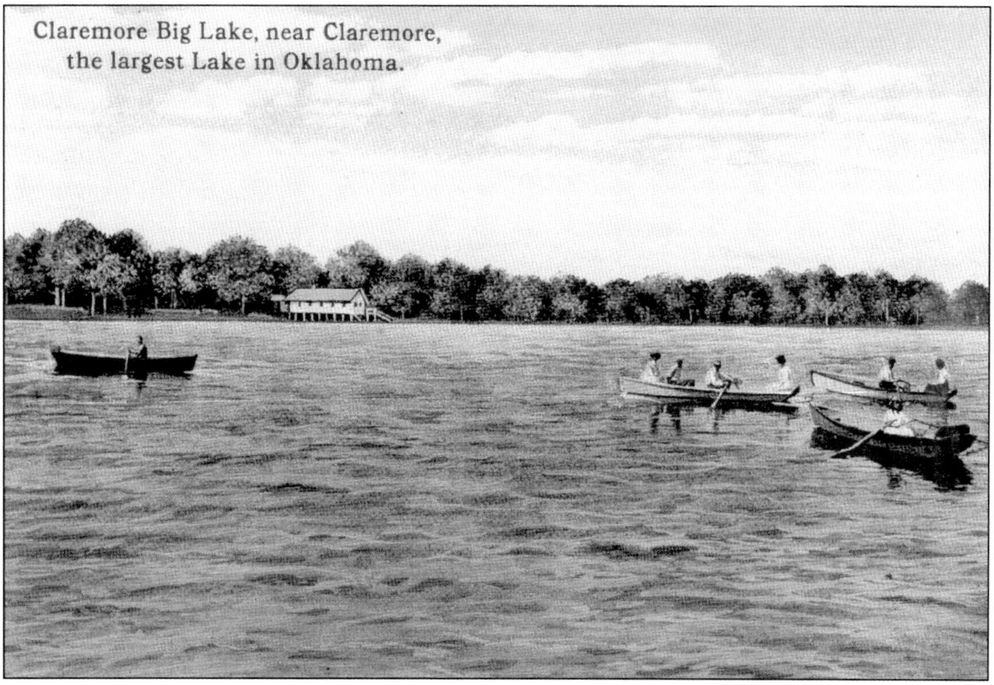


Oklahoma is said to have more actual shoreline than all the Great Lakes. A large portion of that shoreline is in northeastern Oklahoma.

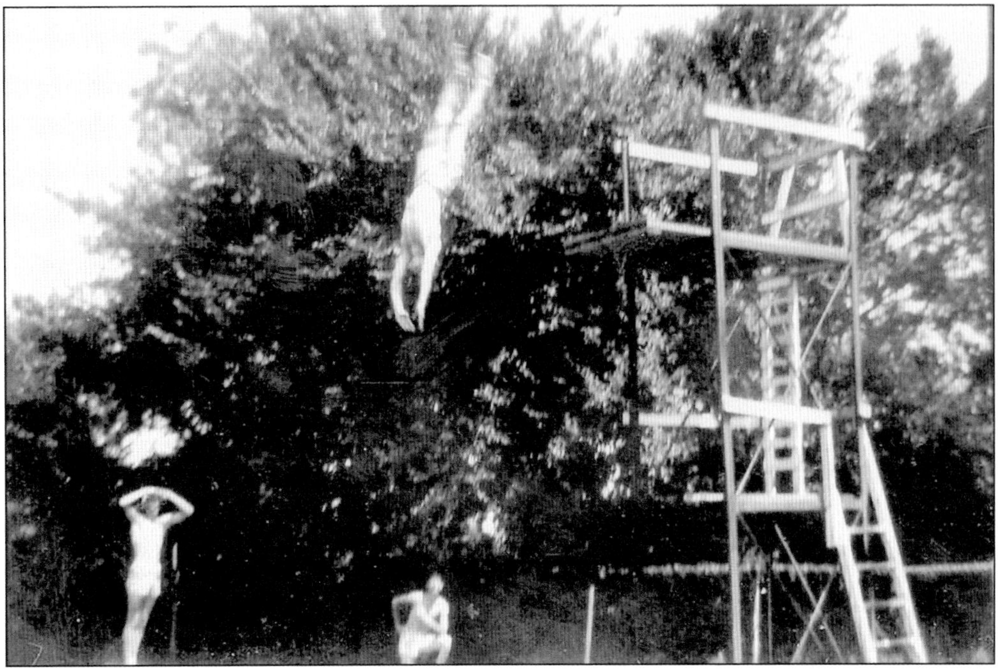

Perrier's Park was located between Dupont Street and Archer Drive, more commonly known as Luther McNames's property. The park contained a large swimming pool called Perrier's Plunge. Bill Crume is shown here diving off the plunge.

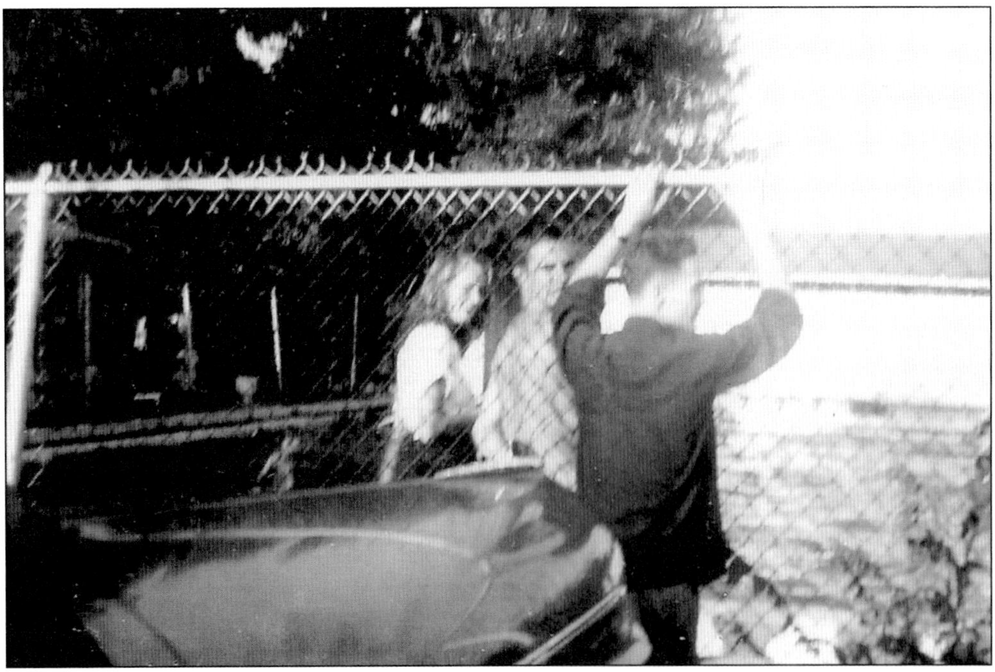

Perrier's Park and Plunge was the teenage hangout. This group of teenagers is gathered around the pool to talk about summer activities.

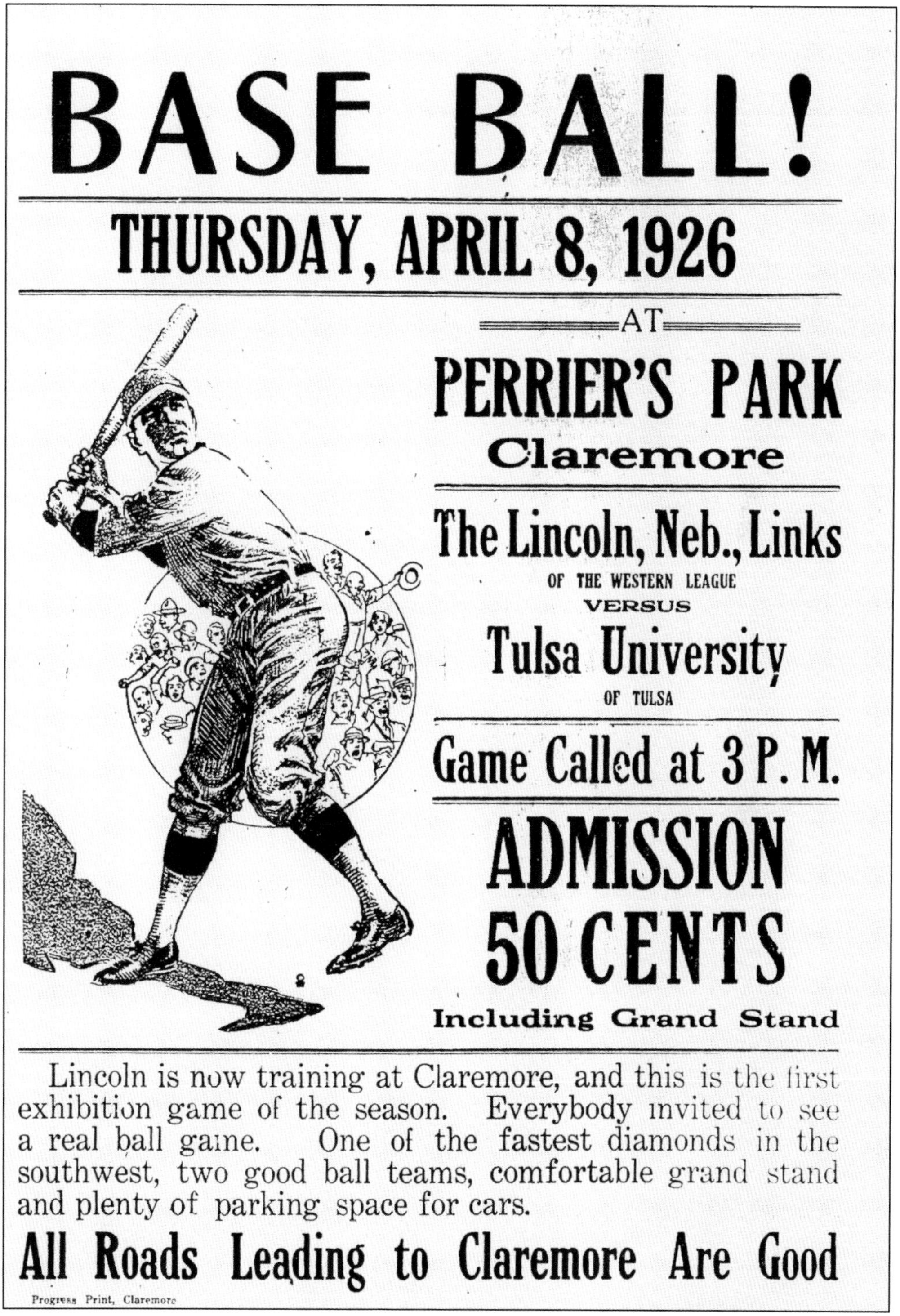


Perrier's Park was also home to Claremore's baseball park. It was billed as the fastest diamond in the Southwest with a comfortable grandstand. The Lincoln Links from Lincoln, Nebraska, trained in Claremore in 1926. This advertisement shows the first game to be against Tulsa University.

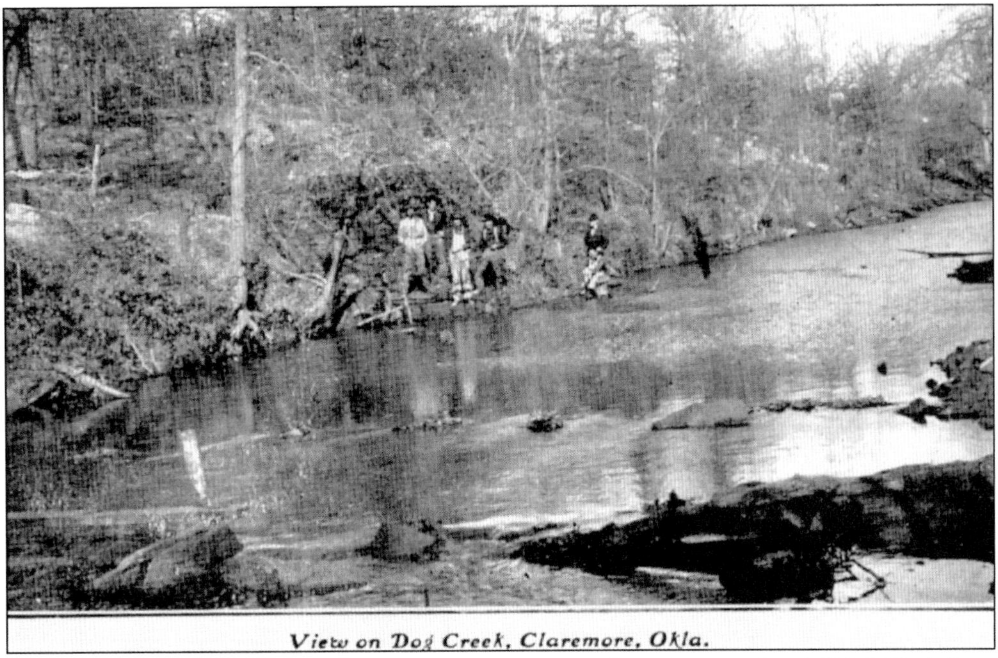


Dog Creek is named for Chief Black Dog, an Osage Indian. A portrait of Chief Black Dog currently hangs in the Smithsonian American Art Museum. Dog Creek feeds directly into Claremore Lake. Area churches frequently used Dog Creek for baptisms in the early years.

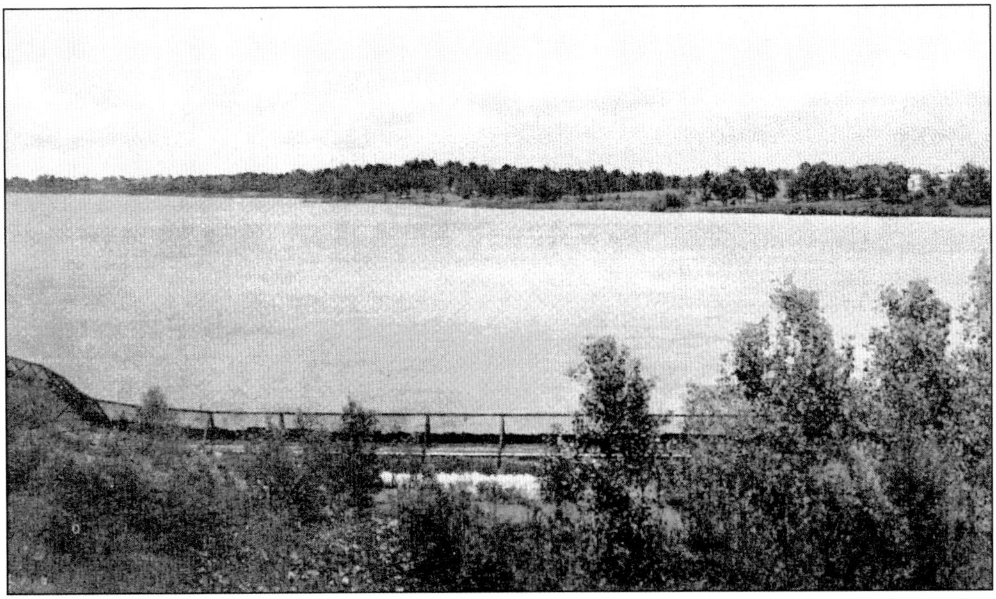

In 1929, a dam was built across Dog Creek. The dam flooded several acres of farmland, creating 500 acres of surface water. Large rock bluffs overlook several points of the lake.

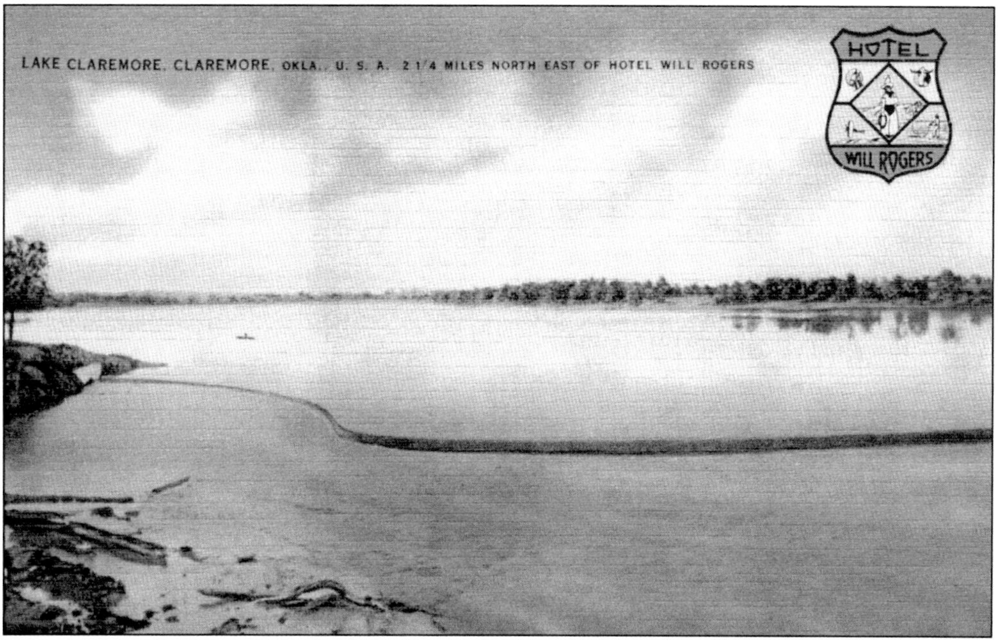


At the time of this postcard, Claremore Lake had 19 miles of rustic shoreline among the wooded foothills at the outskirts of the city. The lake is made up of hundreds of acres of land and continues to provide the city with an unlimited water supply.

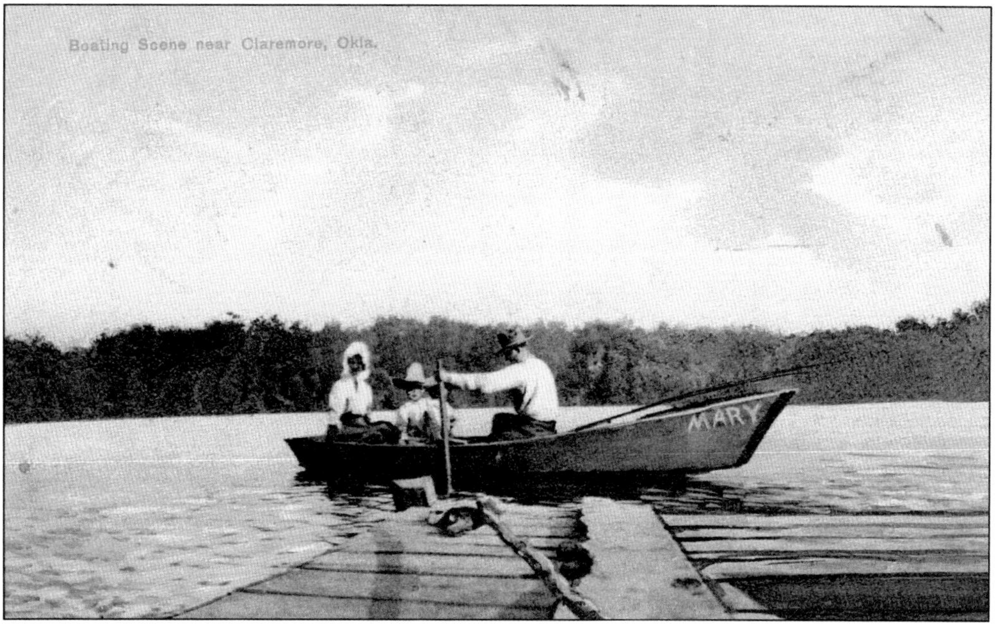


Claremore Lake serves not only as the primary source of water but also as a recreation area for the city. The lake covers 470 acres. Although swimming is not allowed in the lake, recreational boating and fishing are common. At one time, rowboats were available for rental at the lake. The lake abounds with channel catfish and has a bass club that holds a weekly bass tournament in the spring. It is also a stopping ground for pelicans on their migration route, as well as a pair of bald eagles.

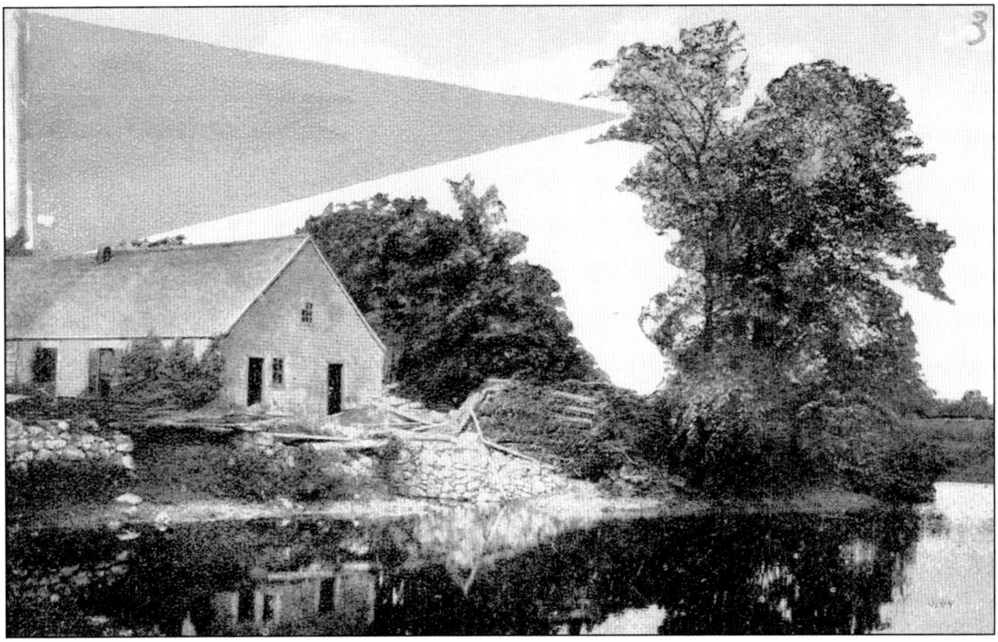

It is difficult to tell where this photograph was taken. However, it depicts a typical rural scene in Claremore at the beginning of the 20th century.

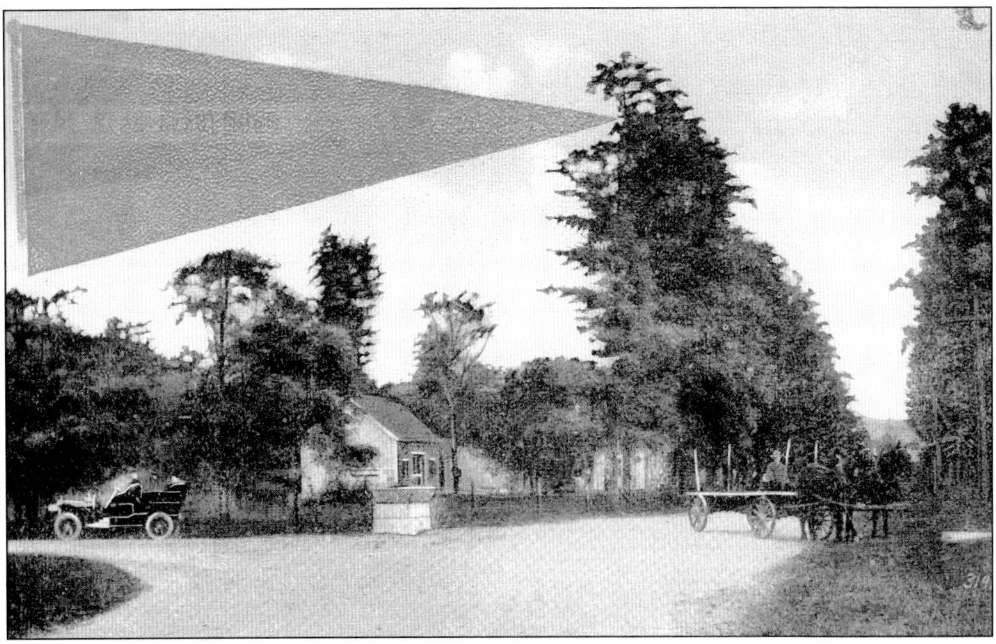

"Oh, what a beautiful morning" in Claremore.

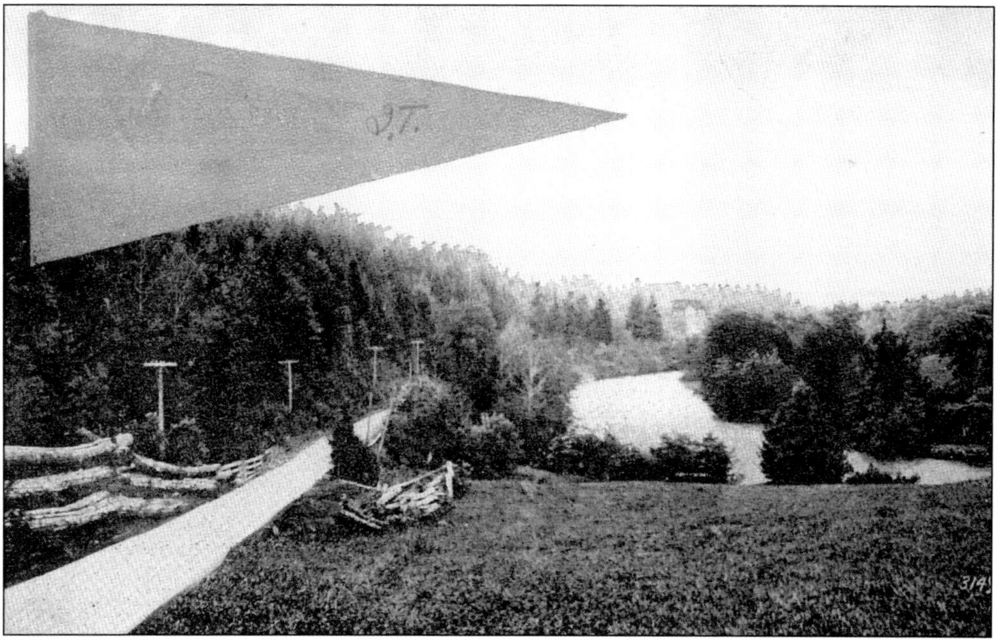

This rural scene appears to have been taken prior to statehood when Claremore was a part of Indian Territory.

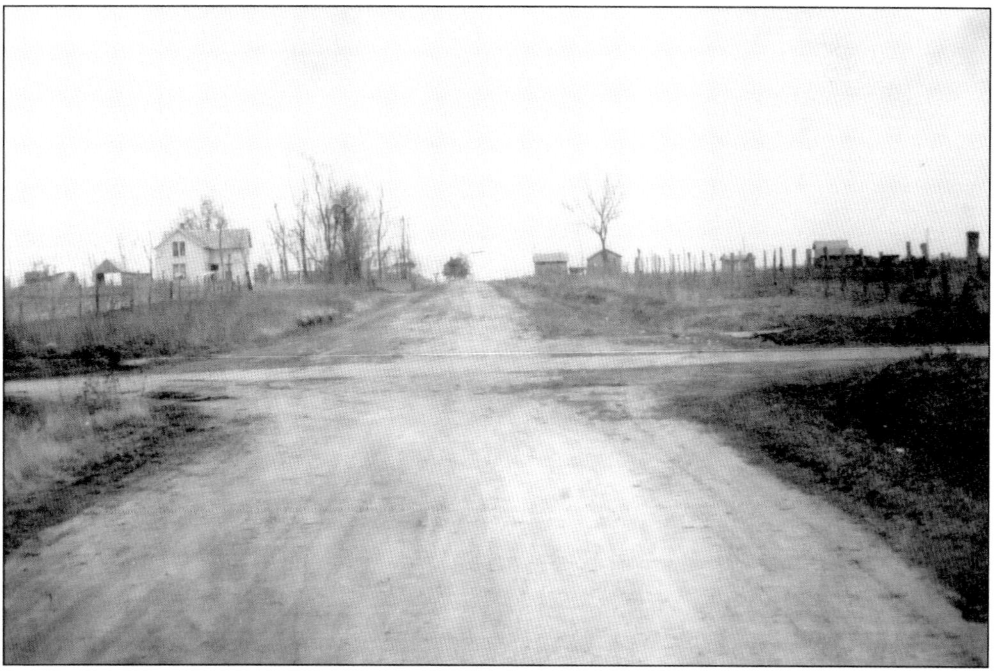

This photograph shows a typical rural Claremore scene.

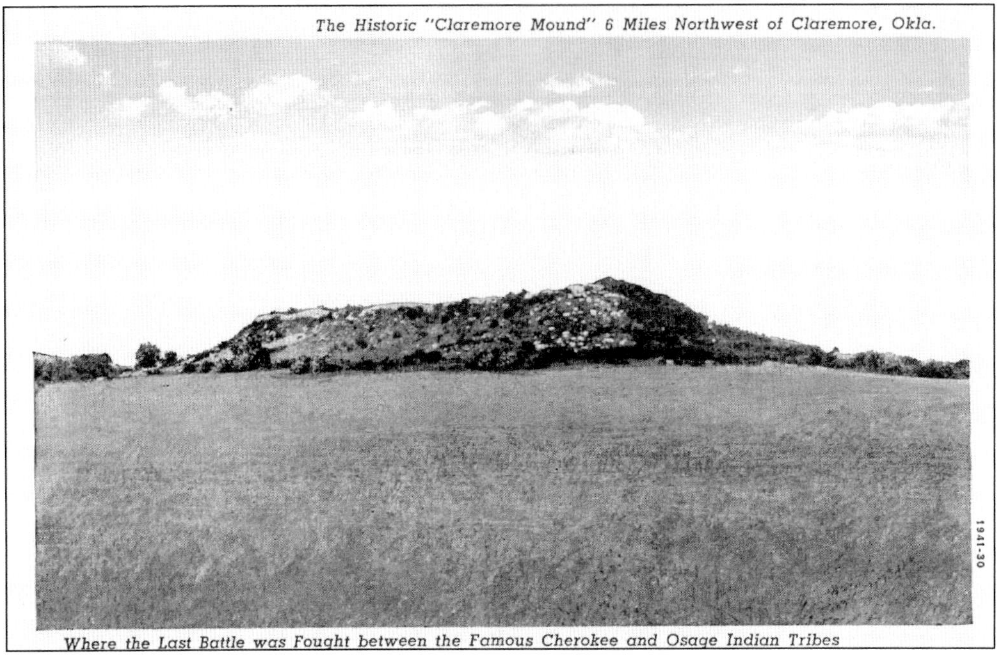


Although Claremore is currently in the Cherokee Nation, it was originally settled by Osage Indians at Claremore Mound. The mound is located four miles northwest of Claremore. Chief Claremont, one of the three principal chiefs of the Osage tribe, built the first official village of Indian Territory in 1802 at Claremore Mound. The Cherokees came to the area around 1808. In October 1817, in what became known as the Battle of Claremore Mound, a band of Cherokees attacked the Osage village while the warriors were away hunting. The Osage suffered great loss, and the town was burned. The Osage were eventually driven out of the area; however, the town still bears the name of Chief Claremont.

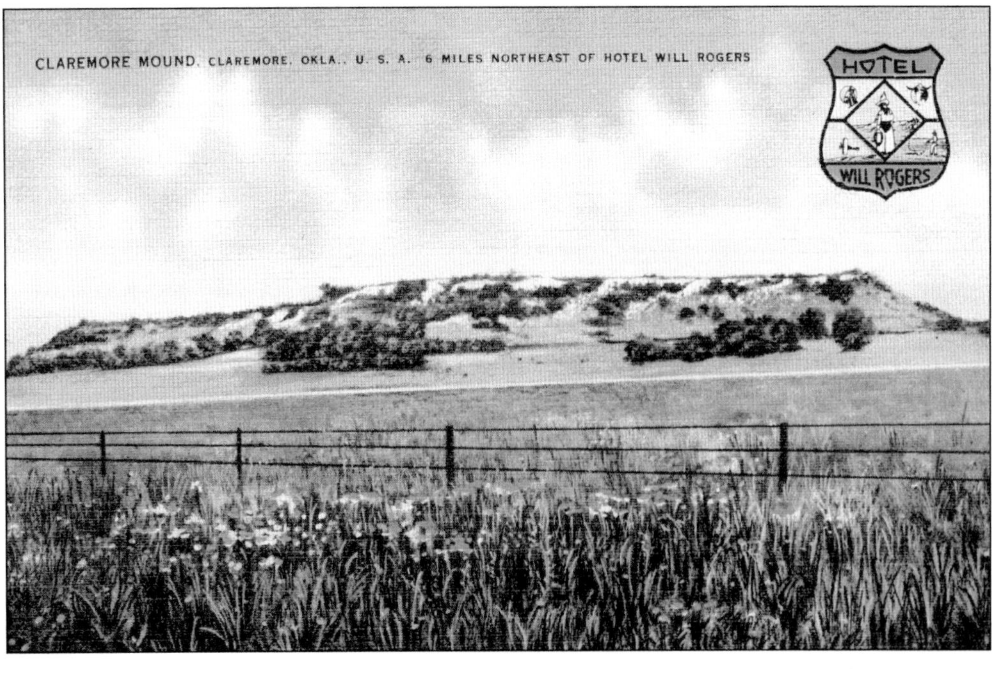

# *Eight*

# Personalities

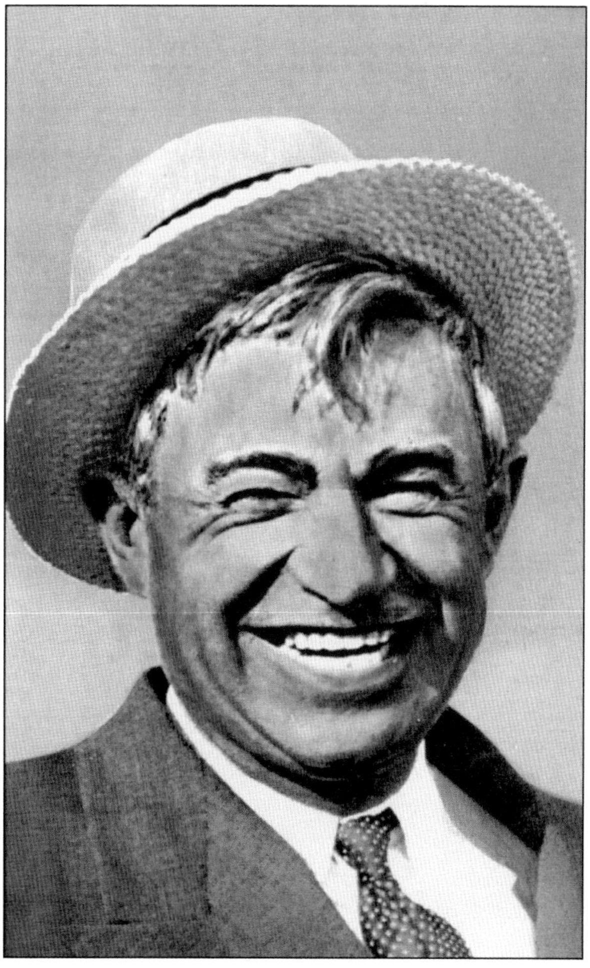

Will Rogers is Claremore's most famous son. Born on November 4, 1879, he was the son of Clem Rogers and Mary Schrimsher. Will was of mixed Cherokee descent. He was a radio personality, movie star, goodwill ambassador, and world traveler. Many people know Will's famous quotation "I never met a man I didn't like."

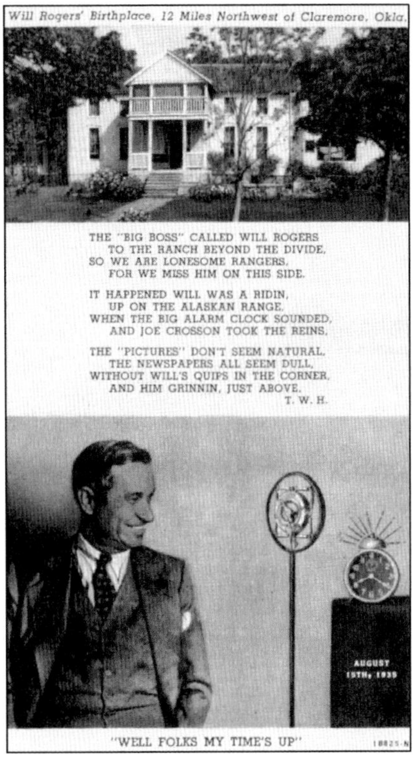


The world mourned as newspapers began to report the death of Will Rogers and pilot Wiley Post on August 15, 1935. An airplane carrying both men crashed in a barren area near North Point, Alaska. The crash was discovered by area Eskimos. The clock pictured in this postcard is stopped at 8:21, the approximate time of Rogers's death.

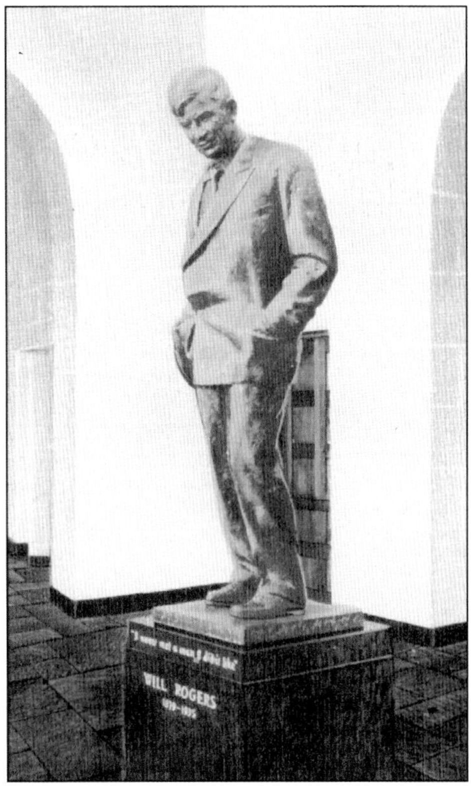


This life-size bronze statue of Will Rogers was created by Jo Davidson. The statue stands today in the rotunda of the Will Rogers Memorial in Claremore. It is an exact replica of a statue that is located in the National Statuary Hall of Fame at the U.S. Capitol in Washington, D.C.

Many people may think Rogers County is named after Will Rogers when in fact it is named for his father Clement (Clem) Van Rogers. Clem was one of the major advocates for Oklahoma statehood. He was one of 55 men selected to write the state constitution. At 68, Clem was the oldest of the delegation. For a birthday tribute to him, the county was named Rogers instead of the intended Cooweescoowee County. Clem was a rancher, banker, senator, and judge, among other things.

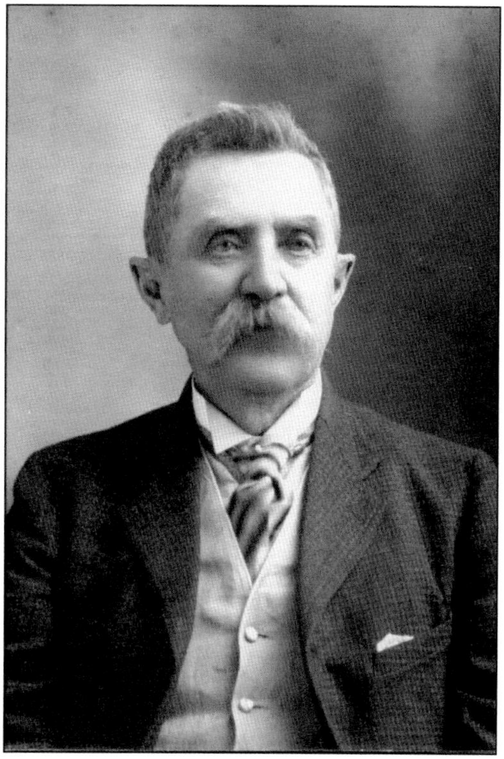

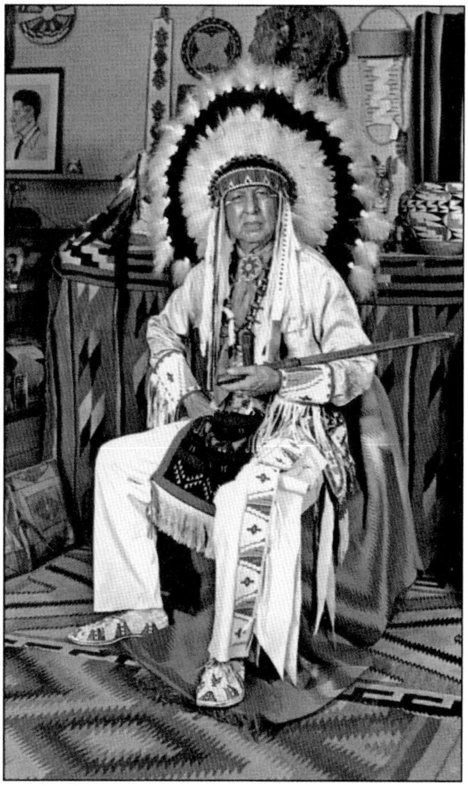

Chief White Robe Hunt was a full-blooded Acoma Indian. He became famous for his fine work as a silversmith. He owned an arts and craft shop for many years on Route 66 just south of Claremore.

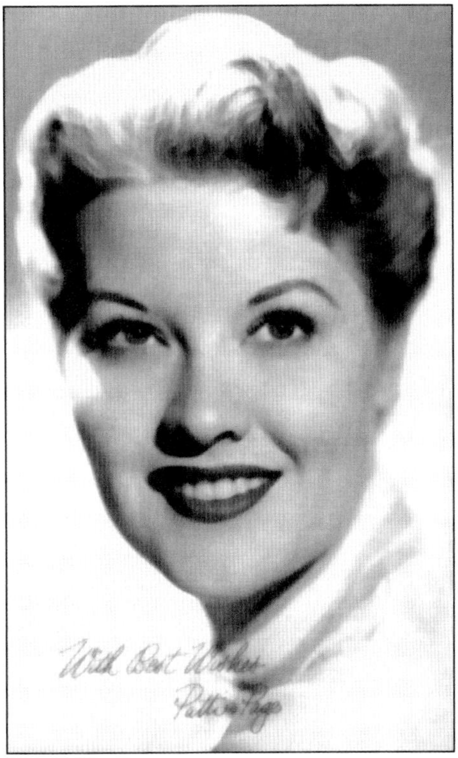


Singer and entertainer Patti Page was born Clara Ann Fowler on November 8, 1927, in Claremore. Fowler was the 10th of 11 children. Her father was a section hand for the railroad, and her mother and sisters picked cotton in the Claremore fields. As a teenager, Fowler got a job singing on a Tulsa radio station show sponsored by the Page Milk Company. She then became known as Patti Page. She is said to have been the best-selling female artist of the 1950s and in 1957 became America's favorite female vocalist. Her recording career spans from 1949 to 1981, and she is known for such songs as "All My Love," "Tennessee Waltz," "Mockingbird Hill," and "Old Cape Cod." She resides with her husband in New Hampshire. Patti Page was the first female to be inducted into the Oklahoma Music Hall of Fame, and a major street in Claremore has been named in her honor.

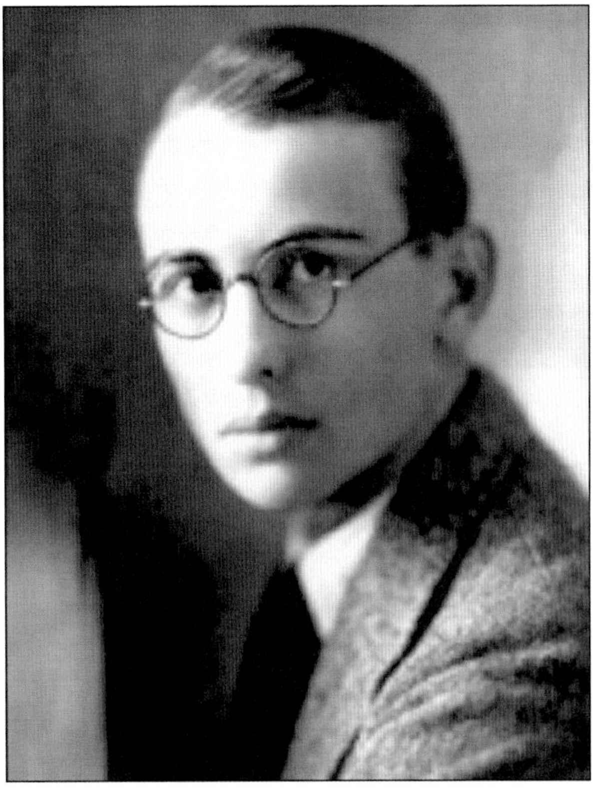

Raleigh Lynn Riggs was born in 1899. Riggs wrote many stories and screenplays; however, he is most famous for his play *Green Grow the Lilacs*. It was this script that Rodgers and Hammerstein adapted into their hit *Oklahoma!* It was based on the Claremore area and its people. The Lynn Riggs Memorial is housed in the old Will Rogers Library. Housed within the memorial is the original "Surrey with the Fringe on Top" from *Oklahoma!* Riggs died in 1954 and is buried in his beloved Claremore. In his honor, a white lilac grows beside his grave.

Stuart Roosa was born on August 16, 1933, in Durango, Colorado. As a young child, he moved to Claremore in 1941. He attended Justus Grade School and Claremore High School. In April 1966, Roosa was selected by NASA to be a member of the astronaut support crew for the Apollo 9 flight. He was the command module pilot on Apollo 14, man's third lunar landing mission. Roosa, along with Alan Shepard and Edgar Mitchell, logged 216 hours in space from January 31 through February 9, 1971, on the Apollo 14 mission. Roosa retired from NASA in 1976, after serving as backup command pilot for the Apollo 16 and 17 missions as well as being involved with the space shuttle program. Stuart Roosa passed away on December 12, 1994, and is buried in Arlington National Cemetery. The City of Claremore has honored this citizen by naming a street and an elementary school on his behalf.

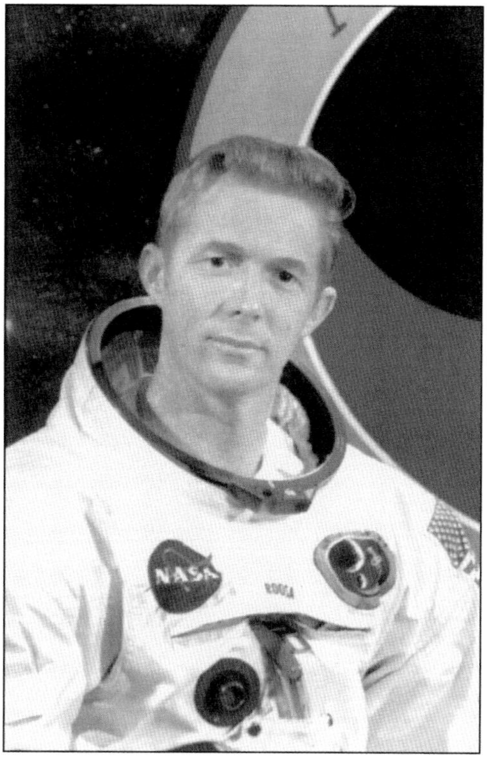


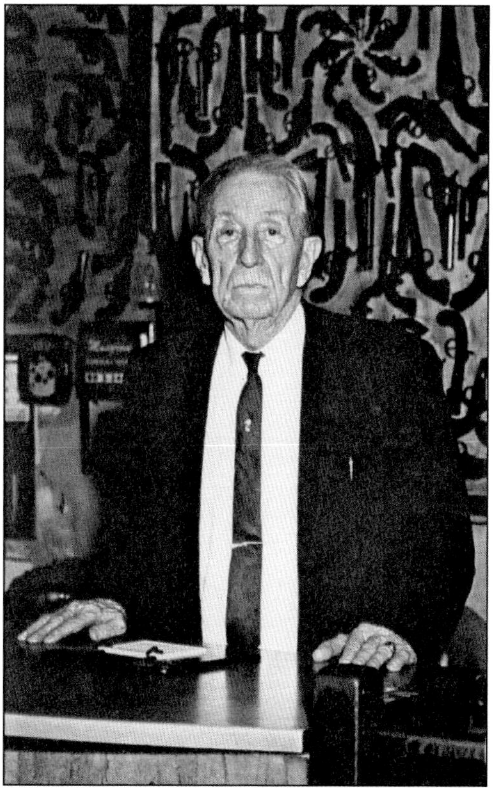

John Monroe (J. M.) Davis was born on June 27, 1887, in Arkansas. Davis began a lifelong hobby of collecting guns at the age of seven. Davis moved to Claremore in 1917, trading his land in Arkansas for the Mason Hotel building. He operated the hotel for 73 years while amassing the largest private gun collection in the world. In 1968, Davis entered into an agreement with the State of Oklahoma to lease his collection of guns and other artifacts to the state for 99 years. The J. M. Davis Gun Museum was erected on the site where the Radium Bath House once stood. Davis passed away on February 7, 1973, and is buried in a crypt inside his gun museum.

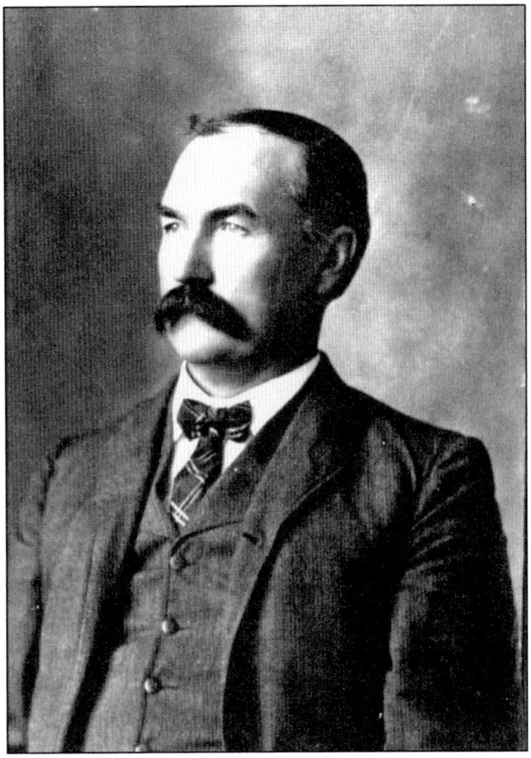

John M. Bayless, along with his family, moved to Claremore from Cassville, Missouri, in 1901. Bayless was known as a banker and a builder. He built many larger buildings in Claremore, including the Windsor Opera House and the Claremore Athletic Association. Only the two bottom floors of the opera house still stand. He also built a three-story private residence named the Belvidere. Unfortunately Bayless died in 1907 just before work on the residence was completed. The family continued to live there until around 1919.

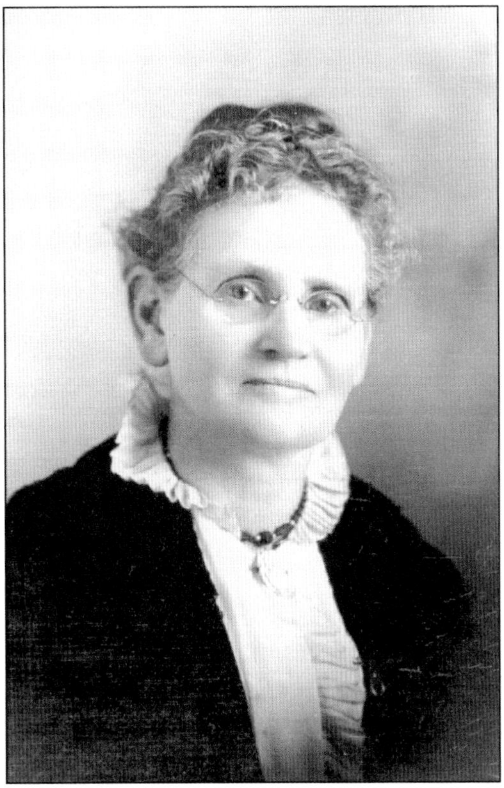

Pioneer women in Oklahoma had to be very strong and able to endure many trials. Mary Melissa Bayless was the wife of John M. Bayless. She came to Indian Territory with her husband in 1901. Pioneer women like Mary, who were willing to follow their husbands, helped shape Claremore and Indian Territory.

# *Nine*

# Fun Cards and Advertisements

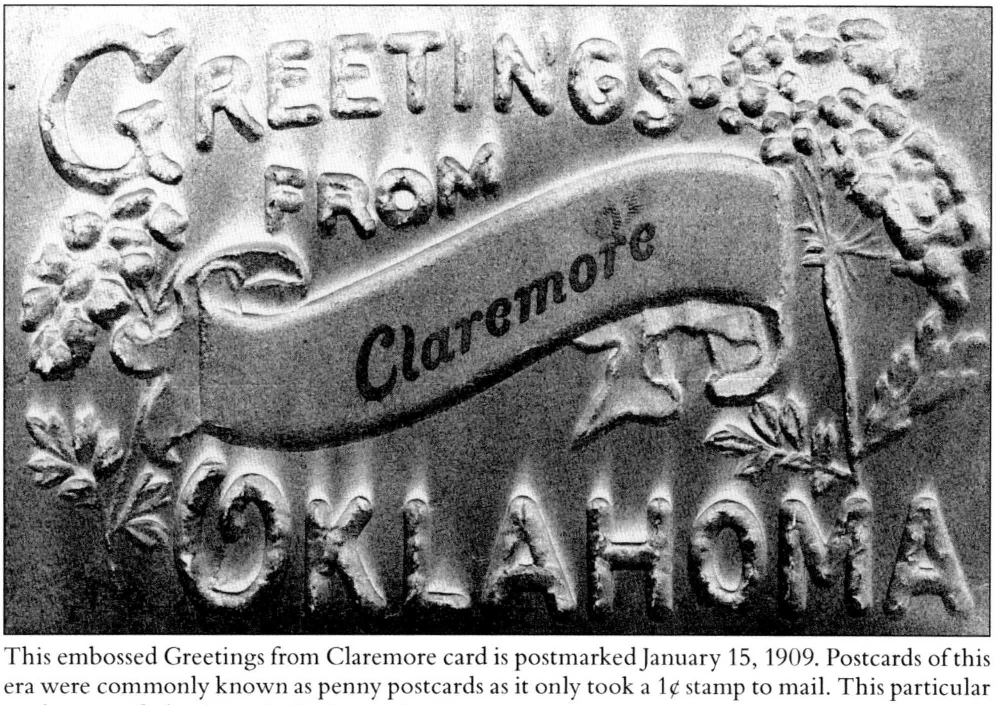


This embossed Greetings from Claremore card is postmarked January 15, 1909. Postcards of this era were commonly known as penny postcards as it only took a 1¢ stamp to mail. This particular card was mailed to Mrs. L. E. Graven in Nowata.

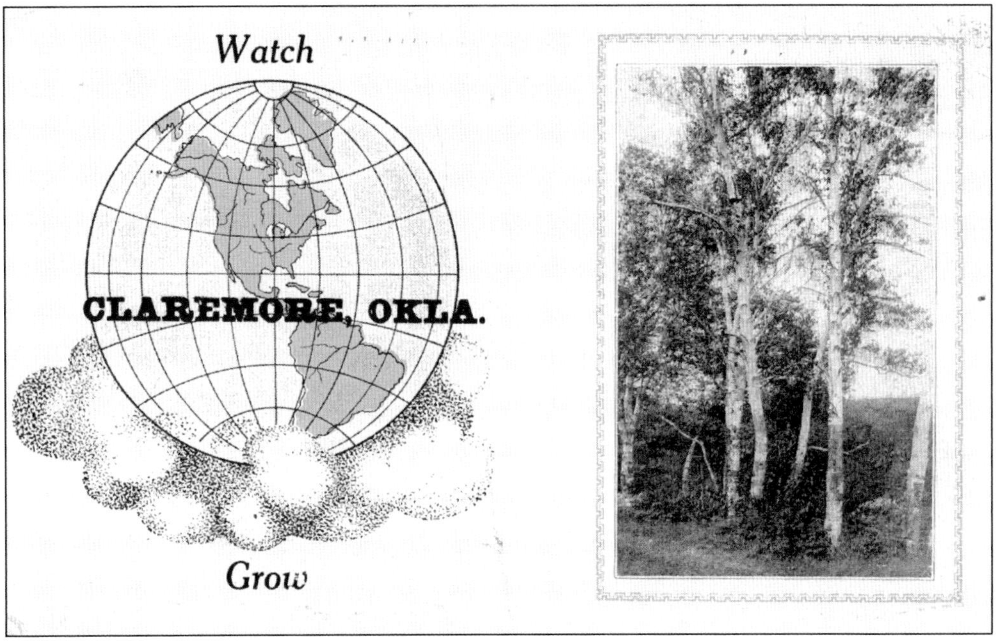


In 1914, Claremore was a fast-growing city. "Watch Claremore Grow" was a slogan that could be heard on the lips of people for miles around.

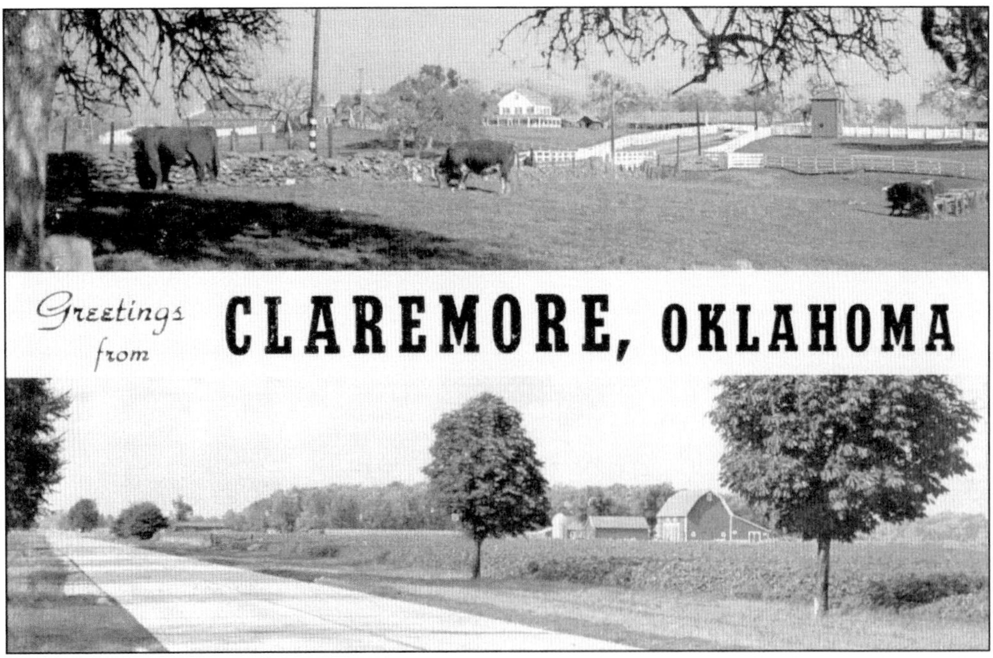


This card depicts agricultural and ranching scenes around Claremore. The fertile soil provided early settlers with a means of providing for themselves and their neighbors.

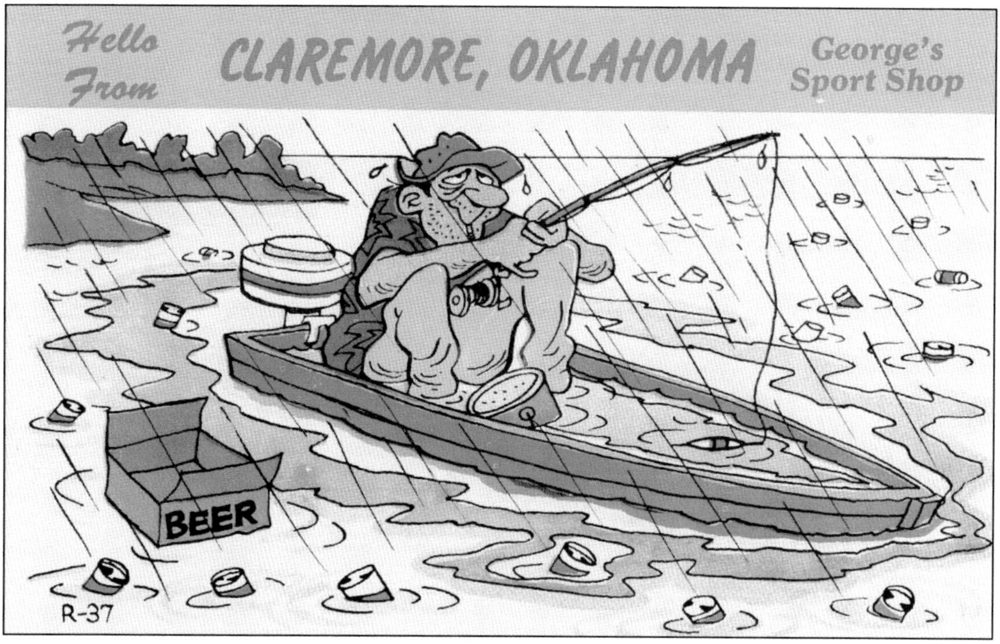


While this is a comical postcard, fishing has always been a main pastime in Claremore. The city's lake and several area ponds provide endless access to a fishermen's dream.

Another 600 sacks of that good mill run bran. Next will almost give you if you take it from the car.

---

| | |
|---|---|
| Rye Flour 48 Lb. sack | $2.90 |
| Large sack meal | 85c |
| Fine Colorado Potatoes, peck | 39c |
| 15c can corn | 12c |
| 15c can hominy | 12c |
| 15c can tomatoes | 12c |
| **Good Coal Oil, per gal.** | **13c** |

# Caspar Lipe's

## Cash Store

Caspar Lipe's grocery store was located in Radium Town. This advertisement was taken from a 1918 copy of the *Claremore Messenger.*

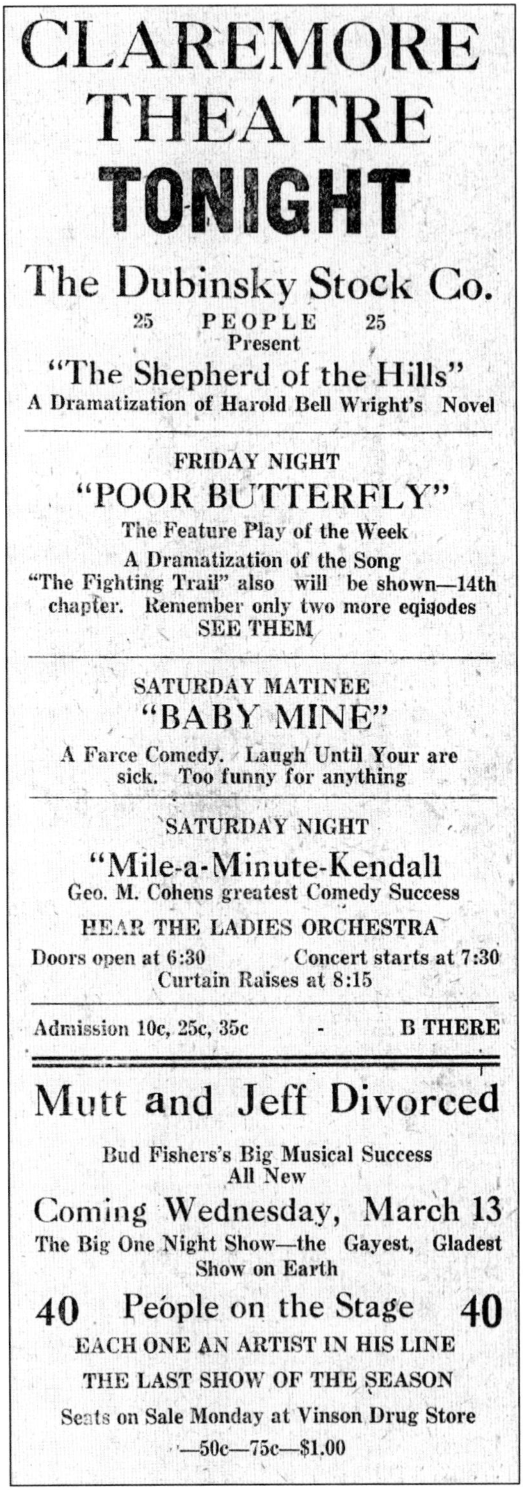

# CLAREMORE THEATRE

# TONIGHT

## The Dubinsky Stock Co.

25 PEOPLE 25

Present

**"The Shepherd of the Hills"**

**A Dramatization of Harold Bell Wright's Novel**

---

**FRIDAY NIGHT**

**"POOR BUTTERFLY"**

**The Feature Play of the Week**

**A Dramatization of the Song**

**"The Fighting Trail" also will be shown—14th chapter. Remember only two more eqisodes**

**SEE THEM**

---

**SATURDAY MATINEE**

**"BABY MINE"**

**A Farce Comedy. Laugh Until Your are sick. Too funny for anything**

---

**SATURDAY NIGHT**

**"Mile-a-Minute-Kendall**

**Geo. M. Cohens greatest Comedy Success**

**HEAR THE LADIES ORCHESTRA**

**Doors open at 6:30 Concert starts at 7:30**

**Curtain Raises at 8:15**

---

**Admission 10c, 25c, 35c - B THERE**

---

## Mutt and Jeff Divorced

**Bud Fishers's Big Musical Success**

**All New**

**Coming Wednesday, March 13**

**The Big One Night Show—the Gayest, Gladest Show on Earth**

**40 People on the Stage 40**

**EACH ONE AN ARTIST IN HIS LINE**

**THE LAST SHOW OF THE SEASON**

**Seats on Sale Monday at Vinson Drug Store**

**—50c—75c—$1.00**

A 1918 advertisement from the *Claremore Messenger* is seen here. The presentation of *The Shepherd of the Hills* was based on the Branson, Missouri, area.

**Walker's Department Store Co.** Sell the Best for Less Why Pay More?

THE GREAT DAY has come. The war has been won for Freedom and Democracy. The world thrills with victory to its finger tips. Feeling long held in suspense has burst its bonds—the purse-strings will be loosened as never before. The demand for merchandise of all kinds—Holiday goods and all requisites, will be the greatest in the history of the world. We therefore advise early buying if you want to get early selection—the late shopper will have to take what is left. So Shop Early—Do Not Wait.

We are showing a very large assortment of sensible gifts, as well as a Wonderful Toy Display in our Basement Store: -:- -:- -:-

Walker's Department Store was located in the bottom of the Mason Hotel.

**Saturday is the last day of our Birthday Celebration**

This event marking the eighteen years of our growth in this city comes to a close Saturday night

EVEN THOUGH we have enjoyed a very mar ked increase in our business, it can readily be understood that selling reliable merchandise at the present time, at prices that are now in force cannot be maintained for an indefinite peri od and so, by reason of the very nature of the values offered, we must bring this anniversary sa le to a close.

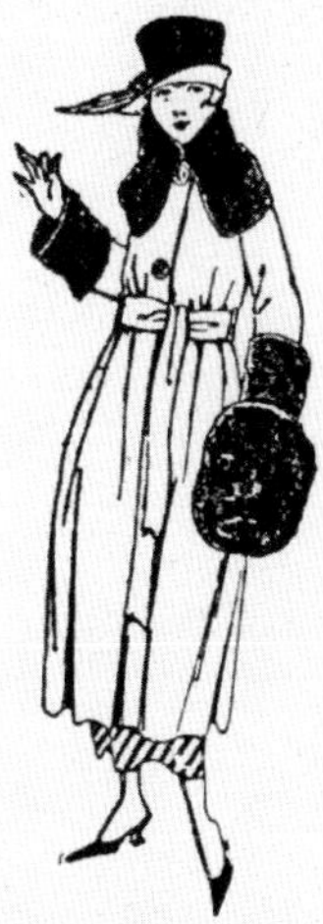

Saturday is the last day and so that t he last days may be as appealing as the first, we have added new lots, and we ur ge you to be here Friday and Saturday to take advantage of the exceptional values.

HERE ARE YOUR SAVINGS

| SUITS NOW PRICED: | Coats now priced: | Dresses now priced: |
|---|---|---|
| $19.75 values at ---$15.00 | $15.00 values now--$11.95 | $15.00 Dresses now $11.95 |
| $25.00 values at ---$19.75 | $19.75 values now--$15.00 | $17.50 Dresses now $13.50 |
| $29.75 values at ---$23.50 | $25.00 values now--$18.95 | $19.75 Dresses now $14.75 |
| $35.00 values at ---$25.00 | $27.50 values now--$22.50 | $25.00 Dresses now $18.75 |
| $39.75 to $45 values $35.00 | $35.00 values now--$27.50 | $29.75 Dresses now $23.95 |
| $50 to $98.50 at 25 pct. Off | $39.75 to $95 values now- - - - - 20 Pct. Off | $35.00 Dresses now $27.50 |
| | | $39.75 Dresses now $29.75 |
| | | $45.00 Dresses now $35.00 |

**Haas**

The Haas Department Store was in business in Claremore since 1901. The Columbia building was built in 1909, and the store moved into that building. The building still stands today at the corner of Will Rogers Boulevard and Missouri Street. It was the old McClellan's store.

## A. H. LITCHENBURG DOES BIG BUSINESS

To Farmers and City:—

I have paid out over $3,000.00 for iron, rags and junk in a little more than a year's time. There is at least half that much left. Yet I am going to pay $8 to $11 per ton for iron and one cent a pound for rags for the next ten days. Bring in all old junk and iron, we will buy it.

**Claremore Junk Comp'y**

A. H. Litchenburg found the junk business to be profitable in 1918.

Statement of the Condition of

## The Farmers Bank & Trust Co.

At the close of business, August 31, 1918., as made to the State Bank Commissioner of Oklahoma.

| RESOURCES: | |
|---|---|
| Loans | $206,167.55 |
| Overdrafts | 606.30 |
| Furniture & Fixtures | 2,500.00 |
| Bonds & Securities | 18,866.96 |
| Warrants | 7,599.12 |
| CASH & SIGHT EXCHANGE | 76,275.73 |
| Total | $312,015.66 |

| LIABILITIES: | |
|---|---|
| Capital Stock | $ 30,000.00 |
| Surplus and Undivided Profits | 4,917.30 |
| DEPOSITS | 277,098.36 |
| Total | $312,015.66 |

The above Statement is Correct,

J. F. FLIPPIN, Cashier

WE INVITE YOUR ACCOUNTS BELIEVING WE CAN RENDER SATISFACTORY SERVICE.

OFFICERS AND DIRECTORS

W. G. RIGGS, ........ President
J. F. McCLELLAN, – Vice-President
J. F. FLIPPIN, ........ Cashier
F. B. CARDEN, ........ Asst.-Cashier
JNO. Q. ADAMS

W. G. Riggs, father of Lynn Riggs, was the president of the Farmers Bank.

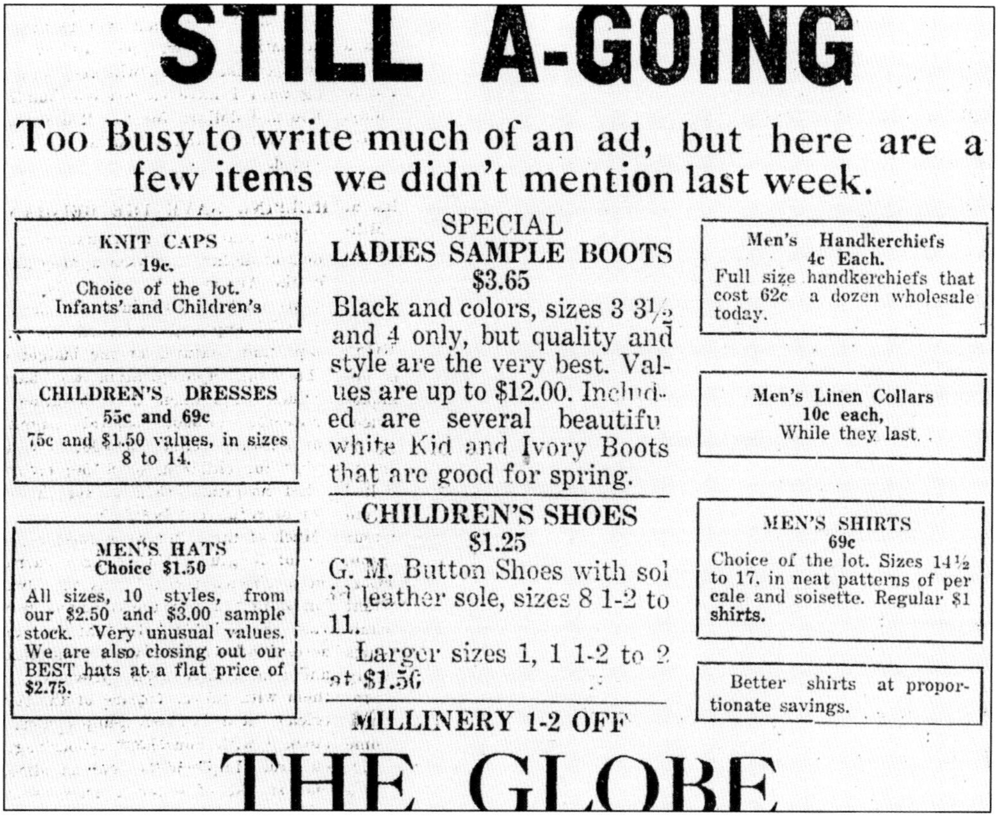


The Globe department store went out of business one week after this advertisement ran in a 1918 issue of the *Claremore Messenger.*

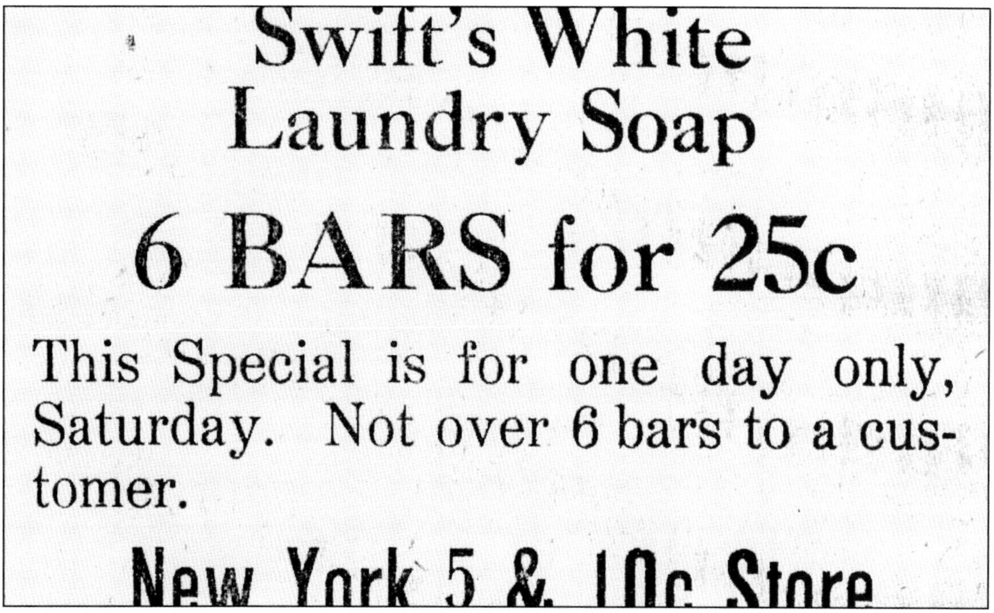


Seen here is a 1918 advertisement for the New York 5 and 10¢ Store. This general merchandise store was located on Third Street, also known as Main Street.

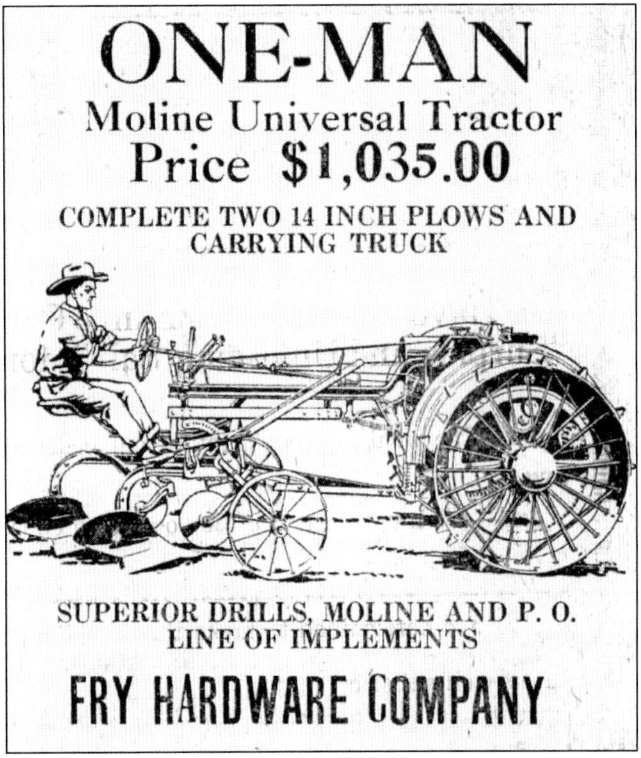


This 1918 Fry Hardware Company advertisement tempted many area farmers.

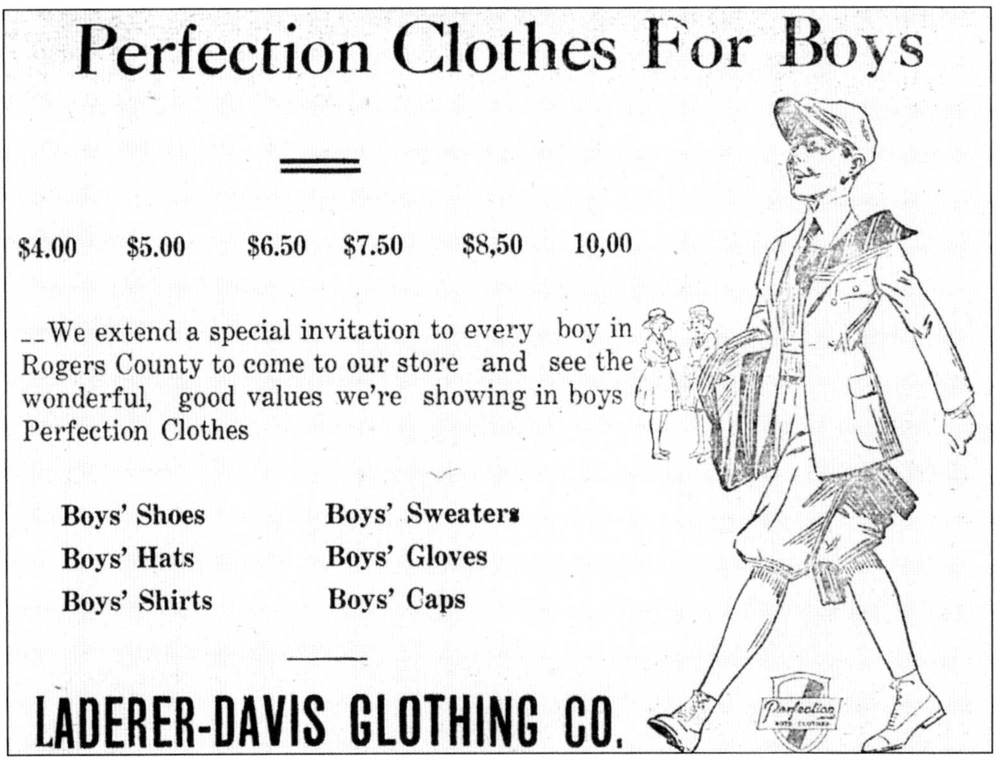


Laderer-Davis Clothing Company sold only men's and boys' clothing in 1918.

The Boston Store was one of the earliest stores in Claremore. It was located in Claremore as early as 1895. In 1895, it appeared to have been located in the middle of the second block of Third Street, commonly known as Main Street, just down from the present site of the chamber of commerce. The owner in 1918 was T. L. Sullivan.

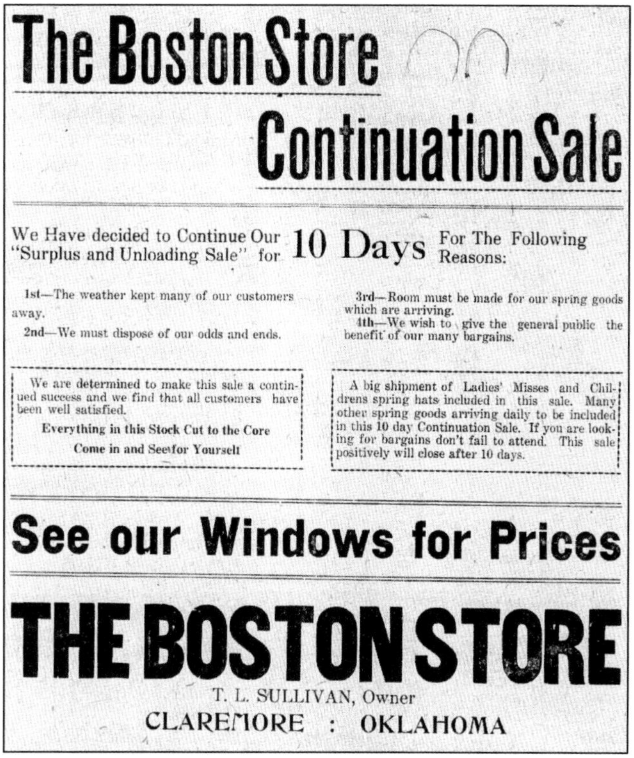


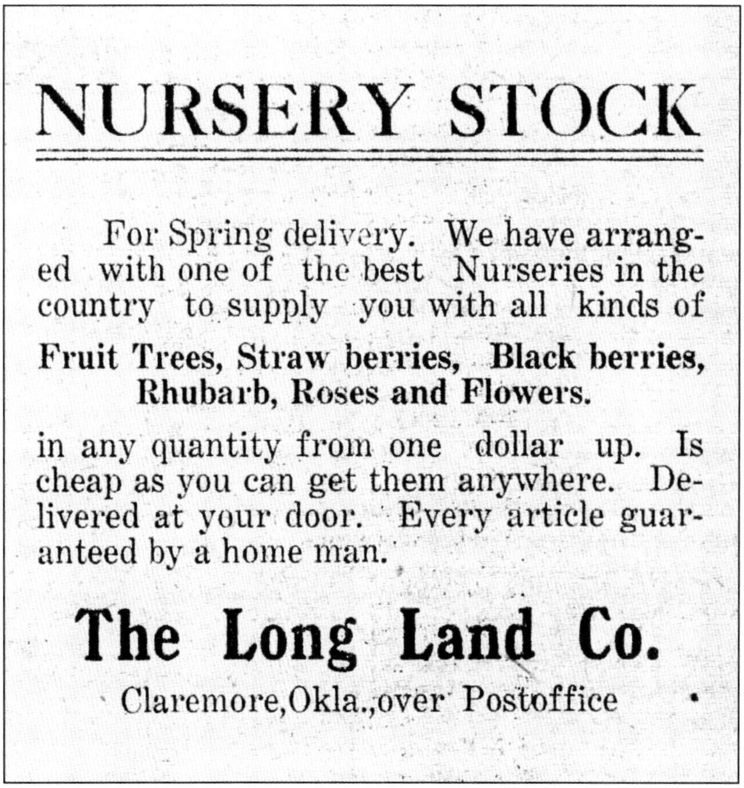


The Long Land Company was located over the post office in 1918. It sold nursery stock such as strawberries, roses, and other flowers.

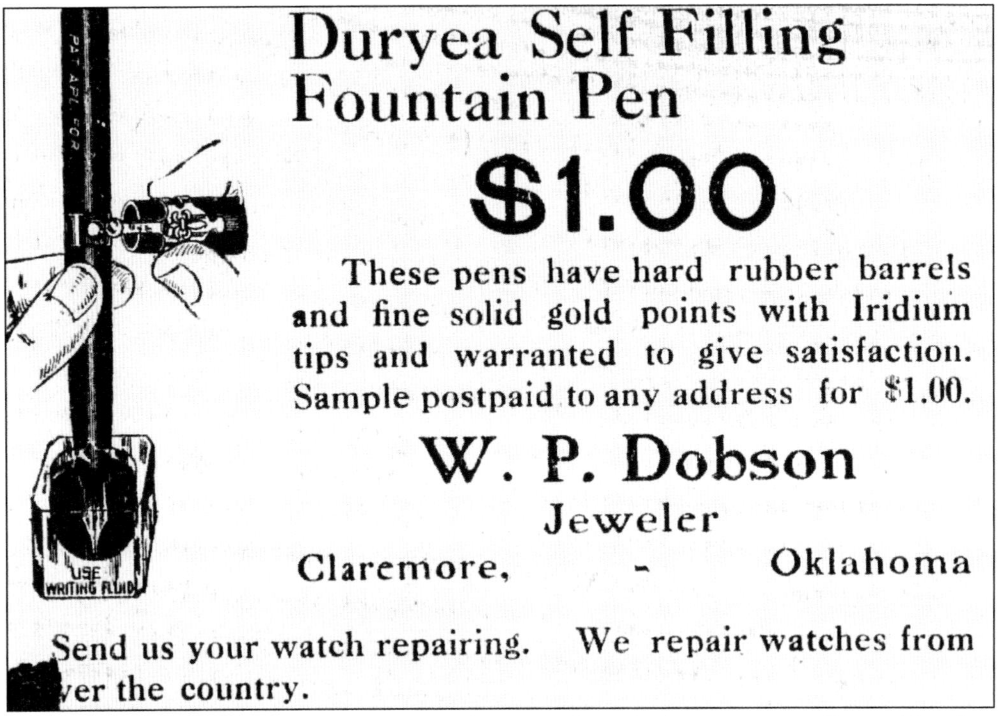


A 1918 advertisement for W. P. Dobson Jeweler is seen here. Dobson was one of several jewelers in Claremore. The store was located at 423 West Third Street, also known as Main Street.

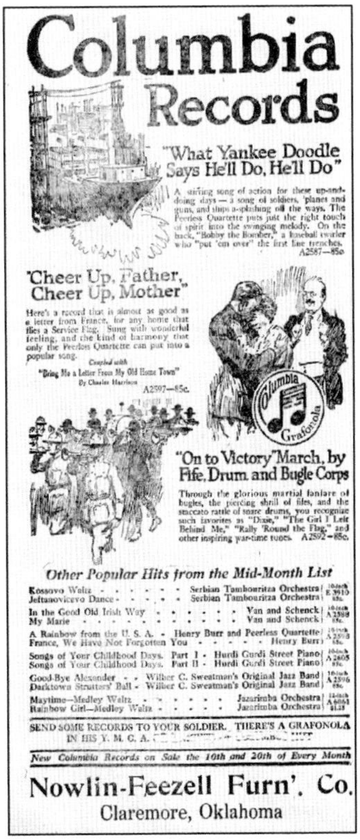


The Nowlin-Feezell Furniture Company not only sold furniture, but according to this 1918 advertisement, it also carried a wide assortment of popular music.

# *Ten*

# Route 66

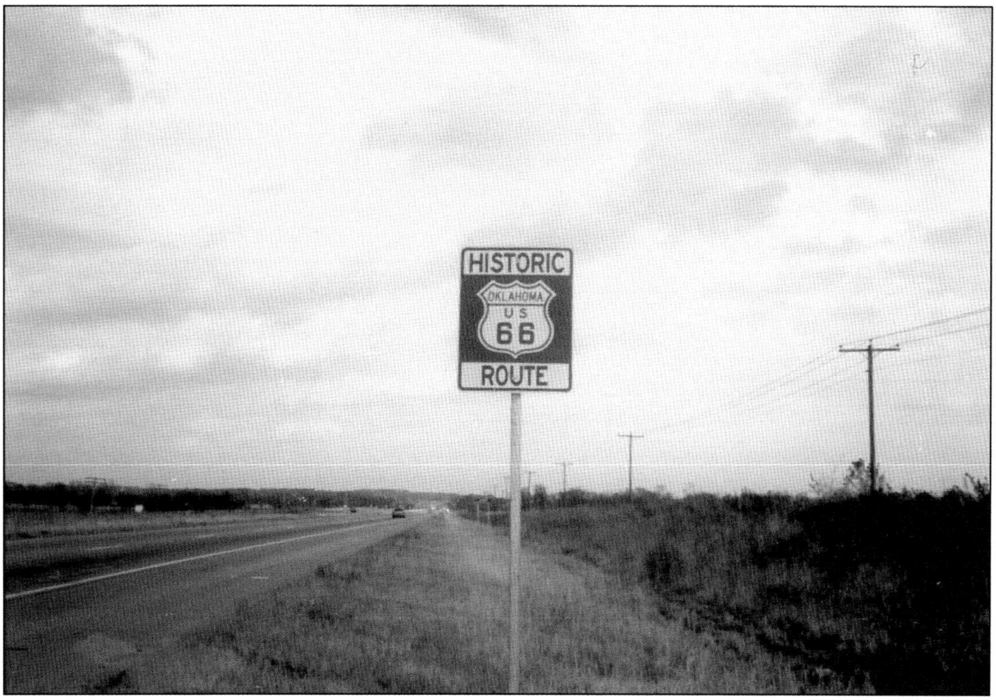


Fully paved in 1936, historic Route 66 connected America through its heartland. Route 66 cut directly through Claremore, bringing more business, including motels, to town. The road was also known as Will Rogers Highway. Tourism was at a high, and people were getting their "kicks on Route 66."

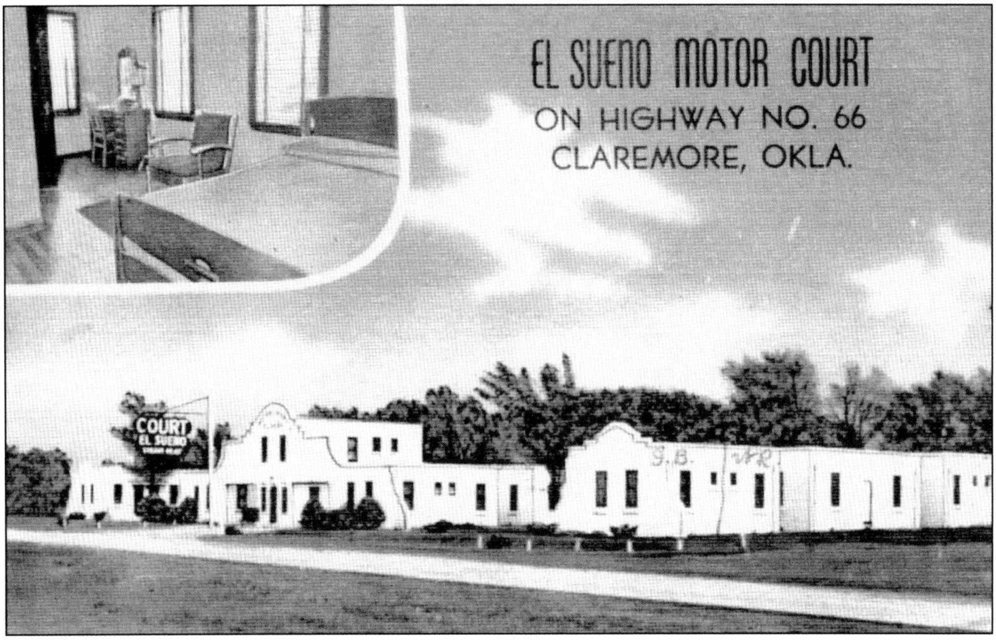


The El Sueno Motor Court (Spanish for shut-eye) was located on Route 66 and was the first motel in Claremore. It was owned by Harold and Christine Sibley. The building still stands but has fallen on hard times. It was recently bought at auction, and the new owner plans to restore it to its original state.

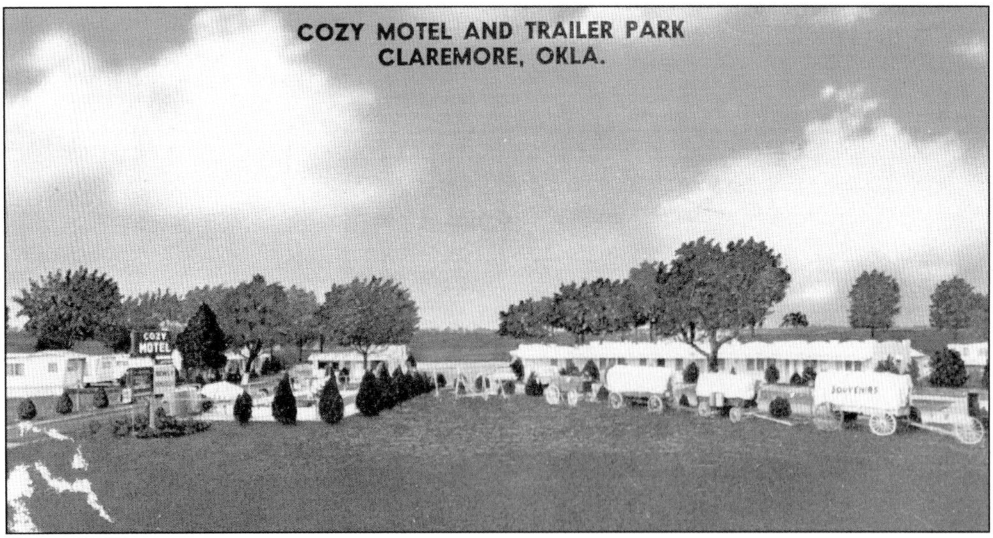


The Cozy Motel was located on the north end of Claremore on Route 66. It boasted 19 air-conditioned units, wall-to-wall carpets, television, and a swimming pool. The motel was easily recognized by its teepees and covered wagons along the circular entrance. Many of the area's children took swimming lessons in the motel pool. Author April Churchill's grandmother spent her honeymoon at this spot.

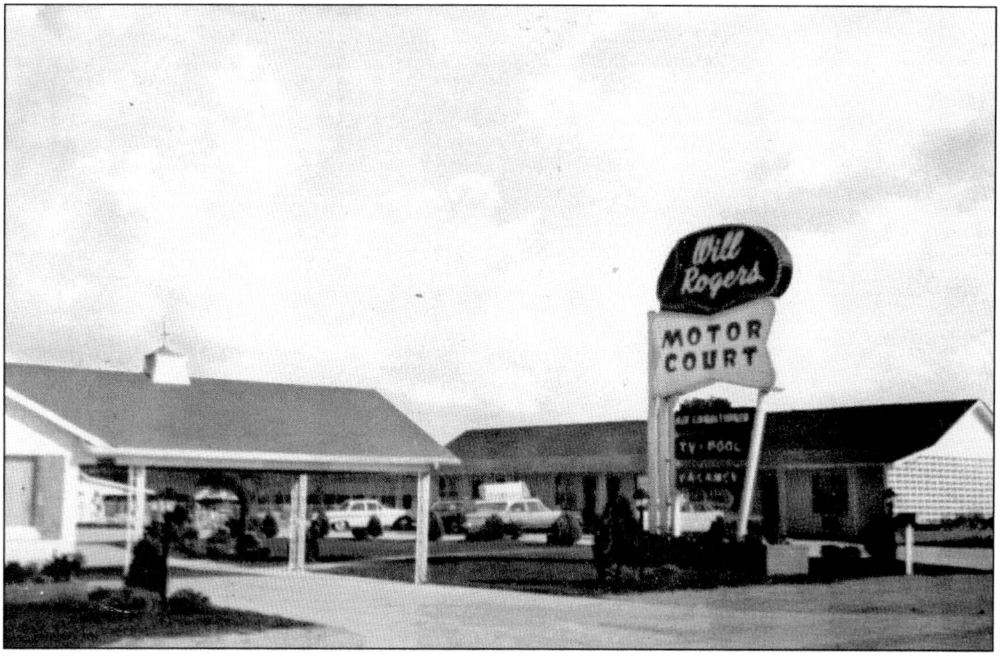


The Will Rogers Motor Court is located on the south end of Claremore on Route 66. It is AAA approved, and the telephone number was RO3-4410. The motor court is still fully operational today.

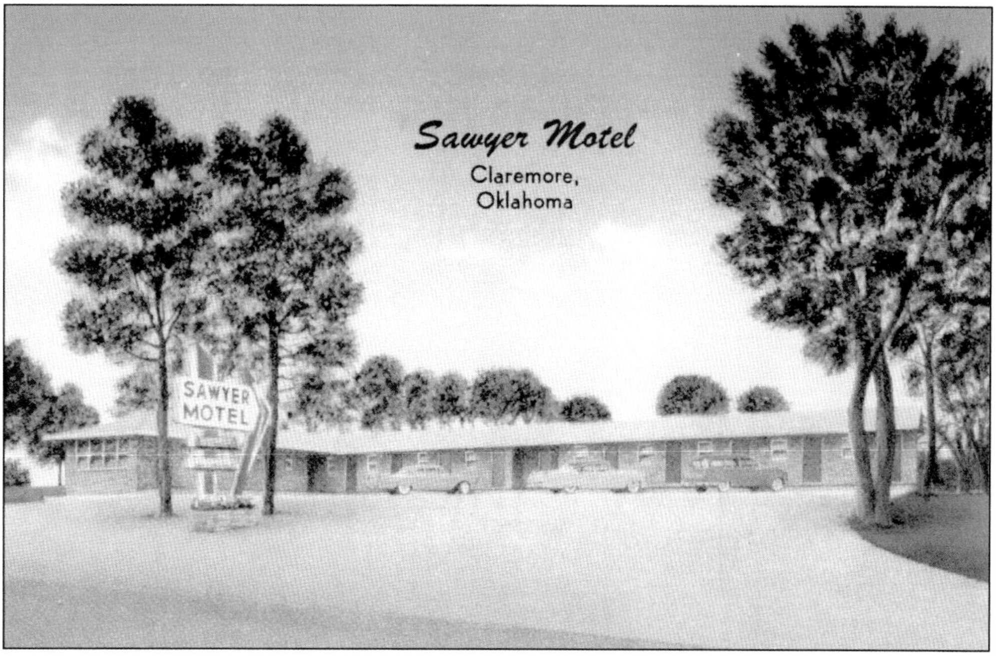


The Sawyer Motel was located on Highway 20 near the Will Rogers Turnpike gate. Highway 20 intersects with Route 66. Since the Sawyer Motel was far enough from all railroad tracks, it was one of the only motels in town that was able to offer no train noises. Anyone who has been to Claremore knows this is valuable, as newcomers can sometimes find it difficult to sleep due to the train noises.

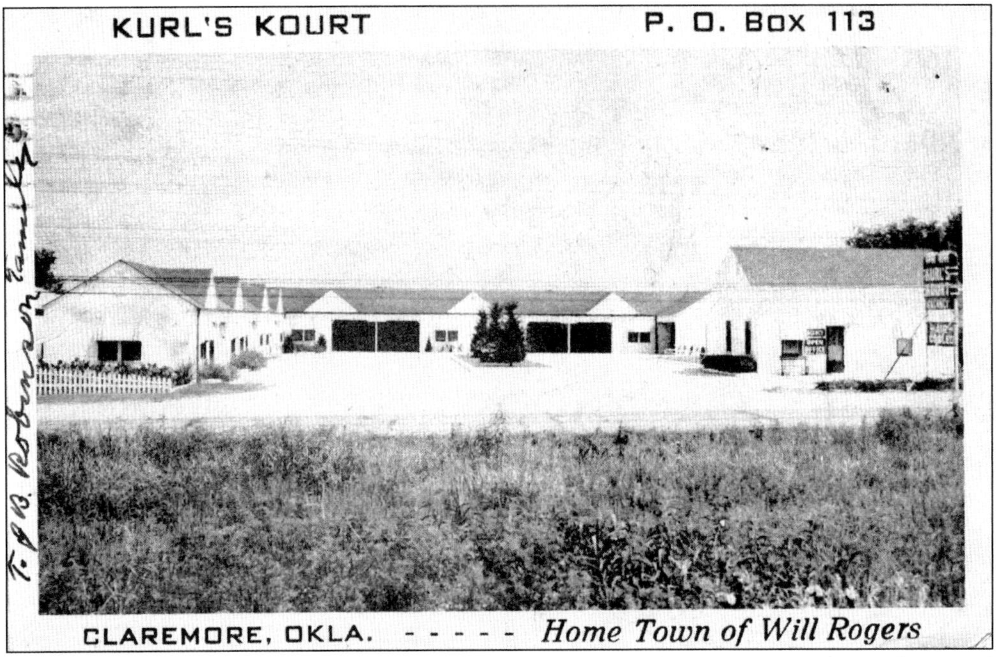


Kurl's Kourt, south of Claremore on Route 66, was owned by J. H. Boucher. The motel advertised family suites, a playground for children, refrigerated air, panel heat, good beds, and tubs. Refrigerated air is a necessity for Oklahoma summers.

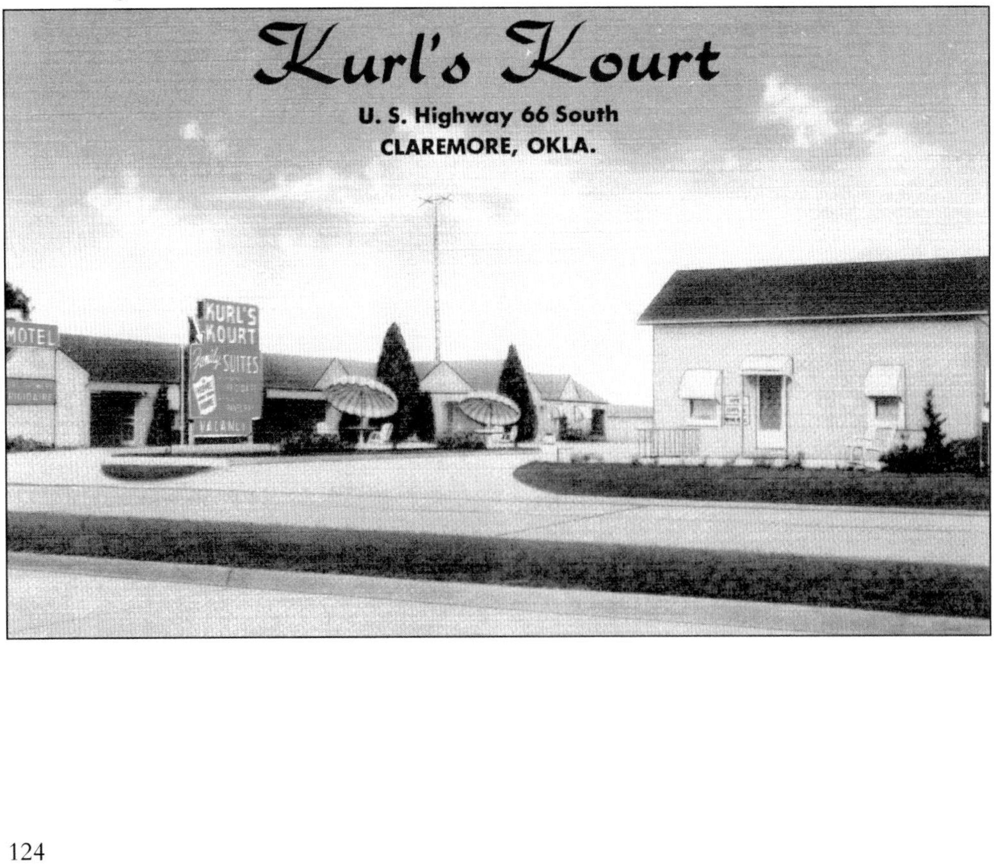

The Oklahoma Totem Pole was built by Nathan Edward (Ed) Galloway just north of Claremore. It is the undisputed world's largest totem pole. Galloway started his tribute to the American Indian in 1937 and completed it in 1948. He built the totem pole using one bucket of cement at a time. The totem pole is 90 feet tall, 18 inches in diameter, and 54 feet around the base. It displays 200 different carved pictures. A total of 28 tons of cement, 6 tons of steel, and 100 tons of native sand and rock were used in the construction. It is the only remaining folk art of its type in Oklahoma and is on the National Register of Historical Places.

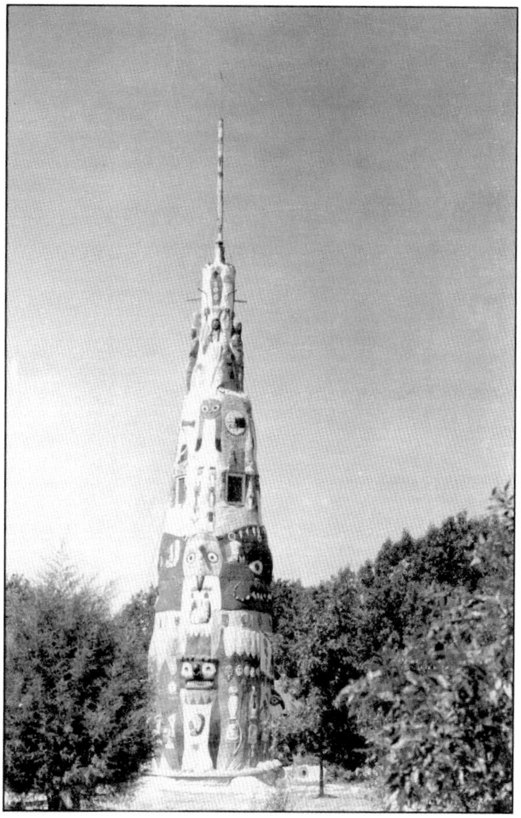

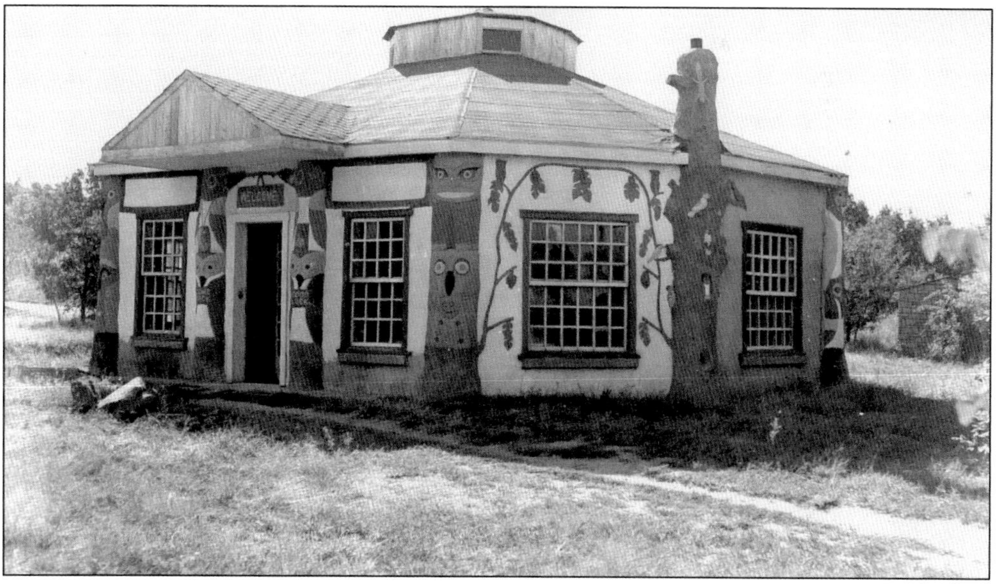

Ed Galloway's wife, Villie, encouraged him to build a museum on the property to show off his furniture, pictures, and fiddles. It was built at the same time as the Oklahoma Totem Pole. It was originally called the Fiddle House as he had made 300 fiddles of different wood types to display wood from across the world. Ed Galloway died in 1962. The totem pole and Galloway Museum are left for generations to come.

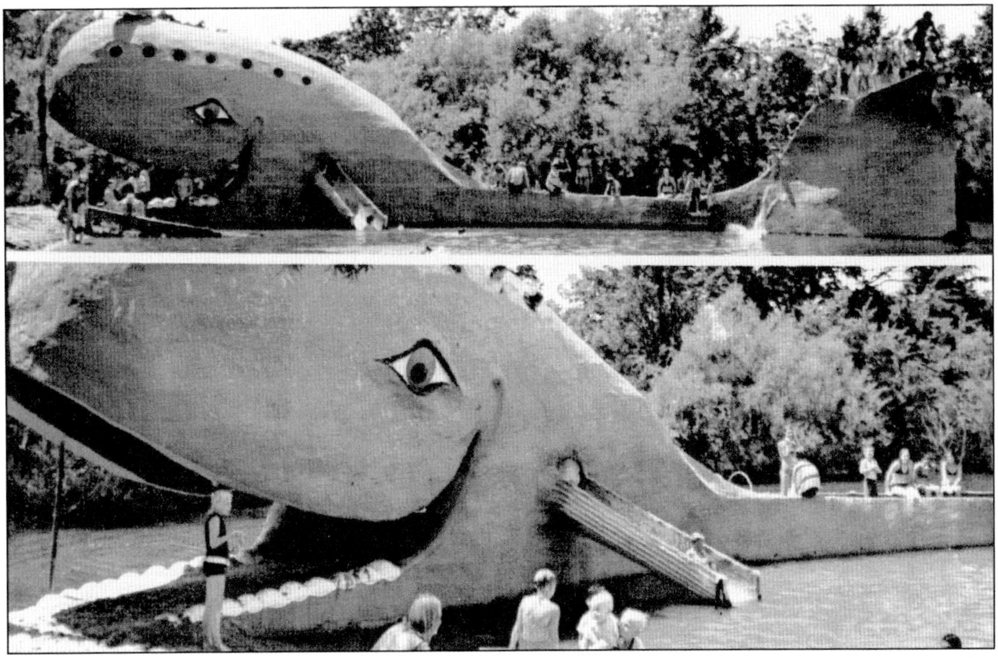

The Blue Whale is located a few miles south of Claremore on Route 66. It was a very popular tourist attraction during the 1960s. It was built by Hugh Davis for his wife, Zelta. The family later opened it for public use.

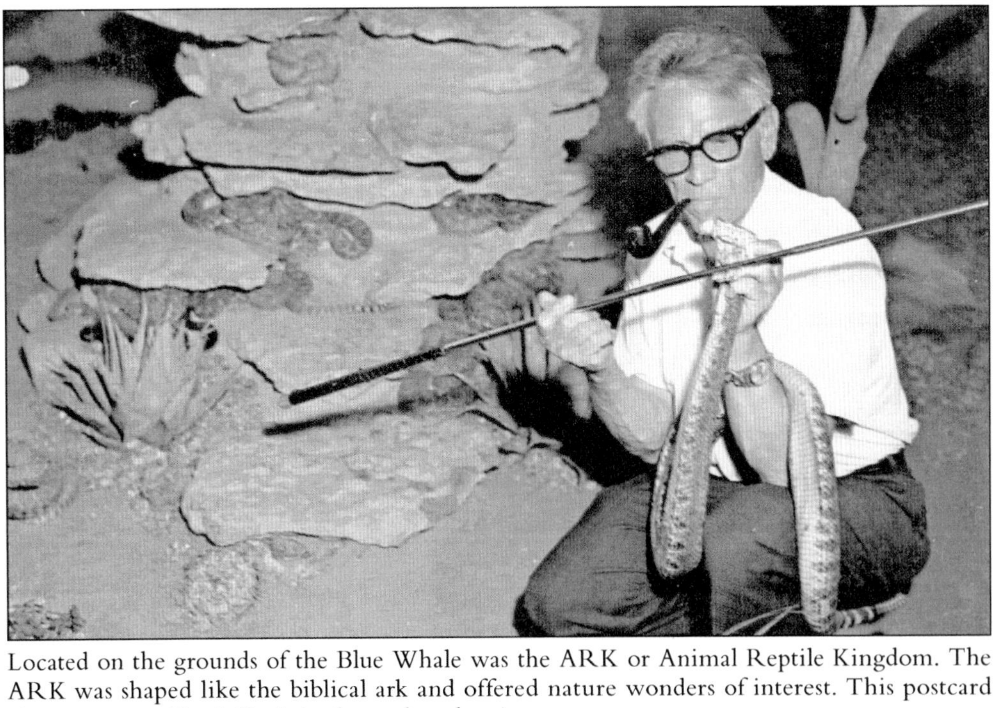

Located on the grounds of the Blue Whale was the ARK or Animal Reptile Kingdom. The ARK was shaped like the biblical ark and offered nature wonders of interest. This postcard pictures owner Hugh Davis in the rattlesnake pit.

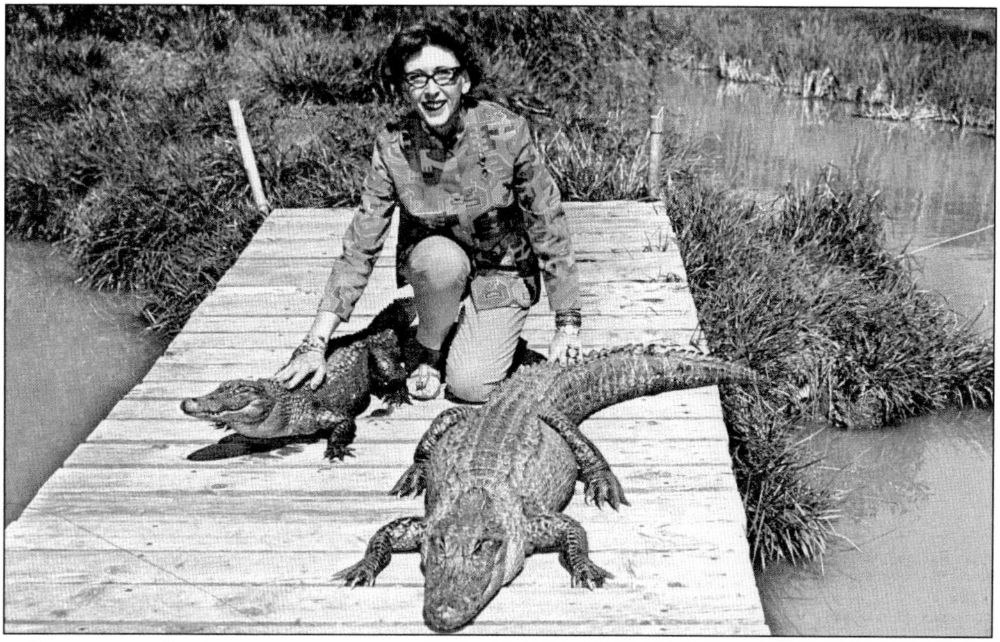

Zelta Davis, wife of Hugh Davis, was the alligator wrestler of Route 66. Alligators were allowed to roam free on the grounds. Zelta led guided walks through the grounds and fed the alligators while giving the tour.

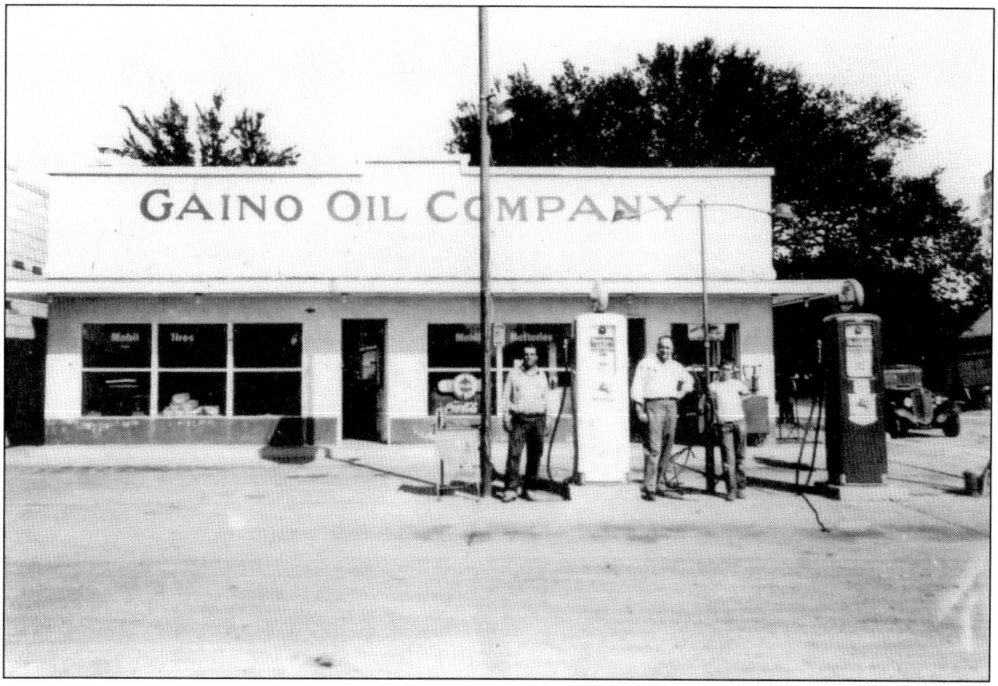


The Gaino Oil Company service station was one of the first gas stations located in Claremore on Route 66. The station was built in 1927 at the corner of First Street and JM Davis Boulevard, the original Route 66.